Rudolf Nureyev

As I remember him

Rudolf Nureyev

As I remember him

Patricia Boccadoro

The Book Guild Ltd

First published in Great Britain in 2023 by
The Book Guild Ltd
Unit E2 Airfield Business Park,
Harrison Road, Market Harborough,
Leicestershire. LE16 7UL
Tel: 0116 2792299
www.bookguild.co.uk
Email: info@bookguild.co.uk
Twitter: @bookguild

Copyright © 2023 Patricia Boccadoro

The right of Patricia Boccadoro to be identified as the author of this
work has been asserted by them in accordance with the
Copyright, Design and Patents Act 1988

Cover image taken during rehearsal in London
Frederika Davis
© Sasha Davis

All rights reserved. No part of this publication may be
reproduced, transmitted, or stored in a retrieval system, in any form or by any means,
without permission in writing from the publisher, nor be otherwise circulated in
any form of binding or cover other than that in which it is published and without
a similar condition being imposed on the subsequent purchaser.

Typeset in 11pt Minion Pro

Printed and bound by CPI Group (UK) Ltd, Croydon, CR0 4YY

ISBN 978 1915853 240

British Library Cataloguing in Publication Data.
A catalogue record for this book is available from the British Library.

*For my daughter Natalie
the little girl who wanted to marry Rudolf*

Contents

Introduction — xi
Prologue — xix
   October 1992 – St Barthélemy, French West Indies — xix
   January 1993 – Paris — xxi

Part I
   The London Years 1964–1969 — 3
   Swan Lake — 5
   Romeo and Juliet — 23
   Marguerite and Armand — 29
   Giselle — 31
   Le Corsaire — 37
   Paradise Lost — 41
   Les Sylphides — 46
   Sleeping Beauty — 49
   Paul Clarke — 50
   Sasha Davis — 51

Part II
   The Intervening Years 1969–1982 — 55
   Petrushka — 55
   The Palais Garnier — 56
   Don Quixote — 64
   Don Quixote – the film — 67

Ivry Gitlis	70
Balanchine	77
Apollo	78
Polyakov	80
La Sylphide	81
Charles Jude	84
Oriental carpets	86
Song of the Wayfarer	90
The Tempest	92
Mademoiselle Julie	93

Part III

The Paris Opera Ballet 1970–1983	97
Serge Lifar	99
From George Skibine to Rosella Hightower	101
Claude Bessy	103

Part IV

Nureyev in Paris 1983–1993	109
Patricia Ruanne	115
The hierarchy	117
Teaching	119
Patrice Bart	119
Genia Polyakov – "Bonjour la danse!"	122
Elisabeth Platel	124
Raymonda	126
Nicholas Georgiadis	128
Nutcracker	134
Journalists	136
Maurice Béjart	141
Washington Square	142
Cinderella	143
Charles Jude	145
Manfred	149

Contents

Young choreographers 150
Sleeping Beauty 152

Part V
1989 to 1993 161
Conducting 166
Back to Russia 168
Minkus score 169
La Bayadère 171
Monique Loudières 178
The illness 179
Agnès Letestu 181
St Barts 182
La Bayadère – the film 185
The BBC film 187
Memorial 190
Maude Gosling 193

Part VI
Legacy 197
Brigitte Lefèvre 197
Manuel Legris 200
Wilfried Romoli 202
Yann Bridard 204
Florence Clerc 205
Carnavalet 207
Saint Petersburg 210

Epilogue 216
Further Reading 218
Acknowledgements 221
About the Author 225

Introduction

What was Rudolf Nureyev like? How well did you know him? Did you actually see him dance in London and was he really the greatest dancer in the world? What did he actually do as the director of the Paris Opera Ballet and how did he change the world's perception of the male classical dancer? These are just a few of the questions I've been asked over the years.

Maybe it's time to share my personal memories of this man and try to explain just how this exceptional being accomplished so much before his untimely death at fifty-four.

The first thing to say is that no dancer I have ever seen matched the grace, power and perfection of Nureyev's work in classical ballet, particularly during those golden years in the 1960s at Covent Garden. He played an exceptional role in the development of the English ballet scene from the moment he arrived there in 1962.

While it is common knowledge that Nureyev breathed new life into the Paris Opera Ballet, being a director of exceptional gifts, what is not known is how, and exactly what he accomplished there that previous directors did not.

And then, was he just a producer of ballets rather than an original choreographer in his own right as has been asserted? Does criticism for his additions and changes to the great 19th-century ballets come from people who have never danced themselves, but profess to know exactly how these works should be performed? It seems to me from talking to him over the years and seeing for myself how he brought these masterpieces back to life, that no one knew the works of Marius Petipa better than he did. Still today there are those, immured in the past, who view with horror any attempt at what they esteem to be unnecessary tampering with Petipa's great ballets, despite the considerable advances in technique as well as the changes in dancers' physiques. Moreover, would audiences today really appreciate seeing these ballets in their original form?

It's time to recognise that Rudolf Nureyev was also a good choreographer and a man of great vision, often underestimated because he did so many other things, dancing in more ballets, with more partners, with more companies in more countries, sharing his art and simply giving more than any other dancer. During the 1960s and early 1970s, he danced tirelessly, giving up to 250 performances a season.

Not least, one of his greatest contributions to the history of dance was how, with his knowledge, glamour and generosity, he totally transformed the image and destinies of all male ballet dancers throughout the world.

The actual seeds of this book probably date back to 1988 or early 1989, when I commented to a friend at the Paris Opera that the pas de deux of the last act of Nureyev's version of *The Nutcracker* was the prettiest I'd seen and that I had been fascinated by his imaginative Shakespearian version of *Romeo and Juliet*.

I suggested it was time that someone wrote a book about his work in Paris, which, having viewed the state of the company before, was nothing short of miraculous. I enlarged upon this, saying that it should be along the lines of *Nureyev: His Spectacular Early Years*, the excellent 1962 autobiography written and edited with the help of Alexander Bland, the pen name of Nureyev's dearest friends, Nigel and Maude Gosling. On his arrival in the West, the Russian dancer had little economic security and to further his career, had, albeit reluctantly, agreed to tell his story himself. I said that it was now time for him to give his own account of his Paris years.

Great was my amazement when some time later I heard that he was interested in the project and was quite amenable to doing it with me. I could scarcely believe it as, with his encouragement, I had only just begun writing about dance for *Dancing Times*, the specialist dance magazine based in London and had had only a couple of features published in *The Guardian*, one of them being based on the Diaries of Vaslav Nijinsky. And although

I had done considerable book editing, I had never contemplated writing a book myself. All the same, I was basically a nobody on the literary scene and for a superstar like Nureyev to contemplate writing a book with me left my head spinning.

Well, I thought, if Nureyev believed in me, then, why not, and with the help of Douce Francois, the lovely young woman whose home in the Rue Murillo had been the dancer's Paris base for many years, I began gradually amassing material and talking to many of those who knew him best, both friends and colleagues.

One evening in her apartment, she went to get his diary and bulging address book and together we pored over it and made a list of those people she knew would give honest answers. I had already met and liked Genia Polyakov, the Russian ballet master he invited to join him in 1983, as well as dancers Charles Jude and his wife, Florence Clerc. Via my friendship with Douce, I had also got to know Nicholas Georgiadis, the distinguished Greek designer and close confidant of all Rudolf's early productions. In addition, living in Paris for several years, I had already met many of the dancers and teachers at the Paris Opera with whom he had worked. Maude Gosling, whom Rudolf regarded as his second mother, emphasised the importance of speaking to his close colleagues, Patrice Bart and Patricia Ruanne.

Since I had lived in London in the 1960s, I had also had the privilege of meeting Margot Fonteyn, and some time later had been introduced to Wallace Potts, two people who played significant roles in his life, and with whom he had shared such special relationships. I then began talking to people, recording conversations, taking notes of what had been said during or after interviews, depending upon whom I'd been seeing. Usually chatting to Nureyev on an informal basis, I never had a camera nor a recorder with me, but everything he said was imprinted in my head and frequently jotted down on paper later. I also began reading through my own notes based on all the productions I'd seen. From my side, things began to fall into place.

The main problem, however, with his work in Paris together with his illness, hospital visits and subsequent upsets with the rigid Opera administration, was for Nureyev to find the time to see me, particularly when he accepted invitations to conduct, and then began work on, *The Bayadère*, which he had set his heart on for so long. At this point, time was running out.

With his death on January 6, 1993, when he could no longer sue, a spate of books he would have intensely disliked came out, focusing on the sensational aspects of his life and founded for the most part on gossip and rumours to the detriment of his artistic achievements. They were probably written by people who had never met him, had never seen him dance, and moreover, knew little or nothing about the world of dance. And then my book project was subsequently put aside when the idea was taken out of my hands and given to the BBC, where it was turned into a prurient documentary, which delved more into his personal life and fight with Aids than with his exceptional achievements. Over the years, more books appeared in which Rudolf's private life and illness, as well as stories of no interest about people he encountered outside the world of dance, took precedence over the extraordinary and unique contribution he gave to dance worldwide. The fact that he was one of the most outstanding artists of the century paled against lurid details of the army of young men attributed to have slept with him.

I recently glanced through some of these books and, in addition to being taken aback by the fatuous gossip they contained, found I disagreed with much that had been written. Events had been taken out of context and, more often than not, grossly exaggerated, so much so that I lost sight of the man I had met so many times.

And then several fairly innocuous details finally convinced me to put pen to paper, so to speak. I was irritated, perhaps unduly so, by an otherwise interesting piece by Mike Dixon, who made the sweeping statement "Nijinsky is the greatest dancer who ever lived" in the February 2020 edition of *Dance Europe*, writing as if he'd seen him perform the week before. Nijinsky is a legend, famed for his exceptional elevation, but all the same, Dixon never saw him dance as Vaslav Nijinsky was born in Kiev in March 1889. His opinion could only be based on hearsay and photographs of the dancer, whose last performance was in January 1919, after which he was diagnosed as mentally insane, sadly spending the rest of his life in specialised institutions. Unfortunately, the rare films of him are barely watchable, while photographs show a delicate, graceful figure, 1.63m tall, far from the image of a 'danseur noble'. His brief career, after training at the Imperial School of Ballet in St Petersburg, was with Diaghilev's Ballets Russes, where he became their most famous dancer. While he did give a few performances of *Sleeping Beauty*, *Giselle* and *The Nutcracker*, his fame grew from his appearances in all Fokine's ballets, in particular *Petrushka* and *Spectre de la Rose*. When I think of Nijinsky today, it's as a brilliant and innovative choreographer as demonstrated by the few timeless works he created, not least his 1913 ground-breaking *Rite of Spring*. That Nureyev was vexed by comparisons with him, I fully understood.

But what did disturb me was a line Ralph Fiennes made the actress who portrayed Clara Saint say in his film *The White Crow*, which dwells upon Nureyev's early years and which was seen by a wide public: "Nureyev was the most selfish man I ever met," declared the lady. I cannot think of a more blatantly untrue statement, as Nureyev was one of those rare people who gave far more than they ever took from life and who had so much more to give. In conversations with all those I have spoken to over the years, as well as in my own experience, everyone considered Nureyev as the most generous person they knew. Whatever else he might have been, and he was many different things to many different people, he was also kind, thoughtful and caring. In all our meetings and conversations he was always gentle and courteous, never failing, for instance, to return phone calls and ensure I had his personal number so I could call him directly for any reason. I can only imagine that Fiennes' inclusion of such a misleading remark referred to the dancer's dramatic 'decision' to remain here.

While it's true to say that Rudolf had fallen in love with Paris, and despite his longing for personal and artistic freedom, I find it impossible to believe that he had cold-bloodedly planned to remain in the West. While I would not presume to know what was in his head at the time, I can only suggest that when he was barred from boarding the plane to London, and with events occurring with such amazing rapidity, he was unable to take any rational decision. The only relevant fact was Dance, which was as important as breathing to him. It was Nureyev's whole reason for living. Not to dance again would have killed him. As a drowning man would automatically resurface to gasp for air, so Nureyev knew in those few fatal moments that returning to Russia, after what was considered his unacceptable friendships with the French dancers, his suspected homosexual tendencies, plus his refusal to become a card-carrying member of the communist party, would spell an end to his career. Nureyev did not so much have a 'career' as a way of life. There was no choice as such for him to make. He was panic-stricken; any possible repercussions on his family and friends in Russia would simply not have entered into his mind at that precise moment in time.

Several detailed versions of his request for political asylum at the Paris airport of Le Bourget in June 1961 exist, but those who wish to get as close to the truth as possible would do best to rely on Nureyev's own words in his autobiography, *Nureyev: His Spectacular Early Years*, where the dancer states very clearly that "he had no choice". When he was told he had to return to Russia, he knew that "something terrible" was going to happen and that, for him, it would be "the end".

This, however, is not the book planned over a quarter of a century ago, but rather a collection of personal memories over the twenty-eight years that I witnessed his career. It covers Rudolf Nureyev's work as a dancer, as a choreographer, as the director of dance at the Paris Opera Ballet, and as a musician. I hope that it will give an idea of what it was like and how it made one feel to actually see him dance, particularly in the 1960s. Beginning in London in 1964 and ending not exactly at his funeral in January 1993, nor at the unveiling of his memorial at the little Russian cemetery in Sainte-Geneviève-des-Bois three years later, but with the legacy he left to the Paris company, as well as to dance worldwide. He changed the destinies of all male dancers, present and future, and after only one year at the helm of the Paris company, he had made it into one of the finest in the world.

When I met him in 1964, Rudolf Nureyev was twenty-six. He was, and remains to this day, the most beautiful person I have ever seen. His was not a fad or bland beauty, marked as it was by a wickedly sharp intelligence evident even at this first meeting. His face was so expressive that one could frequently guess what he was thinking, particularly years later at press conferences at the Palais Garnier that he was obliged to attend instead of being with his dancers in the rehearsal studios.

I still remember, not without some amusement, of how, seated on some sort of raised dais in the richly decorated Main Foyer, he would gaze stony-faced into the distance, facing a horde of journalists who were bombarding him with questions, the answers to which were in the documentation in front of them. In his early years, unaccustomed to demands for interviews in Russia, he would frequently refuse to see journalists, a fact which led him to being described as arrogant and difficult with a certain press. Throughout his life, Nureyev never sought publicity, but with his nonconformist behaviour, he attracted it every which way he turned.

Portrait. 1963.
Frederika Davis
© Sasha Davis

He was more vibrant and charismatic than in any photograph, film or video. In his lifetime, he became the most famous dancer in the world, famous for his dancing and his beauty. Very little was known of his private life. He was certainly the greatest dancer, romantic or otherwise, that I myself ever saw, the likes of which we shall probably never see again, and I fully understand these people who refer to him as a 'demi-god'. He did not simply dance onstage, he inhabited it, taking one's heart and soul with him in a way that simply does not, indeed could not, exist today. He lived his roles. Every time he danced, it was as though it was his very last. He gave everything he had. When the curtain rose on each of his performances, there was an electrical charge in the theatre; there was an enormous wave of excitement unlike anything I have experienced since.

There is also something else of great importance in view of all the nonsense that has been written about him, and that is that I liked him. I liked him very much. He was, as the French say, 'terriblement attachant'. I know that I was privileged to have known him. And since this is a book about the man I personally did know, it excludes all mention of his private life, which in his lifetime was exactly that. There are no vivid descriptions of any 'imperious behaviour' or 'explosive temper tantrums', which, not being a dancer nor one of his lovers, I certainly never experienced. Articles I've read about him proclaim his "arrogance", his "animality", his "mysterious personality" and even his "troubled nature", but frankly, offstage, once I had overcome my initial awe of him, he was nothing but unfailingly gracious. My memories are of a warm-hearted, sensitive and thoughtful person. He might well have been many of the things he has been accused of being; maybe he was, but there again, maybe he wasn't. This is simply an account of the man I remember over the years I observed his career and had the pleasure of meeting on countless occasions.

"Rudolf Nureyev as I remember him"

Prologue

October 1992 – St Barthélemy, French West Indies

"'Put your arms this way, now try like that,' Rudolf suggested as we began working together on ideas for the new ballet, *The Prince of the Pagodas*, that he had in mind."

I was listening to the French danseur étoile Charles Jude, Nureyev's closest friend and confidant, explaining to me how the Russian dancer was using him as a model for the next ballet he planned to stage on his return to the French capital.

"We were on the terrace of his holiday home in St Bart's and he was experimenting with different movements in his research to transport classical dance steps into oriental ones," Jude said. "As my mother is Vietnamese, I certainly look part oriental, which he thought was an advantage. It was fascinating to watch him, and I'm convinced that if he'd continued his work on that ballet and all the others he had been turning around in his head, he could have been the equal of all the choreographers with whom he'd worked. With his immense knowledge of dance, he was capable of anything."

Charles Jude, the man who was virtually Nureyev's adopted son in all but name, was recalling the two weeks he spent with him at his home on the Caribbean island of St Bart's, Rudolf's paradise. After a strenuous three to four months spent at the Paris Opera preparing his production of *La*

Bayadère, Nureyev, as ill as he was, having fought against Aids since the mid-eighties, had persuaded Jude and his wife, Florence Clerc, to accompany him there, insisting that the glorious scenery and ideal climate could only be beneficial to his health. They were joined by Jeanette Etheridge, a Russian friend from San Francisco who was in Paris at the time, and Nureyev's big black dog, Soloria, rescued from a dog pound, who went wild on the island's beaches after being confined in a Paris apartment.

"Rudolf loved the sun and adored being on the beach, and I remember looking at him on that last holiday," Florence told me. "His eyes, normally grey, a grey-blue verging on green, were such a clear sparkling green, so vivid, so full of strength and shining with the gladness of being there. In spite of being so dreadfully ill, which he just brushed aside, his joy of being alive was so intense; all he wanted to do was drink in the natural beauty surrounding him and take everything into his arms. Maybe he was happiest at night just sitting with us on the terrace, not speaking much, but just watching the stars and the sky around him. You didn't need to speak because it was breathtakingly beautiful. Those moments we spent with him were unforgettable."

"Later," Jude continued, "we'd watch videos of orchestra conductors, particularly one of Seiji Ozawa, which he was glued to as it showed the maestro's debuts. Rudolf, who played the piano himself, was in another world and missed nothing. He'd set his heart on becoming an orchestra conductor as early as 1964, his dream being to conduct all of his own ballets, from *Swan Lake* to *Romeo and Juliet*, as well as all those he was planning. He had already conducted *Sleeping Beauty* on four occasions in America the year before, when I was dancing the prince, when he amazed all the musicians in the orchestra by his perfect timing, precision and sensitivity. For me, it was one of the most extraordinary moments of my career. He was fifty-four, and the end of his own career as a dancer was no longer a drama. He intended to replace it in the orchestra pit, and had already accepted to conduct *Coppélia* in Marseilles at Roland Petit's invitation.

"Few people realised that Rudolf, who had enrolled at the Juilliard School in New York and trained as a conductor in Vienna, had already led orchestras in works by Tchaikovsky, Stravinsky, and Prokofiev, the three composers he considered as his gods. His ballet, *The Bayadère*, was over and he didn't want to hear about mounting a fourth act, being more interested in finding other ballets to stage including *Ondine* and *Le Mandarin Merveilleux* as well as *The Prince of the Pagodas*. He was looking to the future, was full of projects, and still had so much more to give to the world."

January 1993 – Paris

Shortly after reluctantly returning to Paris, Nureyev suffered a severe relapse and on January 6, 1993, he breathed his last at the hospital of Notre-Dame-du-Perpétuel-Secours at Levallois-Perret. A grandiose memorial service was held for him at the Palais Garnier on January 12 before he was buried in the little Russian cemetery at Sainte-Geneviève-des-Bois, some 25km outside Paris.

Friends, family and colleagues from throughout the world gathered together, crowding over the balconies and lining the staircase in the magnificent entrance foyer of the Opera Garnier to pay tribute to him. Led by Charles Jude and Francis Malovik, six male dancers carried his pale wooden coffin slowly to the top of the sweeping marble stairs, where it was gently placed on a bier. A spray of white flowers was laid on top. The insignia of a Commander of Arts and Letters, France's highest award for exceptional achievements in the arts, which was awarded to him onstage at the première of *La Bayadère* barely three months earlier, lay on a cushion below him. There was scarcely a sound.

A small string orchestra of eleven musicians then opened the non-religious service, which he himself had requested, with a fugue by Johann Sebastian Bach, his favourite composer. Poetry readings in Russian, French, German, English and Italian from writers he loved, Pushkin's *Eugene Onegin*, *Manfred*, by Byron, on which his ballet by the same name was based, *Faust* by Goethe, *Illuminations* by Rimbaud, and *Rime* by Michelangelo were read by some of his closest friends. They might have been written just for him.

Ninel Kourgapkina, one of Nureyev's favourite partners from his time at the Kirov in St Petersburg, who came to help him mount *La Bayadère*, was asked to read the passage from Pushkin shortly after her arrival. It evoked, she said, the anguish of the exile far from "sad Russia where I suffered, where I loved, there, where my heart is buried".

More verses that were so appropriate and so relevant to the dancer's life were those written by Goethe. "I have crossed this world running and have seized every desire by the hair".

After the slow movement of Tchaikovsky's first string quartet, Jack Lang, the French Minister of Culture, the man responsible for bringing Nureyev to take over the Paris Opera Ballet in 1983, gave a passionate and moving eulogy in which he quoted Baryshnikov's words, picked up by the popular press at the time: "Nureyev had the charisma of a man of the earth and the untouchable arrogance of the gods".

Lang spoke of Nureyev's God-given gifts of beauty and passion as well as his taste for the absolute, concluding with the words that from the pantheon of beauty, "Rudolf Nureyev continues to dazzle and inspire us", commenting that his genius would continue to send out thunderbolts forever.

It could almost be said that Nureyev finally ended his exile when he was taken to the little Russian cemetery at Sainte-Geneviève-des-Bois, where his coffin had already been lowered into Russian soil when I arrived. Standing at his grave, I looked down and gently threw a single white rose tinged with pink upon the gleaming wood below, with immense sadness and disbelief that the life of this exceptional man who had given so much to the world had ended. My memories return to hearing the sharp crunching noise of the gravel under my feet coupled with an awareness of the overhanging rows of tall conifers leading the way to Nureyev's burial site, which, with the rows of ancient orthodox crosses of the graves behind, so resembled the setting of the last act of *Giselle* he had so often danced.

Everyone was wrapped up in their own sorrow, making it impossible to say who was there. The only noticeable arrivals were the children from the Opera school, silent, white-faced and frightened, who were brought by bus. People huddled together in the bitter cold with scarcely a word, moving only to file past the grave and cast small white roses down until the coffin was covered with a thick carpet of white flowers. Saddened and empty, mourners were beyond tears. The very air was heavy with grief.

Part I

The London Years
1964–1969

When I saw his performances at Covent Garden in the 1960s, Rudolf Nureyev was indeed the greatest romantic dancer the world has ever known. I realised that the first time I saw him dance, even though I had not seen many other male dancers apart from David Blair and Michael Somes. Although I remember liking Somes, I never fell in love with his prince. With Nureyev, however, it was quite the reverse; almost the instant he appeared onstage, I adored him. Barely halfway through the first act, I knew that what I was seeing was an 'absolute', and that I would never ever see anything remotely like it again. Nearly sixty years later, I haven't.

While I have long admired the technical perfection of Baryshnikov, would have followed Vladimir Vasiliev and Ekaterina Maximova to the ends of the earth, and fell in love with the joie de vivre of Edward Villella in New York, all of them great dancers and each one unique in their own way, no other dancer I have ever seen possessed the charismatic stage presence, the soft feline suppleness, nor the ability to turn music into movement and emotion of Nureyev.

The two qualities imprinted on my mind for all time were his utter grace and softness. When he leaped, he floated, descending back to earth in slow motion, so softly with incredible ease and control; he seemed not of this world. I remember his long, sweeping, curving backward leaps, followed by those sure, silent landings as he lightly skimmed the floor. It was, above all, the total beauty of each of his movements that bewitched us; audiences were spellbound. He didn't 'jump', he flew. And then hovered in the air. No one who saw him then could ever forget it. His very features were the epitome of romanticism.

He drew us all into his world. It wasn't only Odette, Giselle, Juliet, and Aurora who fell irrevocably in love with him; he also won the hearts of every man, woman and child in the audience. And who amongst us has not, in their wildest dreams, imagined themselves as Medora, with Conrad, that handsome, swashbuckling pirate swearing undying love as he flung himself slavishly, passionately, at her feet? We were all Odette, our hearts in our mouths as he tore his way through the swans at the lakeside in his anguish to reach her.

I remember his close friend Douce Francois making a comment that never fails to make me smile. "Everybody who met him," she told me, "whether they admit it or not, was in love with Rudolf!"

While photographs and films give an excellent idea of what he was like, they in no way convey the sheer force and impact of his physical presence. There were those who complained about the length of time he continued dancing, describing what they called his 'stiff legs' and 'soggy jumps', asserting that he was destroying his own legend, yet they still chose to go to see him, even in roles they knew to be more suited to younger dancers. In contrast, there were many who also saw him dance towards the end of his life, particularly in character roles, even including his interpretation of Carabosse in his own version of *Sleeping Beauty*, who still treasure their memories of seeing a living legend for themselves. Driven by some inner demon, he danced because he had to. He did not dance to please audiences or to amass money, but because it was what he was. We breathe, Rudolf danced. But despite his illness and declining physical powers, the artistry was there at every performance; as long as he danced, Rudolf Nureyev was alive.

For the most part, I have chosen to write about the first time I saw Nureyev dance a role when he was resident guest artist with the Royal Ballet from 1962 to 1977. I didn't see him there after 1970, when his appearances grew considerably less frequent, as I left London to spend two years in the US, anxious to discover Balanchine with the New York City Ballet then at its peak.

Swan Lake

Arriving in London in 1964, I went immediately to see Nureyev partnering Margot Fonteyn in a performance of Nicholas Sergeyev's version of *Swan Lake* at Covent Garden. With Tchaikovsky's immortal score and choreography by Frenchman Marius Petipa and Lev Ivanov, it is the most well-known of all the great 19th-century classical works, telling the story of Princess Odette, who has become the symbol of classical dance.

The ballet tells the tale of how she was transformed into a swan by the magician Rothbart and how she can only regain her human form if a man swears to love her forever. The prince Siegfried, smitten at first sight, is unhappily tricked by Rothbart and Odette is lost to him. Nevertheless, sitting on the edge of my seat, I kept hoping that good would triumph over evil and that the lovers would live 'happily ever after' and not both drown in the lake as I'd been warned. Rather like in performances of *Romeo and Juliet*, when one can't help dreaming that the story will end differently, and that Romeo would not be so quick to take the poison.

When the curtain rose on Nureyev in *Swan Lake*, the exciting newcomer everyone had come to see, he identified so completely with Siegfried that we saw a dreamy young aristocrat, every inch a true fairy-tale prince, appear in front of our eyes and not the outstanding dancer from the Kirov we had heard so much about. In the middle of a cynical 20th century, Rudolf Nureyev made his audience believe that a young man could indeed fall in love with a swan, and that yes, there was magic around that could enable a cruel magician to transform a pretty young girl into a bird, albeit an elegant one. It was Nureyev's exceptional ability to become the person he was interpreting, to make the audience believe he really was Siegfried, which made him unique. It was not only Odette who fell in love with him, it was the whole theatre.

From my seat in the front row of the circle stalls, I remember holding my breath as this slender, extraordinarily beautiful young man with his mop of shiny dark blond hair raised his arms centre stage. Do I recollect feathers drifting down or did I dream that? With that very first port de bras, of extreme beauty, he illuminated the stage. If Rudolf Nureyev had appeared in the ballet in blue jeans, the audience would still have known that he was the prince the moment he arrived.

The downfall to this first unforgettable performance, which I was unaware of at the time, was that this young dancer's presence was so mesmerising

Nureyev with Fonteyn in Swan Lake at the Champs-Élysées Theatre in Paris, November 1963.
© Boris Lipnitzki/Roger Viollet

that one could simply not tear one's eyes away from him. Forget about the poor princesses dancing their hearts out as they vied for his attention, for I could see only him. At the ball, everyone, courtiers and spectators included, only had eyes for him, the peerless, Kirov-trained prince.

In fact, it was not until several years later that I was able to appreciate the ballet as a whole, and watch the six dancing princesses at his birthday party, each hoping to win the hand of the prince. But for my first *Swan Lake*, my eyes were irrevocably drawn to this charismatic figure sitting immobile on his throne, feet crossed elegantly in front of him. Motionless he commanded one's attention.

Elegance is a word I have not frequently come across when glancing through reviews or books on him, but elegance coupled with musicality immediately come to mind when I recall these London performances. Nureyev's Siegfried simply soared through the air in impossibly high, effortless leaps full of grace, with super-soft, cat-like landings after which he would remain motionless for a couple of seconds. I'm not entirely happy about descriptions I've read comparing him to a wild young panther because he was not so much 'wild' in those early days, but rather gloriously free and untamed. He flew. There was something so pure about him as his huge, spectacular jumps electrified the audience, leaving us all breathless.

With the merest gesture, Nureyev captivated spectators the moment he arrived onstage, which is often not the case with other dancers when one tends to wait to cheer for the spectacular codas, the famous solos and grand jetés. Rudolf's hands, each of his arm movements were magical, movements of absolute beauty.

From the very beginning one believed in the story. With one glance at this young stranger, so gentle and sincere, it was obvious that Odette, the sublime Margot Fonteyn, would give him her heart. From her first entrance, she was heart-stopping. She had an inner glow, a radiance that brought tears to one's eyes the instant she appeared onstage. There was such beauty in the simple poise of her head and in her soft, perfect arabesques. Like Nureyev, Fonteyn did not merely dance a role, but inhabited it.

Emotionally and physically, they fitted together; body and soul they were as one. Nureyev would lift her effortlessly high in the air in a fluid extension of their every movement; she seemed weightless. As unbelievable as it was, they just flowed into each other. There was no heaving into the air, no staggering round the stage in one-armed lifts to cheers from the audience.

Quite simply, the two dancers were meant to be together. As Alexander Bland was to write, it was "a match made in heaven". At the risk of repeating myself, no one who witnessed their appearances together could ever forget them.

Odette had been a fun-loving princess until a supernatural being had transformed her into a swan, a swan by day and a princess by night, and in this first act, she implores the prince to love her and promise to remain true in order to break the spell. What the audience saw was a tragic love affair enacted out onstage before its very eyes. So moving, so passionate and so real was their performance that it obviously gave off rumours that Fonteyn and Nureyev had to be a couple offstage as well as on. No one could dance like that otherwise. The love just poured out of them. No one who saw them together in these early days could ever forget the image of Siegfried, crazed with grief after his involuntary betrayal, tearing his way down to the lake to search frenziedly for her amongst the swans.

I don't quite remember whether it was at this first performance or later that I realised I was in the presence of greatness, and from quite early on, I literally did stretch out my hands to hold on to, and keep, all the happiness I was being given. I told myself that I had a camera in my head and what I saw and felt, I would remember for the rest of my life. So be it, as now, well over half a century later, my mind and heart are as clear now as then. The joy I was given has always remained a constant in my life. I knew, and the years have proved me correct, that Fonteyn and Nureyev was the greatest dance partnership the world would ever see. The warmth and radiance of one was intensified by the artistry and brilliance of the other.

It wasn't until much later that I learned their collaboration in *Swan Lake* had not had such an easy start. In Margot Fonteyn's own autobiography, she related how Rudolf hadn't at all appreciated the mime scenes she had been accustomed to enacting in the Royal Ballet's version. He argued that it wasn't done that way in Russia and a full-scale row was only avoided when she reminded him that she had been dancing *Swan Lake* since 1938, the year in which he had been born. At that, she wrote, they both broke down in giggles, and the tension disappeared. Rudolf adopted the mime scene years later when he introduced it into his 1984 production for the Paris Opera Ballet as a tribute to her.

In the 1960s, the public saw that in all their performances Fonteyn and Nureyev were as one, moving in the same way. Nureyev responded to each

Rudolf with his perfect partner, Margot Fonteyn. 1962. Frederika Davis. © Sasha Davis

shift in Fonteyn's portrayal of Odette; they seemed to speak with their eyes. Dance alone expressed what words could not. "We were complementary," Nureyev himself has explained, adding that when they danced together there were no cultural gaps nor age differences between them.

"I think the public was enthralled because we were enthralled with each other, with our every head and arm movement, and with what we did with the part" were the words he used in Patricia Foy's remarkable 1991 documentary, a film centred on the dancer's life and work, and containing archival footage of many of his performances.

It mustn't be forgotten, however, with all we hear about Margot Fonteyn being the epitome of a cool, refined English ballerina, that she was not at all the demure, conventional English rose. With her enormous big brown eyes like liquid pools, dark hair and small, slender build she was not particularly English, neither in looks nor temperament. Her mother was half Irish, half Brazilian, and from the age of eight, Margot had been brought up in China. There was fire under the ice, which rose to meet Rudolf's Tartar passion. Together they were dynamite, for when they danced together there was something so intrinsically special, a magic they spun that has been absent from any other partnership I've seen.

It had not been easy to obtain tickets, extremely difficult to get for this performance, nor for all those I would see over the following years. Rudolf Nureyev was not a permanent member of the Royal Ballet, but was given the title of resident guest artist when he first came to the company in 1962. He and Fonteyn would only dance a certain number of ballets each season, and if one waited for the first day of booking, all their performances would be sold out. Consequently, with three of my friends from university, Sue and Russell Thomas and Beverley Labbett, I skipped class and went to queue for seats on the morning of the day before booking opened.

We were fully equipped with blankets, sleeping bags and thermos flasks of coffee, clutching all the money we had, and full of confidence and determination. Error. When we got to the Opera House, we found to our consternation that huge lines of people already stretched along Floral Street, right round the Royal Opera building and beyond, and from our place in the queue, we couldn't even see the main entrance. I remember feverishly counting the people in front of us, many of whom had been patiently waiting since the previous day. Even though we had arrived some twenty-eight hours before the booking office opened, there were still over a thousand dance-lovers in front of us! Nevertheless, with the number of tickets available to each person for each performance being limited, we reckoned we had a reasonable chance of seats, even if we had to pay more than we had anticipated. No such phenomenon exists today; who would line the streets, wait for hours in drizzly rain, and sleep on the cold hard ground to see a dancer?

Much later, in conversation with Hugues Gall, then General Director of the Paris Opera, I discovered that he too had been one of those camping out on the street, and one day in his office, we both wondered if people would ever again sleep out on pavements in the middle of winter to see for themselves a partnership unlike any other. My passport to happiness in those heady London days was leaving the box-office clutching a fistful of tickets for the legendary pair. Once, I remember hanging on to no less than eleven, one for each of the performances they were giving that season.

Florence Clerc and Charles Jude at the barre, c. 1983.
Personal collection of Florence Clerc

Paris étoile Florence Clerc added her own first experience of seeing Nureyev dance. "I remember when Charles Jude and I decided to go and see him dance in London some time before we were married," she told me. "We were only kids, new members of the corps de ballet in Paris, but when we arrived at Covent Garden, he immediately gave us two seats. After the performance, which left my mind swimming, he took us out to dinner, and upon finding out that we had nowhere to stay, simply took us back to his place as if it was the most normal thing in the world. And he didn't even know me. We sat and watched late night TV with him as though we'd done that all our lives and when we got up in the morning, he'd already left for work and we had his house to ourselves. He was so natural, so genuine, and so generous with everything he had. He would give you anything."

Some ten years later, it was Charles Jude, risen to the rank of étoile, who was to create the role of Siegfried in Nureyev's own adaptation of *Swan Lake* for the Paris Opera Ballet, shortly after he had taken over the post of artistic director there.

Before dancing at the Palais Garnier in Nureyev's initially controversial production, Paris Opera étoile Agnès Letestu told me that she and José Martinez had repeatedly watched the 1966 film of Nureyev and Fonteyn in Nureyev's own, early production of *Swan Lake* with the Ballet of Vienna before their Paris première in the work, precisely because they were fascinated by the way the two dancers seemed to meld together. "We tried to absorb everything they did, and although we never saw them dance onstage, we dared to try to emulate what they were doing, the way they almost became as one," she said.

Agnes Letestu with José Martinez after her nomination as étoile after a performance of Nureyev's production of Swan Lake.
October 1997.
© Patricia Boccadoro

"I can't imagine how incredible it must have been to have actually seen them for real," she added. "Even though dance has evolved since then and we were physically very different, the emotion and ideas remain unchanged. Nureyev's own vision of the work is very different in many aspects except for the love between Siegfried and Odette."

Indeed, after first dancing *Swan Lake* in London with Fonteyn, Nureyev subsequently created a new production of the work for Vienna Opera Ballet in 1964, filmed two years later. Amongst his changes and additions, the role of the male dancer was happily given greater prominence. It mustn't be forgotten that in the days of Petipa, the role of Siegfried was first danced by Pavel Gerdt, the most famous Russian dancer of his time, but a portly gentleman of fifty-one or fifty-two, who is best remembered in dance annuals for his genius for mime. The image of Mr Gerdt staggering around the stage carrying his ballerina aloft is not one we usually associate with the youthful Nureyev, an artist of dazzling virtuosity, who had arrived in London at the peak of his form. Coming from a Russian company where the classics were being constantly renewed, Rudolf took making changes for granted.

He then worked on this 1964 version over the years before his final 'Freudian' work for the Paris Opera in 1984. It was created to replace the Soviet choreographer Vladimir Bourmeister's superficial version, which I saw in the 1970s and which I remember not only for the interminably boring ensembles, but also for the brief appearance of the young Patrick Dupond, fresh from his gold medal at Varna. He stupefied the audience with his bounding jumps, admirably suited to the showy role of the jester, a role which had nothing to do with the original ballet but which had been added on by Alexander Gorsky in 1920 without any meaningful justification.

Nureyev's superb *Swan Lake* is possibly the most typical of his productions, being both theatrical and dramatic with a strong psychological side. He conjured up an entirely dreamlike, supernatural world, where true love and happiness are a distant ideal. The whole story was conceived as a dream, with Prince Siegfried, a reader of romantic novels, trying to escape from the loveless marriage his mother is forcing upon him by entering into a world of make-believe.

The decor by Ezio Frigerio, with Nureyev's wishes in mind, is spectacular

Nureyev's production of Swan Lake at the Palais Garnier, 1994, with Agnès Letestu and José Martinez,
© Colette Masson/Roger Viollet

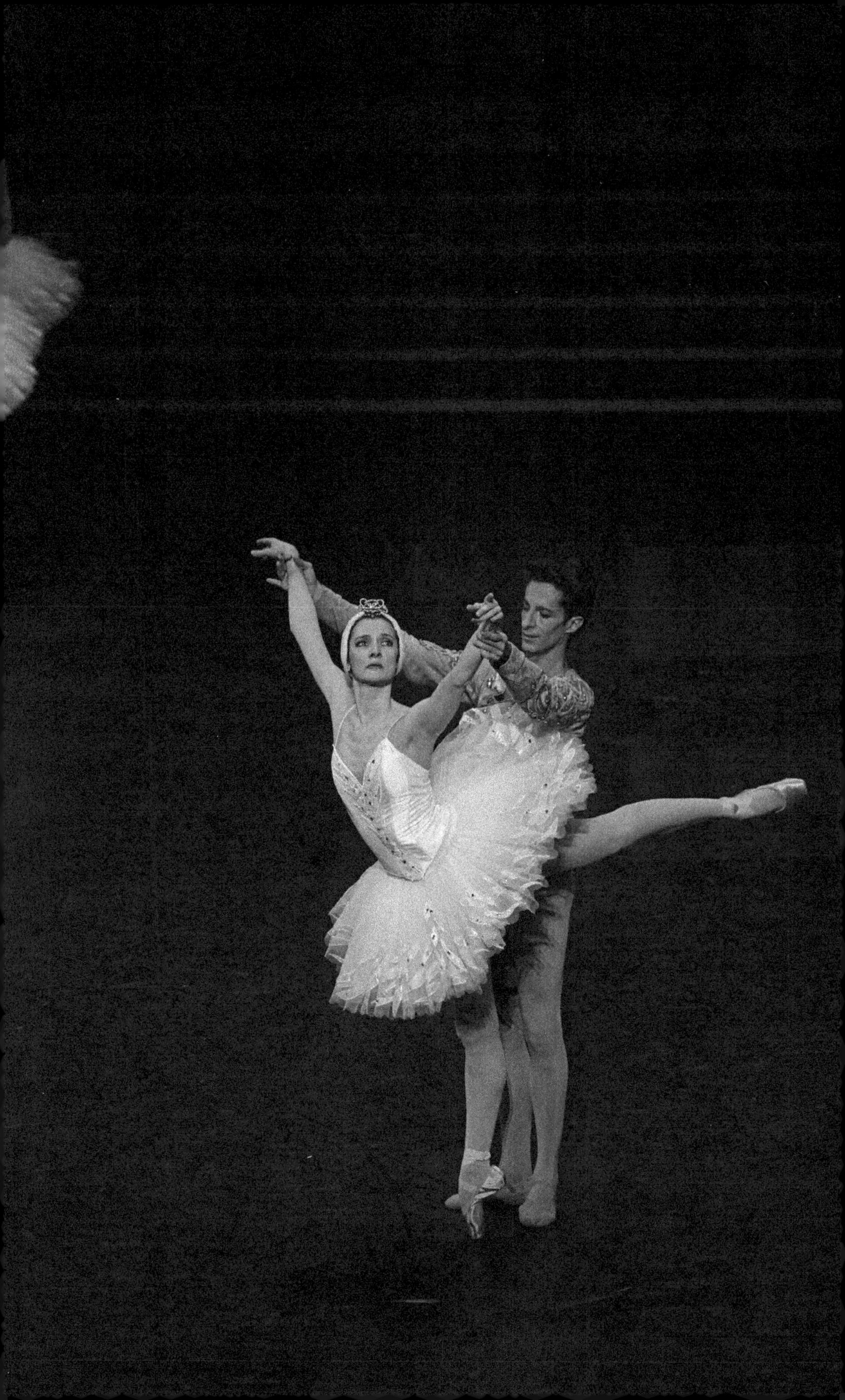

if initially disconcerting, opening as it does within the forbidding grey walls of the palace and representing an enclosed space from which there was no way out. No enchanting lakeside scenery here. However, in contrast to the sobriety of the decor, the pastel-coloured costumes by Franca Squarciapino, each handmade in silks or satins and encrusted with embroidery, are exquisite.

As far as the choreography is concerned, Nureyev's version returns to its original sources, eliminating all the bits added on over the years including the interlude with the jester. Since its creation in 1877, with choreography by Reisinger, which was poorly received, the ballet has been revisited and revised by countless choreographers over the years. It is, however, the full-length 1895 work for the Maryinsky, by Frenchman Marius Petipa and the Russian choreographer Lev Ivanov that is regarded as the 'definitive' one and which forms the basis of the subsequent stagings by companies around the world.

"Rudolf based the ballet on a video we had of the Kirov company, using his prodigious memory as well as adding choreography of his own," the Paris Opera étoile Elisabeth Platel said. Platel, who created the role of Odette, Nureyev's Swan Princess, emphasised that he faithfully reproduced the delicately lyrical White Acts choreographed by Lev Ivanov.

"The first time Rudolf danced *Swan Lake* in St Petersburg," she told me, "he had already tried to convey the melancholy he heard in Tchaikovsky's music by walking around the stage with a mandolin, an idea he developed in London in 1962 when he added what has become known as the melancholy solo towards the end of Act 1."

That solo, a slow, dreamy variation, one of the earliest examples of Nureyev's own choreography, and which has since been incorporated into countless other versions of the ballet throughout the world, is not only extremely beautiful to watch, but is also of great dramatic importance. It sets the scene and, above all, the mood for Nureyev's whole conception of the work, that of a prince who takes refuge from his duties and responsibilities in an imaginary world. It was while watching him dance his own solo in London that I realised that all his movements simply flowed on in one whole unbroken line. He didn't just jump and land, but touched the ground with incredible grace, practically caressing the floor and simply gliding into the next movement. No other dancer I've seen has accomplished that; they jump, take a breath, and then continue. We also sometimes hear a gentle, but nevertheless distracting, thud as they land.

Charles Jude, the danseur étoile who partnered Platel and who subsequently created the main roles in almost all of Nureyev's productions, told me that at first Nureyev had wanted Siegfried to fall asleep in his chair while reading a book at the beginning of the ballet to illustrate that what we were to see was a dream. Young men, he had asserted, do not fall in love with birds and he wanted the ballet to be accessible to all audiences, and not be taken simply as a children's fairy tale.

"It made it logical," Jude said, "that Siegfried's spirit takes off as it were, making sense of the story. The court jester, superfluous, is no longer there, while the role of Wolfgang, his tutor, present in Petipa's early version, is developed and becomes transformed into the evil Rothbart. This dual character thus symbolises a spirit of destruction in opposition to the prince's idealism. Rudolf also makes it clear that the strange, ambiguous Rothbart, a role he developed to interpret himself, is not the only villain in

Rudolf as Rothbart taking a bow alongside Elisabeth Platel and Charles Jude after a performance of Swan Lake in New York, 1986.
© Jacques Moatti

the piece. Siegfried's mother also appears as a force to be reckoned with as she precipitates the tragedy by ordering her son to take a bride."

It was only logical that the youthful Nureyev would not interpret the prince in the same manner as stout Mr Gerdt who created the role over a century earlier and so he developed the part to display virtuoso skills the ageing dancer had long out-lived. Already back in the London days there were those who complained that the appearances of the prince were far too brief. "What?" commented my friend Beverley Labbett as we left the theatre after our first *Swan Lake*. "We paid two pounds, seventeen shillings and six pence to see three jumps!" He should have gone to see the ballet a second time, after Nureyev developed the role of the prince when staging his first full-length *Swan Lake* in Vienna. The male dancer began to take on equal importance as the ballerina, dance no longer being seen as solely the province of women. With Nureyev's arrival, dance began to be an accepted profession for a man.

Nureyev took the interpretation much further in Paris, portraying Siegfried, who becomes the central figure, as a troubled human being. The moody young prince dreams of escaping from his worldly duties and responsibilities via his infatuation with a woman who isn't human and who lives on the shores of an enchanted lake. He is in love with the idea of being in love. He has lost his heart to a figment of his imagination and so a tragic ending, compatible with the nostalgia one hears in Tchaikovsky's score, becomes inevitable. From the beginning the ballet is thus a confrontation between the real and the supernatural world, and one is fully aware that Siegfried's love is doomed from the start. Nureyev's 1984 *Swan Lake* is not, as some have argued, a story of the triumph of evil, but rather that of a man in search of an ideal, yearning for a perfection that can never be reached.

Nureyev introduced and subsequently perfected several new ensembles and dances for the male corps de ballet who had had so little dancing in previous productions. The infamous polonaise for sixteen men, divided into four groups, which so disturbed certain specialists, brings out their virility as well as their superb technique, and gives the male corps de ballet an opportunity to shine in a ballet previously dominated by the women. It is also most exciting to watch.

Nureyev also included the expressive and dramatic mime scene in Act 2, which he had initially refused to do, saying that he would feel silly standing around while Margot Fonteyn told her story in gestures. This, a tribute to the legendary ballerina he adored, does not originate from the Kirov but from Covent Garden.

Not least, Nureyev's version is ideally suited to the Opera dancers. It showcases the work he accomplished with the company's incomparable female corps de ballet, with its academic precision, musicality, and pure unmannered style. All of them, I was told, always had something to do, whether dancing at the Palais Garnier or rehearsing for programmes elsewhere. He made the dancers realise that a fifth position had to be a work of art, and what each one of them did mattered, treating them as individuals rather than as a group, and ensuring that no one felt left out. To make sure they understood that, he brought in Clotilde Vayer as ballet mistress, whose own performance as Odette/Odile remains one of her most treasured memories. Gone were the undisciplined ranks of simpering dancers I'd seen before his arrival, for under Rudolf's watchful eye they blossomed.

"Rudolf would look at them one by one, and do everything he could to make the very last girl at the back even better," ballet master Patrice Bart commented. "He would stop a class or a rehearsal for even the youngest girl, to explain patiently that she was not doing the step correctly and demonstrate to her exactly how it should be done."

By creating roles for everyone to dance and have the opportunity to be noticed, together with his policy of giving early chances to young dancers from the lower ranks, he shaped and guided the Paris company into a new era. Within a year, he had transformed the company beyond all recognition.

Elisabeth Platel told me categorically that Nureyev had brought the grand Petipa back to the company. "What we had before is a shadow of what we have now. He simply eliminated everything that was old-fashioned, all the while keeping the traditional version and only adding on choreography for the male dancers who had so little to do before. His reintroduction of the 19th-century mime scene where Odette introduces herself to Siegfried also tightened up the plot and added dramatic force.

"Rudolf's *Swan Lake* is divine; it's a positive joy to dance. When I created the role of Odette who is a princess and not a bird with ridiculous arm movements, I remember being petrified in case I couldn't manage the steps, but now I wish it could go on forever. Because the choreography highlights any weakness in technique, you have to be very, very precise; you cannot get away with slack work and so it can't be danced by someone who has neither the level nor the understanding. It's why Rudolf's choreography has been criticised. You have to understand his way of thinking and how he wished his steps to be interpreted, each one leading on to the next. I've never enjoyed dancing anything so much in all my life," she continued. "He got rid of all the little feathers we didn't need. It was also amazing how he worked with the musicians and designers to create a work of art. We never had ballets like his before."

Unfortunately, Nureyev's version of *Swan Lake*, with his portrayal of Siegfried as a complex, dreamy young man as opposed to the usual carefree prince they were accustomed to seeing, did not please everyone. Initially, the majority of the dancers revolted, declaring themselves in favour of Vladimir Bourmeister's 1953 version, introduced to the West three years later, and revived for the Paris Opera in 1960. It was a decision they later regretted.

Even the corps de ballet considered Rudolf's production 'heretical' and 'over-complicated', and the situation was only solved by both sides agreeing to a compromise. To persuade them to dance, Rudolf had to promise to stage their much-vaunted version by Bourmeister the following year, but by then they had not only come round to his point of view, vastly preferring his version, but they no longer wanted to dance what they now saw as an old-fashioned staging by Bourmeister! Too late, it had been programmed. Ironically, the same dancers who went on strike at the time and frequently made his life a nightmare are now those who sing his praises the loudest.

Nureyev's personal vision, reflecting the underlying pensiveness in Tchaikovsky's score, hence his lovely melancholy solo, came under attack simply because it was new. There was an outcry, not merely from the Paris dancers, soon to change their opinion, but from British critics, staunchly opposed to anything that they believed was not directly from Russia. What was new and innovative was judged unacceptable.

British ballet, which grew from Ninette de Valois' 1926 Academy and moved to Sadler's Wells theatre in 1931, only became known as the Royal Ballet as late as 1956. The dance world in Britain was therefore relatively recent and unaccustomed to renovating and refurbishing the classics. For *Swan Lake*, and also for *Sleeping Beauty*, it possessed versions compiled by Nicholas Sergeyev after Petipa, which it believed to be the only true Russian ones.

Sergeyev, 1876–1951, had been the régisseur in charge of notation before becoming the company manager of the Imperial Ballet of St Petersburg in 1914. Fleeing Russia in the turmoil of 1919, he had brought with him the written records of the choreographies of Petipa and Ivanov. Arriving in London in 1934, he was therefore acknowledged at the time as being the only person outside Russia who could stage the classical ballets in their original Petipa/Ivanov forms. Consequently, the British were hostile to changing what they had already acquired, insisting on what they considered the 'definitive' versions. However, as in many fields, dance is never definitive but a living art, which Nureyev understood too well. But it just took a few critics with this conservative attitude to propagate the myth that Nureyev, because of the changes he had made, was a 'poor' choreographer despite all the traditional masterpieces he had brought to the West.

"One day," Charles Jude told me, "I questioned Rudolf as to why he included so many difficult, complicated short variations early on in his ballets, not only in *Swan Lake*, but also in *Sleeping Beauty* and *Romeo and Juliet*. He explained that when he was younger and dancing on tour, often for six months at a time, his schedule was so crammed that he didn't have time to train or to warm up before a performance, so he put all his lessons into his choreography. He'd frequently go through a whole lesson onstage during the first act of a ballet while still taking part, so that he'd be able to dance, for example, the demanding grand pas de deux of Act III of *Sleeping Beauty*. It's why," Jude continued, "the steps of his short variations always include what we call the petite batterie with a pirouette or two, because everything was calculated to arrive at the final pas de deux in order for him to be perfectly prepared for the great leaps or he couldn't have danced it. A dancer cannot simply stroll onto the stage and wait his turn to dance the grand pas de deux at the end. When dancers today complain they can't do the steps, they are merely saying that they are unable to accomplish Rudolf's warming-up exercises!"

One can't help wondering what all those critical of his 'fussy' choreography would have thought had they known that the origins of much of his short variations were in fact warming-up exercises. Looking closely, there are innumerable examples of this in many of his other works, including during the waltzes at the beginning of *Swan Lake*. Usually, the prince has nothing to do but be present while the company dances, but in

Nureyev's version, he devised a variation composed of petite batterie, which prepared the dancer's legs. He continued with the exact steps necessary to prepare the rest of the body, and then, when one watches carefully, there is a fairly rapid variation just before the famous slow solo, which uses up all the dancer's surplus energy, leaving them totally relaxed to perform the lovely 'melancholic' variation.

"It is a very difficult solo," Charles Jude continued. "The dancer has to stay en équilibre, and in fact, we are so exhausted at the end of all these quick movements and speed that Rudolf added beforehand, that we have just enough time during the polonaise to regain enough breath to perform it. But at this point, I discovered that I was perfectly warmed up, my surplus energy was gone and I knew exactly what I had to do and how to do it. It was extraordinary how Rudolf Nureyev prepared himself, and us, to dance in his ballets."

But as a choreographer himself, Nureyev's early downfall was that he knew too much. He'd worked with all the greatest choreographers in the world, from Martha Graham to Cunningham and Jerome Robbins, and with Roland Petit and Maurice Béjart. He knew and had absorbed so many steps that at the beginning, he didn't know where to call a halt. It always seemed that he was afraid to miss out a step, so he crammed everything in, which wasn't always, choreographically speaking, the best thing to do.

Happily, the reverse was true regarding the richness and diversity of the costumes, scenery, and staging chosen for his own wonderful vision of *Romeo and Juliet*, created for Paris in 1984. Watching it is like turning over each page of Shakespeare's play in technicolour. He had read and re-read the work incessantly, missing nothing, so much so that philistines, with scant knowledge of the drama themselves having obviously never read it, actually accused Rudolf of inventing certain scenes himself, as demonstrated by the comments that came from people who objected to the choreographer's inclusion of Juliet's bedroom scene with Death. Yet it was William Shakespeare himself and not Rudolf Nureyev who wrote Juliet's lament:

"I'll to my wedding bed
And Death, not Romeo, take my maidenhead."

Nureyev merely staged what the great bard had written.

Romeo and Juliet

Nureyev, who created the role of Kenneth MacMillan's Romeo, with Margot Fonteyn as Juliet, for the Royal Ballet in 1965, finally mounted his own version of it for the then London Festival Ballet in 1977, the same year he left Covent Garden. On a first viewing, when I saw him dance with the English ballerina Patricia Ruanne, I wasn't totally convinced by the ballet, finding parts of it heavy-handed, with its blood-stained bodies in the crypt. It was also staged at the vast Palais-des-Sports in Paris, a venue far from ideal for dance, where I was disconcerted to discover the lack of a balcony. *Romeo and Juliet* without a balcony? Moreover, the Palais-des-Sports, seating 5,000, had always struck me as a venue for sports events, and it was certainly better suited to a circus with dancing bears, dogs and ponies rather than to classical ballets.

However, seven years later he reworked it for the Paris Opera Ballet where it premiered at the prestigious Palais Garnier. In addition to the play, Rudolf had been reading every review and book he could lay his hands on, and had been constantly turning around ideas for his own version. He wanted to put it into the context of the time it was written, when death, disease and violence were rife in both Elizabethan England and Renaissance Italy. Only a few years before Shakespeare wrote the play, all the theatres in London were shut down as disease spread, and the early references in his play probably refer to the Black Death or bubonic plague, which began in the 14th century when *Romeo and Juliet* was set. Millions died.

Shakespeare, born in 1564, lived with the plague all around him, and as scholars know, his own son Hamnet died at the age of eleven. Epidemic disease was part of his life and his plays frequently evolved from his awareness of how precarious life was. Thus in a prologue to his ballet, Nureyev introduces three cloaked figures crouching on the ground playing with dice, symbolising fate, while carts piled up with dead bodies come trundling across the stage.

The ballet, set to Prokofiev's wondrous score, then opens upon a large-scale cinema-like fresco bursting with life, colour and passion, the setting being the magnificent golden palaces and sun-drenched squares of Renaissance Verona. It is a super-production with opulent scenery and costumes by Ezio Frigerio aided by Mauro Pagano, and packed with exciting and dramatic dancing for the ensembles, pas de trois, and pas de deux, as well as a refined and elegant, if somewhat surprising pas de quatre, contemporary in style, performed by Juliet, her parents and her suitor, Paris, the young nobleman her parents were forcing her to marry.

The choreography, highly expressive throughout, allows Prokofiev's vivid score to dictate the course of the action. Nureyev lets the music itself set the mood and tell each dancer what to do, while at the same time, the steps give them freedom of interpretation. No two dancers give the same performance. As Nureyev himself told me, his version, directly inspired by Franco Zeffirelli's 1968 film, which he showed to the dancers during rehearsals in addition to Shakespeare's play, recounts the story of an immature boy who grows into a man after meeting Juliet. And while Juliet, wilful and impetuous, remains the dominating motivator of the tragedy, Nureyev carefully built up the differing characters of Benvolio, Rosaline and Paris. Choosing to emphasise the social conflict of the feuding families, he also developed the personalities of the vindictive Tybalt and the light-hearted, spirited Mercutio, the two champions of the rival clans. The youth and innocence of the two adolescents are in contrast to the bawdiness of Juliet's nurse, who, as Shakespeare intended, is also an individual in her own right. They all emerge as distinctive characters within the violent brawls of members of the Capulet and Montague families in the market-place.

It was no secret that Nureyev greatly admired Jerome Robbins' film of *West Side Story*, and some aspects of it find an echo in the remarkable crowd scenes, excellent character dances and exceptional sword fights, which are most alarming when performed by outstanding interpreters. Upon seeing the ballet for the first time, with a superb Patrick Dupond in the role of Romeo, my thirteen-year-old daughter almost fainted as the fighting appeared so real. We were sitting in a front row seat at the left-hand side of the stage and had to make a quick (temporary) exit. Dupond's interpretation of Nureyev's Romeo was one of his most memorable roles.

Rudolf Nureyev's version of *Romeo and Juliet* is not only the most dramatic and most technically difficult ballet inspired by the story of the star-crossed lovers; it is also a creation full of humour, generosity, theatricality and provocation. It is a magnificent work with just that touch of vulgarity, which the American writer Anna Kisselgoff summed up as being "pure Nureyev", forgetting perhaps that it was also pure Shakespeare.

When the ballet was filmed by Alexandre Tarta over ten years later, the doomed teenagers were interpreted by the slight, fair-haired Manuel Legris, a dreamy and poetic Romeo, partnering the beguiling yet wilful Monique Loudières, with Charles Jude, unforgettable as the quarrelsome, hot-headed Tybalt. This was the cast requested by Nureyev. Legris and Loudières, pushed to their limits, took every risk possible with their sweeping leaps and heart-stopping lifts.

Possibly more than in any other of his productions, Nureyev's *Romeo and Juliet* is a ballet where he put all aspects of the theatre together, very much in the style of Roland Petit and Diaghilev before him. Not only is it his own choreography throughout, but he also worked with the painters, the set-designers and musicians to create a work of art. He told me on more than one occasion that the spectators who came to see a performance saw with their eyes, but that they had to eat too. If they didn't eat, they would be hungry when they left the theatre.

He wanted to give people a spectacular production so they would leave the theatre satisfied. His concern was to give audiences a glimpse of beauty in the dancing, the music, the costumes and the scenery as well as in the emotions. I remember him saying to me years ago that he had given many romantic ballets shape and content because he believed they were essential for the perpetuation of classical dance in the future. His story of the star-crossed lovers is no exception.

The 1995 video, *Romeo and Juliet*, with choreography by Rudolf Nureyev, filmed with the Paris Opera Ballet, is a co-production between Bel Air Media and La Sept-Arte NVC Arts.

Nevertheless, there are those nostalgic for the golden years of Covent Garden. Many still sigh with longing over Kenneth MacMillan's very different version of *Romeo and Juliet*, created twenty years earlier in 1965, with the sumptuous decor and costumes by Nicholas Georgiadis, immortalised on film with Fonteyn and Nureyev the following year. They left their mark on it for all time, as was the case with so many of the works they danced.

Nureyev's first appearance in *Romeo and Juliet*, with Margot Fonteyn as Juliet, was heart-stopping. Although he and Fonteyn danced at the premiere of the ballet, the first time I saw Kenneth MacMillan's adaptation of the story of the doomed adolescents was at a matinée performance when the leading roles were performed by Antoinette Sibley and Anthony Dowell. Dowell, one of the Royal Ballet's most outstanding dancers, was happily cast as Benvolio in the 1966 film.

However, upon seeing the ballet for the first time, I had no idea that the work had been created around Lynn Seymour partnered by Christopher Gable, and was built around the famous balcony scene. Nevertheless, as much as I had enjoyed Sibley and Dowell in the central roles, I was determined to see Fonteyn and Nureyev in the work, and it came as an emotional shock when I did. I had never seen anything like it before.

Fonteyn and Nureyev in MacMillan's Romeo and Juliet, Covent Garden 1965.
© Dundee University, The Peto Collection

Unaware of the furore around the first night cast, which by rights should apparently have been danced by Seymour and Gable since MacMillan had created the ballet around Lynn Seymour, I only knew that with Fonteyn and Nureyev in the Balcony scene, I was witnessing something beyond belief. For that impassioned pas de deux, preceded by Nureyev's solo, marked me for life. Even now, if I close my eyes, I can still see Romeo, alias Rudolf Nureyev, hair in the wind, the sleeves of his white silk shirt billowing out as he sailed through the air in the moonlight under Juliet's balcony before she ran to join him. Margot Fonteyn flew down Georgiadis' steps so fast, I don't know how those little feet managed to follow her body. They were a couple of teenagers in the passionate throes of first love. The audience was transfixed; not a sound could be heard.

Fonteyn and Nureyev in MacMillan's Romeo and Juliet, Covent Garden 1965.
© Dundee University, The Peto Collection

Would their love have developed into a mature, adult love, caring only for each other forever? Burning passion such as theirs could not survive, and Nureyev instinctively understood that Romeo's love for Juliet was something quite different from the quest for an ideal that Odette represented.

Romeo's solo and the ensuing pas de deux with Juliet was nothing less than an outpouring of raw emotion from two adolescents pitted against an unrelenting society. Fonteyn's Juliet, defying all convention, flung herself with total abandon into Romeo's arms. With his boyish charm, Nureyev, an incomparable Romeo, was everything a naive young girl could dream of.

Tragedy or not, one left the theatre, after some thirty or so curtain calls later, uplifted by the greatness and beauty of the performance. The words of Alexander Bland spring to mind again when he wrote that Fonteyn and Nureyev had a special gift of being able to translate classical movement into

Rudolf as James declaring his love to Fonteyn in La Sylphide in rehearsal. 1963.
Frederika Davis
© Sasha Davis

romantic emotion. The fire and passion of their partnership has never been equalled.

We all knew beforehand how the story would end, but nevertheless, maybe this time… The 1966 film, with Fonteyn and Nureyev, and Anthony Dowell and David Blair as Benvolio and Mercutio respectively, is wonderful but is still far from giving the emotional impact of what it actually felt to be present. Such was the partnership, that it again gave credence to the rumours that no two people could possibly dance like this if they were not as passionately involved in real life. Was this then a love affair played out onstage? Fonteyn herself has spoken of there being a special attachment between them, a deep affection or a certain ideal of love, referring to Rudolf as a 'magical being'. Certainly, seeing Nureyev dance with countless successive partners, nothing ever remotely equalled the impassioned relationship that occurred onstage in those exciting irreplaceable London years.

Marguerite and Armand

If MacMillan had created the role of Juliet around Lynn Seymour, then Frederick Ashton had had Margot Fonteyn in mind as the ill-fated heroine of Alexandre Dumas fils' 1848 book of *The Lady of the Camellias* for some time. Ashton had been intrigued by Dumas' own poignant real-life love for the 19th-century courtesan Marie Duplessis, who died of tuberculosis at the age of twenty-three. With the arrival of Rudolf Nureyev on the scene, he had his ideal Armand. Duplessis had already served as the inspiration for Verdi's Violetta in *La Traviata* and for the Garbo film *Camille*, as well as for countless stage plays and other ballets.

Now given the name of Marguerite Gautier, she and Armand Duval, Ashton's fictional characters, fall helplessly in love, but their subsequent idyll is broken during Armand's absence by the arrival of Duval's father, who convinces the young courtesan that with her immoral way of life, she is ruining Armand's future as well as his sister's chances of marriage. Breaking her heart, he thus induces her to return to her old way of life. Initially believing that Marguerite no longer loves him, Armand leaves, only learning the truth when he returns and finds her dying, and she breathes her last in his arms.

Set to a sonata by Liszt, the choreographer created a ballet for them in 1963, an important landmark in Nureyev's career as it was the first time

A rehearsal of Fonteyn and Nureyev in Frederick Ashton's Marguerite and Armand, Covent Garden 1963. The choreographer refused for the work to be performed by any other dancers in their lifetime.
© University of Dundee, The Peto Collection

a role in a full-length ballet had been created for him. Sadly, for family reasons, I had to leave London when it was programmed and subsequently never had another opportunity to see it. It was a work I only saw on film; two friends were extremely happy to benefit from my tickets. All I know first-hand of the ballet is when the Greek designer, Nicholas Georgiadis, told me how Nureyev had seized a pair of scissors at the dress rehearsal and cut off the coat-tails of the jacket that the designer Cecil Beaton had given him, with the excuse it hampered his dancing. Beaton, he recalled, was most displeased.

The ballet, which tells the story of the dying Marguerite in flashbacks, in the form of five pas de deux, has fortunately been filmed in its entirety, but during the two dancers' lifetimes, when they performed it around the world, Ashton refused to let the work be danced by any other artists. However, it was revived by Covent Garden in 2000, and then subsequently interpreted on the 10th anniversary of Nureyev's death at the Palais Garnier by Sylvie Guillem, one of Nureyev's favourite dancers, partnered by Nicolas Le Riche.

Giselle

If Siegfried's love for Odette could be said to be infatuation, and a hopeless passion of two adolescents fighting against overwhelming odds marked the story of the teenage lovers, then a different kind of love, tender, sincere and, if fate would have had it, a lifelong love could and should have been the outcome of Nureyev and Fonteyn in their interpretation of *Giselle*. The evening that I saw their performance was another never to be forgotten experience.

However, before starting to put down my memories of the first time I saw Nureyev in *Giselle*, with its haunting score by Adam and as near as perfect choreography by Coralli/Perrot, I felt I should share the reaction of my twenty-year-old self, who wrote the following words in her five-year diary shortly after returning home after the performance:

> *"Saw Fonteyn and Nureyev in 'Giselle'. It was fantastic, fantastic, fantastic! Nureyev was fantastic! Fonteyn was fantastic! Met them afterwards. They were fantastic."*

Those words, albeit over fifty years later, remain as true now as they were then, excepting that having spent the greater part of my life writing about dance, I've learned to be a little more explicit. What I saw enacted before my eyes, in those heady London days, was a gentle love story between a romantic young man and a pretty young girl that went tragically wrong. A Romantic ballet rooted firmly in the 19th century, *Giselle* is a work full of grace and generosity, with its story of love, involuntary betrayal, and forgiveness, at least in the version danced by Fonteyn and Nureyev.

Fonteyn, a delicate, lyrical Giselle, was enraptured by the slender youth she had fallen in love with. The moment the curtain rose, the complicity between them was obvious. They were teasing and playing light-heartedly with each other, totally at ease and enjoying the simple pleasure of just being together; the first act was a joy to see.

There were soaring leaps of total beauty, which seemed to defy gravity, by a young dancer who truly hovered in the air at the highest point of his jump. Everything in his dancing was so natural and so effortless. Each gesture, each movement was of such grace, at one with the score; music was translated into movement. This was not the first time, and far from the last, that I realised that Nureyev could turn poetry into motion.

They were a girl and a boy, Giselle and Albrecht, the latter escaping from his restricted life in his mother's castle, exchanging clothes with his valet in order to pass as the ordinary young adolescent he longed to be. In doing so, he had met and lost his heart to an unsophisticated, trusting young girl, and his crime, if crime there was, was to disregard their difference of class for fear of scaring her away. He was as innocent and as inexperienced as she was. Unhappily, their love affair provoked the jealousy of the gamekeeper, Hilarion, himself in love with Giselle, who exposes Albrecht's true identity, and in doing so, precipitates her death.

As I sat and watched events unfold, I didn't believe that the social context, where noblemen didn't marry peasant girls, ever occurred to Albrecht. Unlike in other productions I saw later, he wasn't a calculating young aristocrat out to seduce the first susceptible young girl he found, but just a boy deeply in love. Losing his head as well as his heart, he had no control over his feelings. Immature, thoughtless and naive he might have been, but a cold-hearted seducer he was not.

When fate caught up with him and he was recognised by a hunting party escorting the princess chosen to be his bride, he was so taken aback to be

Rudolf in rehearsal as Albrecht at Giselle's tombstone, London 1962.
© Bridgeman Images

brought face to face with her in such an unlikely place, that his first reaction was to stammer out excuses for his presence there. How was he to realise that his slight deception would end in tragedy? In that fatal, split-second moment of confusion as he turned away from Giselle, she believed he had deceived her, and having always suffered from a weak heart, she died from the shock. Albrecht's fault was not because he didn't love her, but that he concealed the fact that he was a nobleman, blinding himself to the fact that marriage between them was socially impossible.

In the second act, Albrecht, heart-broken by her death, has been found by the Wilis, a group of supernatural women betrayed by their fiancés before their wedding day. They consequently sought revenge by dancing to death any man they found between dusk and dawn. As these vengeful ghosts are dancing him to exhaustion, Giselle appears, transformed into an ethereal being, and pleads repeatedly to the Queen of the Wilis to save his life before returning to her earthly grave for eternity.

Dancing together, their lines were a natural extension of the other, their jumps landed in unison, their heads were at the same angle, their bodies as well as their hearts were complementary. No longer totally human, but part woman, part spirit, Fonteyn barely touched the ground. Rarely had I experienced such moments of utter grace and beauty. As dawn broke, Nureyev was dancing as though in a trance, his leaps lower and lower, weaker and weaker, softer and softer, his arms trembling by his side until I really thought he had died too. Part of him had.

If I had only been able to see one performance of Nureyev and Fonteyn in all my life, then it would have to have been *Giselle*.

In Covent Garden that night, every woman, man and child in the audience remained silent as the curtain came down upon a grief-stricken, exhausted Albrecht, and those not in tears or sobbing quietly into handkerchiefs could be counted on the fingers of one hand. A dancer present at rehearsals told me that even then, Fonteyn and Nureyev had seemed to be dancing "for real", and he remembered that everyone present had tears streaming down their cheeks at the end.

After a moment or two, the theatre exploded. People went wild. Flowers rained down from the balconies and bouquet after bouquet was flung onto the stage from the orchestra stalls. Curtain call after curtain call, and the applause, roars, bravos continued, as if a third act had been added on to the ballet. People at the back of stalls left their seats to run

Fonteyn and Nureyev rehearsing Act II of Giselle, London 1962.
© University of Dundee, The Peto Collection

forward to stand cheering in front of the orchestra pit, still throwing flowers which joined the bouquets raining down from the seating above. Not a soul left the theatre, but gazed enthralled at their idols, Nureyev kneeling at Fonteyn's feet. There was something so intrinsically special in their partnership, a magic that I have never seen recreated by any other couple. Not before nor since have I witnessed such a rapturous reception after any ballet, theatre or concert. As far as Nureyev's interpretation of the role goes, onstage with Margot Fonteyn, it was inconceivable he could ever have betrayed her, no matter how fine an actor he was. For, to tell the truth, he was not acting. He truly believed he was Albrecht; he was truly deeply in love with Giselle.

Thanks to the advice of a dancer friend familiar with the ballet, I had bought seats right at the front. They were almost onstage at the far right of the auditorium above the orchestra, seating which does not exist today. Not only did those seats project us into the centre of the action, but we almost had Albrecht land on our knees as he flew diagonally across the stage in a series of impossibly high grand jetés from Giselle's grave on the left, landing barely a metre away from where we sat on the right. He was strong, he was powerful, he was passionate, yet at the same time, so vulnerable. Never will either of us ever forget the expression on Nureyev's face, the wild rapture of dancing that transported him to another world. He was transfigured; he was unbelievably beautiful.

Dance to Rudolf Nureyev was not merely a passion; it was greater than life itself.

It was also on this occasion that I met him offstage for the first time. My friend Sue Jones and I had ourselves floated slowly on air out of the theatre, and as we lingered past the stage door, out came the dancer by himself, smiling at the gathering of admirers waiting for him, and patiently signing autographs. My first impression of him at this meeting has never left me. In spite of his fame and phenomenal beauty, this was a man with a natural unforced charm (I think he would intensely dislike my use of that word, but charm he had), warmth and good humour. Now dressed in his everyday clothes and devoid of make-up, he was greeting the small crowd, joking with them, and thanking them for coming. We halted, reluctant to leave and bring an end to the evening as we watched him disappear in the darkness round a corner, but as we turned and slowly began to make our way to the London tube station, a small car crawled its way towards us through the sodden cabbage leaves, rotting sprouts and other squashed vegetables littering the ground, with Rudolf at the wheel.

Nureyev drove cautiously up to us, presumably from where he'd been parked by the old Covent Garden open-air market; it had been drizzling, and the sweepers had not yet finished their clearing up. Coming to a halt when he saw us, my friend, who also happened to be extremely attractive, tall and slim in the style of Swinging London, saw her opportunity and quick as lightning, jumped onto the bonnet of his car, announcing, "My friend over there would like to speak to you!" I was hot with embarrassment, as well he knew as he turned away from her, leaned across to where I was standing on the other side of the road and wound down his window, poking his head out. He gave me that famous irresistible smile with a "What you want me to say?" in his inimitable husky Russian accent.

He was without question the most beautiful person I had ever seen, but confronted with a pair of laughing blue-grey eyes reflecting the colour of his gorgeous Russian-style fur hat in the winking light of the street lamps on that damp London night, my courage left me. I suspect that my face told him more than any words could say, and I certainly was unable to ask him anything! The first words I ever spoke to him were to thank him for giving me so much happiness. Prophetic words. In later years, I often wondered whether he remembered that meeting, but never dared to ask. One just never knew what his answer would have been to such a question. But at the time, I had the impression of having met a rather shy, caring, fun-loving person, an impression that was to prove true, be it only one side of his complex, complicated personality, over meetings during the next twenty-nine years.

Le Corsaire

Another evening at Covent Garden with Nureyev and Fonteyn that remains burned in my mind was their performance in the shortened version of *The Corsaire*, to a score by Drigo and reworked virtuoso choreography by Petipa and Chabukiani, with more than a few 'touches' by Nureyev himself. Curiously, the film *An Evening with the Royal Ballet* credits the choreography to Nureyev alone. It was a pas de deux from a ballet based on Lord Byron's poem of the same name, undisputedly associated with him since he had interpreted the work for the 1958 Moscow National Classical Ballet Contest, following which he had been offered contracts as a soloist both at the Bolshoi and the Stanislavsky Ballet company. However, upon being invited to dance *Laurencia* with the Kirov's senior ballerina, Natalia Dudinskaya, in St Petersburg in the company he had dreamed of all his life, there was no hesitation. The Kirov it was.

Le Corsaire was a ballet on which he was to forever leave his mark. Again, I remember my seat: third row centre stalls.

Although the ballet lasted only a magical twelve minutes, the rapturous almost hysterical acclaim continued for well over half an hour more, with flowers and bouquets raining down from the seating above, as had become usual with each of their performances. Fonteyn and Nureyev had a most incredible rapport with those London audiences who just would not let the pair go and it got to the point when their curtain calls really did become a final act to the ballet they'd been dancing. The curtain calls, as in this case, sometimes lasted longer than the ballet itself. The cheers, the never-ending applause and the stamping of feet would mingle in a single deafening roar. In later years, in other theatres with other dancers, I often thought back to this when audiences applauded the performance they'd seen with genuine enthusiasm, but then were all too ready to scurry off home as soon as the curtain fell. This never happened at any Fonteyn and Nureyev performance, when spectators were invariably reluctant to leave the theatre, often sinking back in their seats after the final curtain in order to get their breath back! Returning to reality was never easy.

First conceived as a full-length work and in the repertoire of both American Ballet Theatre and the Bolshoi, *The Corsaire* tells the story of Medora who is sold as a slave girl to the lecherous Pasha Seyd, but is rescued by the handsome, swashbuckling pirate Conrad, who is passionately in love with her. In its shortened form, frequently performed as a show-piece throughout the world, it is full of huge, soaring jumps and intricate twisting turns in the air, which, with Nureyev's exceptional grace and softness contrasting with his long, powerful, high grand jetés, had the audience gasping for breath as he hovered motionless in the air, legs crossed beneath him as if for all the world he was sitting on one of his own oriental flying carpets.

"But he's flying," my granddaughter gasped recently, the first time she saw him dance on the DVD of *An Evening with the Royal Ballet*.

Rudolf in Le Corsaire, London 1962: 'An evening with the Royal Ballet'.
© courtesy Ronald Grant archive/Mary Evans

Rudolf in Le Corsaire. First performance in London, 1962.
Photograph taken in Paris, early 1970s.
© Francette Levieux/CNCS

No one present on that occasion in London could ever forget the sheer impact of seeing this seductive, bare-chested young man blaze across the stage, silken trousers billowing, his dark blonde hair surmounted by a golden circlet, as he launched into a bewildering solo full of tremendous, twisting leaps, contrasting with the graceful, oriental softness of his arms. His heart was bursting with romantic fire as with a final flourish he flung himself down at Fonteyn's feet in a fusion of total submission and sensuous arrogance before the delicate tranquillity of the woman he adored. This was a love raised to the level of worship. No dreamy prince or thoughtless young nobleman here.

Then after, as always, he would acknowledge the bravos and cheers of the audience with a slow bow from the waist, often raising one arm and then the other, his eyes sweeping round the theatre. In later years I was to see this same variation performed by many dancers on different occasions, but never ever with the same romantic fire, never remotely with the same intensity, and never ever with the same supple grace. In fact, I never saw Conrad again. No other dancer I have ever seen combined the expressive beauty of Nureyev's body together with his magnetic, sensuous charm.

What the audience also witnessed was the unique partnership with Margot Fonteyn, a combination of her cool, refined authority with the hot-blooded, temperamental Tartar. We saw an impassioned love story enacted out onstage, which once again gave credit to the rumours that two people could not possibly dance this way unless they were also intimately involved offstage. No matter that Fonteyn was married and rumours were rife that Nureyev was in love with the Danish dancer Erik Bruhn. There was a physical current that passed not only between the two dancers, but which was projected from the stage to the spectators. There was a connection between the couple onstage and their audience, albeit fleeting.

Paradise Lost

Paradise Lost, commissioned in 1967 by Covent Garden from the French choreographer Roland Petit, proved to be quite a different experience, and one I was in not too much of a hurry to repeat despite the spectacular choreography.

Petit had already worked with Nureyev the preceding year, when his 1946 ballet, *Le Jeune Homme et La Mort*, had been filmed with the Russian dancer.

Set to Bach's *Passacaglia and Fugue* with a libretto written by Jean Cocteau and created for Jean Babilée, one of the first, forceful contemporary classical dancers, it tells the story of a young man driven to suicide by his faithless lover. Full of everyday movements charged with electricity, it was something quite new for Nureyev, more used to dancing the traditional princes in classical ballets, and consequently Petit adapted it for Rudolf's more classical technique. To my knowledge, Nureyev never danced it onstage, certainly not in London.

However, with *Paradise Lost*, Petit wished to go much further away from ballerinas in tutus, Tchaikovsky, and the Petipa style in general. He therefore set his ballet to a score by Benjamin Constant and completed it with an eye-popping 1960s decor by the Realist painter Martial Raysse, as an added attraction for a forthcoming American tour. Petit had decided to create a contemporary work for the star couple, breaking away from their romantic classical style, and producing a work in tune with the nightclubs of Swinging London, a fusion of classical ballet, flashing lights and pop art.

Naive as I was, I hurried to Covent Garden with the preconceived idea that the ballet was based on John Milton's immortal poem where the central theme was the fall of Man via the revenge of the evil archangel, Satan. Satan, having been cast out of Heaven by God, plotted to destroy his maker's creation of perfect happiness of Man and Woman in the Garden of Eden. Adam, provoked by Eve, was seduced into eating an apple off the forbidden Tree of Knowledge. Indeed, a grandiose theme.

Wrong. The work was not directly based on Milton's poem, but rather on one by the French writer Jean Cau, and what we saw was a modern retelling of Milton's story of Adam and Eve. To begin with, I recollect being taken aback by the costumes, seeing the slight, exquisite frame of Margot Fonteyn, the 'grande dame' of the Royal Ballet, attired in an unflattering sort of tutu, which pulled uncomfortably across her crotch. It was a sort of miniskirt made out of white vinyl, and I wondered how on earth she could move in it, let alone dance. It seemed so out of keeping to see her, the essence of refinement and femininity decked out in this plastic mini skirt, more mini than skirt, and decidedly shorter than my own, as I remember glancing down. I was wearing a pale blue, high-necked Mary Quant mini. This was Carnaby Street, the Beatles, and here we were at Covent Garden confronted with a work in keeping with London in the Swinging Sixties. Why not? Why not indeed, but this was Fonteyn and Nureyev.

It was also the first time I regretted my front stalls seat, giving a bird's eye

Fonteyn in her 'mini-mini' with Nureyev in Paradise Lost, taken at the
Palais Garnier in Paris in January 1967.
© Colette Masson/Roger Viollet

view of all the pseudo sexy, acrobatic and complicated movements invented by Petit, which I would have preferred to see from the amphitheatre. Although time has blurred any clear remembrance of the actual choreography as such, including the presence of any other dancers, I recall being fascinated watching this legendary pair in the turning, twisting, backwards and forwards arabesques and slow somersaults, completely alien to anything we'd seen before. To tell the truth, they were magnificent! Moreover, I had the impression they were really enjoying themselves. The fact that the only clue to what all this activity was about was the title seemed almost irrelevant.

There were abundant flashing neon lights, spectacular leaps and bounds from Nureyev and one unforgettable instant when he ran swiftly round the stage before throwing himself head first through a gap in the red, giant-sized Andy Warhol style lips at the back of the stage. It was quite weird to see a pair of legs waving around in the air. The sudden appearance of Fonteyn onstage also took one aback as she inexplicably popped out of Nureyev's side, the only indication that she was perhaps Eve.

One left the theatre somewhat bemused. Fonteyn was stunning in a role so contrary to everything I'd seen her in before, while Nureyev was mesmerising, his power, lightness, and sheer weightlessness accomplishing feats an Olympic gymnast would have been proud of, and yet, despite the compelling beauty of the two dancers, the dominant emotion one was left with was one of mingled surprise and emptiness. From the joyful expression on his face, it was evident Nureyev was revelling in the choreography, but then the words of a film I'd recently seen came to mind: "What's it all about, Alfie?" I never got round to asking Roland Petit the same question.

Surprisingly, the ballet was so well-received by critics and public alike that Petit was invited to create a second work for Fonteyn and Nureyev the following year, and so, undeterred, back I went to see *Pelléas and Mélisande*. Perhaps learning a lesson from *Paradise Lost*, I made sure my seat was much further back, with the consequence that my clearest souvenir remains that of Jacques Dupont's extravagant decor. While I retain memories of leafy foliage mingled with Mélisande's long, undulating hair, the choreography and accompanying intricacies of the ballet itself have faded. Ostensibly the work, set to a score by Schoenberg, was woven around the love story of the hero, the heroine, and Pelléas' jealous brother. But the only memory I have of the dance itself is of the pair of dancers dragging each other around the stage on their bottoms.

It gives me far more pleasure to recall the magic of the hauntingly lovely *Kingdom of the Shades*, taken from Petipa's great 19th-century masterpiece *The Bayadère*, music Minkus, which Nureyev mounted for the Royal Ballet in 1963, the first of his big, beautiful reconstructions. He'd danced the role of Solor, the Indian warrior, in St Petersburg in 1959 and again in Paris in 1961, and the ballet, never seen in the West before, showed the extent of his phenomenal memory. He had not only absorbed his own roles from his years with the Kirov, but also those of all the other dancers as well.

The London audience was transported the instant the curtain rose on an unending stream of the spirits of long-dead temple dancers in glistening white tutus, as one by one, hypnotically repeating slow arabesques, the dancers descended from a ramp at the back of the stage on their journey down from the heights of the Himalayan mountains. It is a showcase for the corps de ballet, one of the loveliest white acts in the history of dance; a pure classical jewel.

Unaware at the time that the ballet was simply the third act of *La Bayadère*, a full-length four-act ballet, I found it even more astounding when Nureyev as the faithless Solor ran on, to witness the emotion emanating from the performance of such a short piece, ostensibly written as a vehicle for the corps de ballet, but taken out of context and tagged on to the end of a programme of three other short works. What was also most unusual was the tide of mounting fever inside the theatre beforehand. The audience was as if electrified even before its stars came on, and went wild at the end. It was in vain that the company fielded excellent young dancers in the preceding works presented, for everyone was geared up to and waiting to see their two idols in this now famous show-piece. Word had got around that if there was only one thing to be seen in London that season, it was Fonteyn and Nureyev in *The Kingdom of the Shades*, first staged by the Royal Ballet in 1963.

Fonteyn and Nureyev in The Kingdom of the Shades. 1963. Frederika Davis
© Sasha Davis

I eagerly anticipated seeing the complete ballet… but had to wait for almost thirty years, as Covent Garden rejected Rudolf's dream of mounting it in London, reluctant to entrust a full-length work to a twenty-five-year-old boy. Frederick Ashton had invited 'the boy' to reconstruct a short work, but that was as far as it went. London's loss proved to be Paris' gain, for a magnificent version of the ballet, complete with the original score, was eventually programmed in the French capital in 1992, barely three months before Nureyev's death.

Les Sylphides

It was quite soon after my arrival in London that I saw Nureyev with Fonteyn in *Les Sylphides*, and yet again, it was a moment when they made time stand still for all who were there. The ballet, a suite of exquisite, dreamlike dances, takes place on a moonlit stage while the rest of the world gradually drifts away. Suspended in time, I could have remained in my seat forever.

I had never seen the ballet before, knew nothing about it, had no programme, and so never knew that the 'hero', so dreamily poetical, was indeed a poet. I just remember feeling a spiritual uplifting, such deep happiness as I gazed in disbelief at Fonteyn's softly flowing movements and lovely expressive face. As for Nureyev, each of his movements to Chopin's immortal score was grace itself. I recollect being mesmerised by the sheer, effortless beauty of his arms and hands. He was soft, weightless, mystical, yet at the same time so impossibly romantic that it was hard to realise that something so excruciatingly beautiful as their dancing could exist. I was so deeply marked by such a spiritual experience that it remains one of those rare ballets I have never been able to see again. The Sylphides in their long white tutus had cast a spell and taken spectators to other realms.

I later learned that the ballet, choreographed by Michel Fokine, had been brought to the West by Diaghilev and had been in the Royal Ballet's repertoire since its early beginnings. The work has been immortalised in the film *An Evening with the Royal Ballet*. It was seen by Alice, my four-year-old granddaughter, who immediately discarded her 'Maisies' and 'Doras' in favour of watching 'the poet in the forest with the fairies' instead. She remains totally enraptured by it and has since begun dance lessons.

Nureyev and Fonteyn in Les Sylphides:
'An evening with the Royal Ballet' 1963.
© courtesy Ronald Grant archives/Mary Evans

Over time, my memories have all but eliminated Nureyev's roles in Ashton's short works, ballets such as the revival in 1968 of *Birthday Offering*, which was on one of the last occasions I saw Fonteyn and Nureyev dance together. Unfortunately, all I retain of this work, set to a fairly unremarkable score by Glazunov, is of Rudolf Nureyev rushing aimlessly around the stage in various tricky, rather pointless steps. One could admire his quick-fire footwork, but little else. I later learned that it had been created in 1956 to celebrate twenty-five years of British ballet, but the main purpose it served when I saw it was the occasion it gave to see the legendary pair dancing together.

Neither do I remember much about Ashton's 1968 *Jazz Calendar*, set to a score by Richard Rodney Bennett, and performed by fourteen dancers, apart from the fact that Rudolf wanted so much to be seen as just one of them. But he wasn't. Although it was based on the children's nursery rhyme 'Monday's Child', the audience was waiting patiently for the sequence 'Friday's child', where the child is "loving and giving". On the evening I went, he partnered a young dancer, Marilyn Trounson. But as hard as Nureyev tried to be an integral part of the company and blend in, he didn't, he couldn't. With that expressive face he had, plus his incomparable training, he stuck out like a sore thumb! He was simply better than anyone else. The moment he stepped onstage, all eyes were on him. Worse. Everyone was just waiting to see him, the superstar despite himself.

Apart from Nureyev and Trounson, the only other parts of the ballet I remember were the effective stage designs by Derek Jarman, which, like *Paradise Lost* the year before, again typified London in the days of the 'Swinging Sixties'.

It must be said that Nureyev did not simply "dance princes", to use Balanchine's dismissive words. He interpreted and lived each 'prince' differently each and every time I saw him. Fascination, idealism, even obsession personify his love for Odette, a love doomed to disintegrate because it never really existed.

Not so Albrecht's love for Giselle. Having broken away from the heavy restraints of his life in the castle, Albrecht cast aside his sword and cloak, and wandered out to be himself. One can have little doubt, given his interpretation of the role, that in other times, Albrecht would have loved, cared for and cherished Giselle for the rest of his life.

Not so the duplicitous Solor, hero of *The Bayadère*, out for the main chance as soon as he was confronted with the prospect of a lucrative future as the Rajah's son-in-law. The exquisite pas de deux of the *Kingdom of the Shades* is nothing less than that of a guilty man pleading for forgiveness and wanting back that which he has lost.

Sleeping Beauty

Of all Petipa's ballets, *Sleeping Beauty* is the classic story with the handsome prince marrying the pretty princess and living happily ever after. In *The Nutcracker*, Clara is a child and the ending but a dream, whereas in *Raymonda*, I have long thought that the heroine's heart lay more with the seductive Saracen knight, killed in a duel, than the unknown nobleman she was destined to marry.

Created by Marius Petipa for the Maryinsky in 1890, *Sleeping Beauty* is, in Nureyev's own words, "the ballet of ballets", the apotheosis of the Maryinsky/Kirov style, which, for reasons unknown, I first saw in Paris and not London. Rudolf danced the ballet all over the world and with many different partners, usually his own version which he first mounted for La Scala in 1966, when Georgiadis set the work in 18th-century Versailles. It was a ballet he perfected over the years, developing the role of the prince, but without changing a step of Petipa's choreography. He mounted productions in Vienna, Berlin and Canada before his final, sumptuous production for the Paris Opera in 1989.

As the handsome Prince Desiré in his reworked 1975 production of *Sleeping Beauty*, decor and costumes always by Nicholas Georgiadis, seen a few years later at the Palais-des-Sports in Paris, he partnered Eva Evdokimova, the American Swiss-born ballerina. Here he personified Balanchine's image of the perfect fairy-tale prince, and I believe the whole auditorium fell in love with him. It was certainly the case for my six-year-old daughter, who, gazing ecstatically up at his face at the end, declared she would marry him when she grew up. With that idea in mind, she began dance lessons the following week.

No one who saw Rudolf Nureyev in the coda of Act III of *Sleeping Beauty*, wherever it was in the world, and whether the Tartar dancer was twenty-six, thirty-six or forty-six at the time, could ever forget him. As soon as I hear the music, I can still see him erupting onstage in my mind's eye, dominating space and electrifying audiences, the epitome of romanticism. However… the perfect cast for *Sleeping Beauty* isn't always obvious, for how often have I heard a ballerina bewail the partner she was cast to dance with and how, upon awakening after one hundred years, instead of the love at first sight demanded by the libretto, she had felt like running away from the kiss of some insipid young man. That would never have happened to Nureyev.

Nor would that have happened to the handsome nineteen-year-old British dancer Paul Clarke, who had hoped so much to dance the role of the prince at the Royal Ballet himself. Tragically, his dream was not fulfilled as shortly after he had moved from Covent Garden to the then Festival Ballet to take up the post of principal dancer, his life, at twenty-eight, ended abruptly with a heart attack.

Paul Clarke

I first met Clarke after he had given a performance of *The Two Pigeons* in Manchester alongside David Wall and Alfreda Thorogood. All three of them, together with Patricia Ruanne, formed part of the Royal Ballet's then second company, when promising young dancers would go on tour. Back in London, when not dancing himself, Paul would be watching other performances, and on the occasions I was there too, we fell into the habit of chatting to each other in the crush bar at Covent Garden. As our friendship grew, we would discuss every aspect of the performances we had seen, from the choreography and casts as well as to the way the orchestra had played, which was not always to our liking. He was thrilled to have danced the pas de six in a 1968 performance of *Swan Lake*, where he said that it had been so hard to drag his eyes away from Fonteyn and Nureyev.

"There is simply no one like Rudolf Nureyev here; he is just outstandingly better than anyone else," I recall him saying. Paul told me about the initial resentment from some of the older male principals who saw their noses being pushed out. "But for us younger members of the company," he said, "his presence was amazing. He completely changed the way people viewed male dancers, and I can't over-emphasise the impact of his extraordinary performances… his suspension in the air at the height of his jump beggars belief! He hung in the air. I was right there. I saw it; I was watching from the corner of my eye."

Paul knew how much I loved Nureyev and so talked about him, telling me everything the fiery Tartar had brought to the British dancers, and not only by just being there in class where he was always trying to be one of them when he was so much more. I remember him laughing as he said that. He related how Rudolf was so ready to help them, to share all his knowledge and give them advice so that they could also have the benefit of his wonderful training. Even those dancers who were envious of him learned so much.

It was after Clarke had danced in John Cranko's *Pineapple Poll*, which we both found disappointing despite the fact we both admired Cranko, that he began to urge me to write about dance, the first person to do so. But, inevitably, our conversation would return to Rudolf Nureyev, to whom, Paul believed, Covent Garden owed an immense debt. I recall him saying fervently how grateful he was to be there at that time. Everyone, he told me, benefited from his presence. "It was as though he cast a spell on us all" were the words he used, and which I noted in my five-year diary.

Certainly, such was the fervour of Nureyev's presence in the company, that a whole new audience of people who had never set foot in a theatre before was brought to dance. He was ballet's first pop star. As Clarke put it, audiences were transfixed by him; they came to see him, mesmerised by what can only be called his incomparable stage personality.

He repeated everything that had already been said before, of the endless curtain calls and bouquets of flowers cascading down from those seated up top, one being deafened by the thunderous shouts and cheers, not only after one specific performance, but after them all. Sometimes, he recalled, Nureyev would run back onto the stage and at other times stroll slowly, but almost always a huge grin would creep across his face, as he'd raise his arm in a sweeping gesture to acknowledge his audience. But the first person he would turn to was always Margot Fonteyn.

Sasha Davis

Sasha Davis, the daughter of Frederika Davis, one of Nureyev's favourite photographers, was also present during London's Golden Years. She recounted some of her mother's stories to me, recalling the many occasions she met him at her home.

"My mother loved him," she said, "and the liking was reciprocal. He trusted her, he smiled in amusement when she had her camera out, and was always joking with her. He used to come to our house and was so much fun, which wasn't always the case when he was in rehearsal and some of the other dancers weren't working properly. Then we saw his prickly temperament! The lovely man we knew at home became someone really not nice when some dancers weren't listening to him.

"I also remember my mother telling me that when she first saw him dance in the 1960s, she had never seen anything like it before. It was totally unbelievable. She said that there was no one remotely like him at Covent Garden. He brought another dimension to the classics. With his work he was a perfectionist, constantly striving for perfection with himself and with others, but there was a wariness in him that extended to journalists as well as photographers, particularly as regards the pushy, self-assertive ones, the opposite to my mother."

That he appreciated Frederika Davis, described by her daughter as a gentle, softly spoken person, is obvious in the number of natural, relaxed photographs she was able to take offstage and on, several of which I'm fortunate to publish in this book.

Part II

The Intervening Years
1969–1982

Petrushka

I happened to be in Paris towards the end of 1969, at the same time that Nureyev was appearing at the Palais Garnier with the Paris Opera Ballet in Fokine's *Petrushka*, a ballet that has justifiably been part of the company's repertoire since 1948. Great was my delight when I discovered that my future mother-in-law, knowing about my love of dance, had bought tickets for his performance... the ninth row of the orchestra stalls. However, the poor woman, who had seen Nureyev dance on his arrival in Paris in 1961, was, unlike myself, bitterly disappointed. "But he danced like a bird when I saw him before," she whispered, shifting uneasily in her seat as she gazed in dismay at the misshapen, pathetic figure shuffling across the stage, disbelieving me when I assured her, that yes indeed, it was Nureyev.

Whether she remembered him from the Bluebird pas de deux, or had witnessed his unforgettable interpretation of Solor in *The Bayadère* in 1961 when he appeared with the Kirov company, I never did find out, but what was clear is that she had imagined Petrushka to be some sort of exotic Russian prince! What she didn't expect was to see her god, Rudolf Nureyev, in the role of a spurned, broken-down and broken-hearted clown. For my part, although I have never considered Petrushka one of his greatest roles, I watched, mesmerised, as the cruel little drama unfolded.

How on earth had this powerful, electrifying dancer, a glorious 19th-century prince, managed to transform himself into this plaintive, rejected creature, his strong-featured handsome face unrecognisable beneath layers of heavy distorting make-up? By what alchemy was he able to cast a blow to one's heart, so that all those who were watching suffered almost as much as he did upon witnessing his unrequited love affair and subsequent demise?

Petrushka, created in 1911, one of the most Russian of Russian ballets, is set to choreography by Fokine, a strident and controversial score by Stravinsky, and evocative set designs by the painter Alexandre Benois. Opening on the day of a fun fair, with its roundabout, Ferris wheel and puppet theatre, in a market square in St Petersburg, it tells the story of three puppets who are given a fictional inner life. Petrushka is in love with the ballerina, who in turn is in love with the Moor, a gross, boorish character who, in a fit of jealousy, ends up killing our unsung hero. It is far from being a mere fairy story, for the work is rooted in the real world as well as in the Slav soul, with the joyful crowds at the fair in dramatic contrast to the heartless events taking place within the little theatre.

One is left with the sensation that his soul triumphs at the end, as throughout Nureyev's moving performance, Petrushka's spirit remains indestructible.

However, that was not the only feeling that I got as I gazed around the imposing, lavishly decorated Palais Garnier. Apart from Nureyev's performance, I had been taken aback by the lacklustre dancing I saw from the French company, particularly from the corps de ballet, the heart of any company. Fresh from the golden years of the Royal Ballet in London and spoiled as I was by the performances of Fonteyn and Nureyev, I was surprised by the mannered and frequently technically weak dancing I'd witnessed.

The building, which Nureyev was to call his "Palace of Dance", is more than impressive. It is magnificent, and my first thought upon leaving was that this splendid theatre deserved a company to match.

The Palais Garnier

While the Paris Opera Ballet can trace its beginnings back to 1669, under King Louis XIV, it wasn't until 1858 that Napoleon III, Bonaparte's nephew, chose to build a grandiose lyric and dance theatre, one which would amply reflect his glory and the prosperity of his reign. After scrutinising more than 170 projects, including one by Barry, architect of London's Royal Opera House, Baron Haussmann, Prefect of Paris, entrusted the project of the new Opera to thirty-one-year-old Charles Garnier, whose design was unanimously declared the most suitable. Garnier, who had studied at the School of Fine Arts in Paris before spending five years in Rome, and had also built the Casino of Monte Carlo as well as the Observatory of Nice, was inspired by the Grand Theatre of Bordeaux and the elegant French and Italian residences of the 17th and 18th centuries.

The theatre, or more correctly, the palace, was meant not only to be seen, but to be seen in, and took fourteen years to be completed. Work had been slowed down by the water-logged ground, and the large reservoir, built twenty metres under the stage, was later metamorphosed into an underground lake, providing the setting for Gaston Leroux's *Phantom of the Opera*.

Garnier's vision was labelled baroque because of its gorgeous ornamentation. He hired the finest craftsmen and the most accomplished mosaicists of his day. No fewer than thirty renowned painters and seventy-three sculptors decorated the seemingly endless exterior and interior facades. Garnier himself is said to have designed the eight ton chandelier in the auditorium with its 400 lights, described by him as being "a burst of fire and diamonds". Notwithstanding his description, when taking my seat nowadays, I still steal a cautious glance at the lighting, thankful I am not seated below it…

Outside, high on the rooftops, the monumental building is dominated by a beautiful bronze statue of Apollo, god of the sun, music, and patron of the arts. It's not only symbolic and decorative. In the centre of his golden lyre, which the god holds high over the city, there is a lightning conductor, making him the protector, not only of the building, but also of the dance troupe below. The statue, restored some years ago together with its two accompanying Muses, was completed for the inauguration of Europe's most magnificent Opera house on January 5th, 1875, in the presence of the French President MacMahon, King Alphonse of Spain and the Lord Mayor of London.

Garnier oversaw all the work himself, instructing the artists and creating his dream of a harmonious, glittering and magical 'Palace of Dance', and defending them when scandals arose, as when a bottle of ink was hurled at Carpeaux' statue of a dancing group on the front facade at its unveiling

The Palais Garnier front and Grand Foyer

in July 1869. "Too erotic!" the crowds roared. Six years earlier, Garnier had proposed four subjects for the front entrance: harmony, completed by Jouffrey, drama by Perraud, music by Guillaume, and dance by Carpeaux. All the sculptors composed groups of three figures, excepting Carpeaux who worked secretly under a wooden hoarding to create a masterpiece of four lascivious Bacchae dancing around a central figure with yet another figure lying prostrate at its feet.

"It's an insult to common decency" the press complained, but when the 1870 war with Prussia broke out, it gave them something else to think about, and the unfinished building was used as a hospital. In 1964, the original statue was moved to the Orsay museum where it can be seen today, to be replaced by a copy made by Paul Belmondo, father of the late popular French actor Jean-Paul Belmondo.

Also in 1964, that long-ago scandal was replaced by another. De Gaulle's Minister of Culture, André Malraux, commissioned the seventy-seven-year-old Marc Chagall to paint a new ceiling in the auditorium, no doubt considering the original, by Lenepveu, dull and, quite frankly, nondescript; a view I share. Chagall's ceiling, spectacular and luminous, but much criticised at the time as being out of keeping with the rest of the building, has today become almost as famous as the theatre, but less for the scandal it caused at the time, and more for the lyrical beauty of the work. In fact, it is truly worth one's while to buy a ticket for 'up top' in the amphitheatre or upper galleries just to gaze one's fill at the sumptuous painting.

Chagall's masterpiece, for which he refused all payment, is a tribute to the great musicians and composers of opera and ballet scores, to which he added his own favourites, Beethoven, Gluck, Verdi and Bizet above the chandelier (hence the attraction of viewing the work from the amphitheatre). Mussorgsky (*Boris Godunov*) and Mozart (*The Magic Flute*), are depicted in blue, Rameau and Debussy (*Pelléas and Mélisande*) are in white, Wagner (*Tristan and Isolde*) and Berlioz (*Romeo and Juliet*) are in green, while two of Nureyev's favourite dance composers, Tchaikovsky (*Swan Lake*) and Stravinsky (*Firebird*), are in yellow and red respectively. I doubt that Nureyev minded too much that Prokofiev, his third musical god as far as dance was concerned, wasn't represented. He was too pleased to take over the harmonious, glittering and magical 'Palace of Dance'.

However, Martine Kahane, the former curator of the Opera's Library and Museum and head of the Cultural Service, was none too happy. "The

Farewell performance of Manuel Legris at the Palais Garnier, with a glimpse of Chagall's ceiling.
© Sébastien Mathé

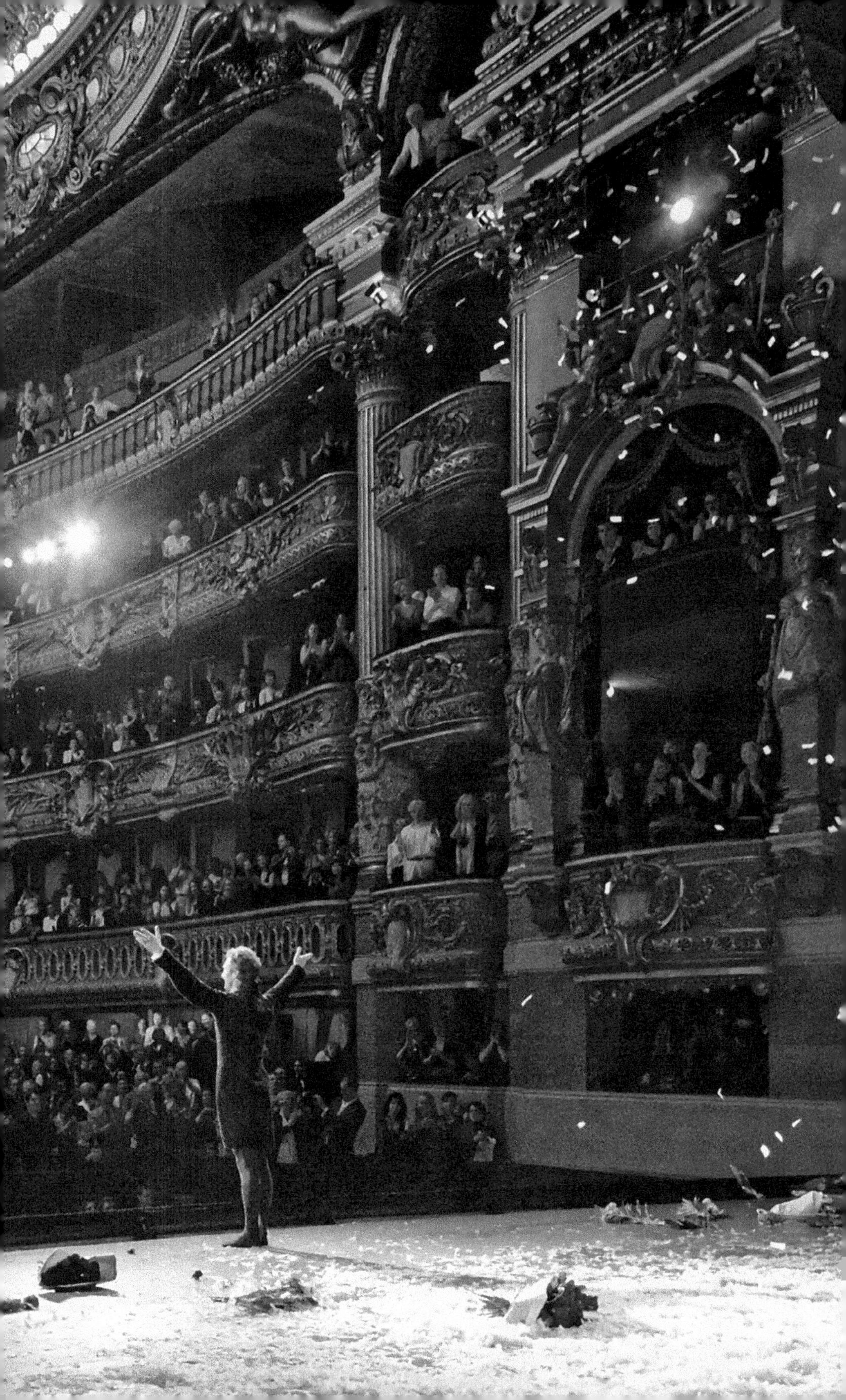

colours are too garish," she told me. "They tend to make the rest of the theatre look drab. The Opera is 19th century and, moreover, Chagall painted on a plastic surface a few centimetres on top of the original ceiling by Lenepveu which illustrates the Muses and the Hours of the Day and Night, a work I doubt we'll ever see again.

"Unfortunately," she said, sighing, "it's here to stay, and it's a pity. No one will be able to see Lenepveu's ceiling until the work by Chagall is taken away, maybe in 300 or 400 years' time, so it's not our problem…"

Behind the scenes there are twelve miles of long dark corridors, many of which lead to a labyrinth of dressing rooms, and yet before Nureyev's arrival as artistic director in 1983, there were only five small rehearsal rooms, a fact that goes partially to explaining the mediocre level of the company before he came.

The splendour of the public areas is also a reminder that the Palais Garnier was built not only for dance and lyric opera, but was a fashionable meeting place for Le Tout Paris. During La Belle Epoque, it was not infrequent for opera goers to stroll around the magnificent Grand Foyer, itself inspired by the Hall of Mirrors at Versailles, or the splendid Foyer de la Danse at the back of the stage, while the corps de ballet performed to give the ballerina a rest between appearances.

The Foyer de la Danse, described as a gilded jewel box and decorated with over fifty portraits, was technically a meeting place as well as a rehearsal room. Situated at the back of the main stage, it is used for the company's grand défilé, which opens each season, and can be opened up for exceptional decor, which was the case with Nureyev's 1985 production of *The Nutcracker*. Myriads of golden butterflies, symbolising dance, flutter along the walls, chased by cupids frolicking among the ornate vine-encrusted columns, while bells, pine cones, masks and lyres crowd every corner. Legend has it that these butterflies did not represent the ballerinas but rather the 'abonnés' who hovered incessantly around them, and that is why Serge Lifar, who laid the foundations for Nureyev's later renovation of the troupe, closed this area to the public.

The monumental Main Staircase is particularly impressive and is possibly the most sumptuous attraction, classically built, and opulent as the times demanded. It is lavishly decorated and notable for the handrails in onyx imported from Algeria. And just as Nureyev was criticised for his choreography packed with so many steps, so was Garnier before him for his excessive use of ornament, for the staircase is composed of no less than thirty-three different kinds of coloured marble. I have frequently amused myself in attempting to count them all on various occasions. The dark green marble was imported from Sweden, red marble from Finland, black from Denmark, brocatelle from Spain, granite from Aberdeen, purple from Italy, yellow from Siena and white from France. Their smoothness and rich softness is in striking contrast to the more vivid, showy mosaic that covers the ceiling of the Avant Foyer.

Garnier had travelled extensively in Italy, visiting Rome, Venice and Florence, as well as Constantinople where he had admired the mosaics. To fulfil his dream of gorgeously coloured scenes in a gold background, he brought two mosaicists, the Facchina brothers, from Venice. They taught their techniques to French craftsmen from the Manufacture de Sèvres, a porcelain works that was the only building in Paris with this lavish style of decoration. The small cubes of enamel (glazed ceramic) were imported from Venice and a new technique used to fix them on the ceiling. They were assembled on sheets of paper and the square thus obtained cemented on the ceiling, while the paper holding the small, jewel-like coloured stones was simply washed away.

Their charm and beauty was only enhanced by their small irregularities. The figures, designed by Salviati, were painted by de Curzon, but the overall design was by Garnier, who considered the mosaics and the marble the Opera's most outstanding features. Indeed, first gazing at the chandelier and then at the mosaic ceiling, one left a performance at the Palais Garnier with a stiff neck, particularly in the 1970s when the splendour of the surroundings outshone the productions onstage.

Once at the top of the staircase, one reaches the sumptuous Main Foyer, opulent, majestic and grandiose. It is a festive gallery, which vies with the Hall of Mirrors in Versailles, and boasts one of the last painted ceilings in Paris. Taking the artist, Paul Baudry, eight years to complete, it is inspired unsurprisingly by music, as Baudry was also an accomplished violinist. He had studied painting under Antoine Sartoris, and had spent time studying Michelangelo's frescoes in the Sistine Chapel, so this was a ceiling to be admired from afar.

The walls of the refreshment room, known as La Rotonde du Glacier, are decorated by eight superb tapestries representing tea, liqueur, coffee, orange juice, and then, no one knows why, a tapestry of fishing and hunting.

The whole interior is dominated by the motif of Apollo's lyre, the symbol of music, in addition to a multitude of other motifs borrowed equally from classical Greek tradition to the Renaissance. Added to Garnier's own imagination, they all illustrate biblical, mythological and allegorical scenes. If the lavish statues and eagles show Napoleon lurking nearby, then the foliage, flowers, masks and lyres evoke poetry, music, and drama, while the waving palms remind one that all we see is in order to glorify the greatest of the world's composers.

Would the level of the company ever match the splendour of its surroundings? Little did I know that I would have to wait for almost a quarter of a century for that to come true. When it did, it was certainly worth the wait.

Don Quixote

In 1970, I left London for New York, anxious to discover the magic of Balanchine and his New York City Ballet. Even though I was to fall in love with Gelsey Kirkland and Edward Villella, a man as charming and handsome offstage as on, the ballet that marked me the most in 1971 was Rudolf Nureyev's own fun-loving, large-scale production of *Don Quixote*, which I actually saw in Boston when he appeared there with the Australian Ballet, partnered by Lucette Aldous in the role of Kitri.

It was over the next decade, left with fewer performances in London, that Nureyev would appear in productions with countless

Rudolf in 1972 at Heathrow airport wearing a favourite black leather outfit, his hat being made of fake fur. © PA images

lesser known companies, giving them engagements they probably would not have had without him. His guest appearances drew in a paying audience who went to see this superstar they'd heard about, but it wasn't only the international publicity that they got when they were invited to go on foreign tours, but more that Rudolf's presence set an example to the whole troupe. When he was there, the level of the dancers rose. He galvanised them. Such was the case with the Australian Ballet, which, despite being an excellent company, would probably not have been invited to tour the US had Nureyev not been guesting with them.

Nureyev had read *Don Quixote*, Cervantes' famous novel, from cover to cover. So he knew exactly what he wanted when he commissioned John Lanchbery to 'lighten' the Minkus score for Petipa's 1870 ballet, which was centred around the love affair of Kitri and Basilio, an episode taken from the second volume of the book. His *Don Quixote* is a light-hearted work, an excuse for high spirits and brilliant bravura displays of classical technique set to a joyous score, telling of the adventures of Basilio, a penniless Spanish barber, and Kitri, the innkeeper's pretty daughter. Unfortunately for the pair, Kitri's father has determined that she is to marry the foppish but wealthy Gamache and it is only with the help of Don Quixote that everything ends happily ever after. At least one hopes so, as Kitri was an inveterate flirt, and Basilio a handsome philanderer!

Happily, from my third row seat in the Boston theatre, I revelled in every moment of the work, as did each member of that fortunate audience. Nureyev had already triumphed in the role of Basilio with the Kirov in Russia and, using the St Petersburg base, had already mounted his own version of it in 1966 and again in 1970 for the Vienna State Opera Ballet, to which he had made extensive alterations and additions. It was, moreover, a role in which he could demonstrate his gifts as an actor/dancer, revealing his own mischievous spirit as well as his comic talents.

Since then, it is a ballet that I have seen so many times I feel as though I could dance each role myself, but the production that remains the most vivid in my mind is the 1971 version, with Nureyev full of fun, sparkling joyously through Barry Kay's adorable if highly impractical decor.

Nureyev had seen the perky Australian ballerina Lucette Aldous in London in Ballet Rambert's staging of *Don Quixote* before inviting her to join him in his own version, and the ballet opens with the diminutive Aldous sitting nonchalantly eating an orange before bursting onto centre stage. Nureyev then zooms into the action, cleverly sidestepping the live chickens, ducks, and donkeys who got there before him and adroitly avoiding the odd squashed tomato fallen from the market stalls. It was a miracle he didn't skid, slide, and fall. There were also rabbits hopping around and I noticed one area of the stage was littered with bird feathers. From the very beginning, the audience was chuckling; the decor certainly set the scene.

Despite the clucking birds, including one chirping happily away in a cage on the side of the stage, one gazed mesmerised at Nureyev's high, soft, weightless leaps. In fine form, he jumped, he floated, he flirted and he laughed out loud in glee. We held our breath as he carried the feather-light Lucette Aldous triumphantly around the stage in that famous one-armed lift, and how the audience exhausted itself laughing. They adored him! At one point as he hovered suspended high in the air, the intake of breath from spectators was so loud that upon landing, he simply stopped dancing and leaned forward looking at us all, his hands on his knees, and joined in the ensuing roars of laughter. People cheered even louder. He was thoroughly enjoying himself, the whole cast was enjoying itself, and consequently, the audience was having the time of its life!

The ballet also gave rein to a side of Nureyev I hadn't seen onstage before as he presented a Basilio full of charm, humour and vitality. No lonely, lovesick prince here. He plays around and teases all the girls, mesmerising his audience with his quicksilver, dazzling footwork, and his very presence electrified the whole company who danced for the sheer joy of dancing. One is swept from the swirling peasant ensembles and high-stepping toreadors in the market square to the wild gypsy dances in their moonlit encampment and then back again to the village tavern to the inevitable happy end and flamboyant wedding festivities.

Such a lightweight plot was never intended to be more than an excuse for displays of superlative dancing from the corps de ballet as well as the stars. By the final act, no longer a Spanish barber is he, but rather the prince that Nureyev was, as his magnificently trained body gave a dazzling virtuoso display in perfect keeping with the music, which, in Basilio's defence, and composed as it was by the Austrian-born musician who served as the Official Composer of Ballets to the St Petersburg theatre, owed more to its Slav origins than to Spanish dancing.

With music by Minkus, arranged and conducted by John Lanchbery, choreography and staging by Nureyev after Petipa, and with exceptional, unconventional decors and set designs by Barry Kay, it is probably ballet's most high-spirited comedy, which was shortly immortalised on film.

Don Quixote – the film

The 1972 film is not only the best of the dance films Nureyev has appeared in, but it is also artistically one of the finest dance films made, with Robert Helpmann as co-director, Geoffrey Unsworth as director of photography, and Bill Hutchinson as art editor. Nureyev's lifelong friend, the gentle and unassuming Wallace Potts, whose passion was lighting and editing, was assistant director.

Rudolf was determined to give audiences a different experience from simply shooting the ballet from the front of the auditorium. He had been disappointed time and time again with films which didn't live up to his expectations, and once behind the camera himself, he allowed dance to tell the story, moving the camera fluidly in and around the action, so it showed the audience what was important at each stage of events. The camera follows the dancer, who has neither head nor feet chopped off. He succeeded in making the film a different experience from that seen sitting in a theatre, experimenting with interesting overhead shots, close-ups of the interpreters and unusual angles, which in no way deterred from the dancing. There was no filming from the orchestra pit, which he abhorred, nor at any time did the camera move away from the feet and arms of those dancing as so often happens in films today. "He was like a child with a new toy," Lucette Aldous commented at the time.

The Australian Ballet is a strong company, the dancing exhilarating, Nureyev himself sparkling and outrageous, but most of all, the sheer fun of the work has been captured.

First released in 1973, the film thereafter inexplicably disappeared, and on a brief trip to Paris, Janine Burdeu, head of ABC Video in Melbourne, Australia, told me the story of its resurrection. "By chance," she said, "I happened to come across an old copy of it and even though it was faded and scratched, the performances were so exciting it gave me goose-bumps. I was determined to see it properly," she continued, "so I found the master tape, which wasn't much better, and then I finally managed to get hold of the original 35mm negative from Pinewood Studios."

She explained how she had spent the next four to five years tracking down the original film, which had been discovered in various cans stored in houses and farms around Sydney as well as in London, before beginning to restore it.

"One camera was out of focus," she recalled, "and this hadn't been rectified at post-production, while the lighting varied from scene to scene and from one camera angle to another. In addition, the sound-track, although recorded in stereo, was unbelievably in mono, unthinkable for a re-release. Some shots even included shuddering and we discovered that two different film stocks had been used, presumably because they were in a hurry and running out of money.

"The aim throughout the restoration was to stay as close as possible to what Nureyev would have wanted, and with that in mind, the film was recoloured frame by frame. New technology reduced the shudder, and the sound-track was synchronised to the video with the sound effects of the donkey clopping and fingers clicking added later. And then," Burdeu enthused, "I unearthed a film of the film actually being made, which intrigued me as much as the film itself. Nureyev had wanted it made but they were all in so much of a rush that it got lost and forgotten about. So that too has been put together giving a fascinating glimpse of the mammoth undertaking.

"It was filmed, you see, in the midst of summer, on an enlarged stage in a deserted hangar at Essendon Airport, Melbourne, where Nureyev's spectacular Spanish numbers for the whole company had them swirling in circles around the huge village square the designer had created. They formed intricate patterns while performing all the characteristic and newly invented steps for the production. It was a crazy time," she added, "with the set builders working half-naked because of the high temperature which was touching forty degrees."

She also commented on the fascinating rehearsals with John Lanchbery conducting the orchestra, and Nureyev, whose plane had only landed the day before, running here, there and everywhere, systematically checking everything in sight.

Lucette Aldous was even more explicit, Burdeu said, recalling the boom of planes overhead and the utter pandemonium around her, with the seventy dancers, fifty extras, one mule, two horses (and their droppings), twenty-four pigeons, thirty chickens, and a parrot flying round, and that without counting the four tons of fresh fruit and vegetables that arrived every day for the market scene.

"But for the rest of the cast," Burdeu continued, "it was the horrendous smell of the fish, including the giant-sized lobster brandished around by Sancho Panza, not so fresh after several days in the heat, that was their strongest memory."

"The dancers treasured every moment with Nureyev," she said. "They would do anything for him, and the level of everyone rose when he was there. The whole company was galvanised by his energy, brilliance and sheer sense of fun and none of us will forget his magnificent bravura display in the last act."

Over those four weeks of filming, Kelvin Coe would dance Rudolf's part while the Russian dancer filmed, and then Rudolf would dance, often until eleven at night, after having been there since seven in the morning. He would simply say to those there that he danced his best when he was tired. And because they were running out of time, he choreographed the scene at the gypsy encampment in the moonlight on the spot. If the classical 'dream sequence' is pure Petipa, then the lovely pas de deux in the moonlight beneath the sails of an old windmill is pure Nureyev. Dance-lovers will recognise that the music he chose for that, also by Minkus, comes from the composer's score for *La Bayadère*. Nureyev also developed the comedy, introducing an element of Commedia dell' Arte, particularly noticeable in the pseudo 'death' scene where Basilio gains the hand of his belle!

As the last shots of the 100,000 feet of film were being put in the can ready to be sent to London for editing, Nureyev, leather trousers over dance tights, was already heading for New York. Limited by time, he couldn't go back over scenes again, nor was he there for the dubbing. The restoration of this film full of charm, which used advanced technology to eliminate technical faults, now seems like nothing less than a miracle.

Over ten years later, Nureyev reworked the entire production for the Paris Opera Ballet, which, as splendid as it is, no longer has the slender, slim-waisted thirty-four-year-old star at its leaping brilliant centre. But then, neither does it have bird droppings, squashed tomatoes and oranges rolling around on the floor. His ebullient view of Petipa's *Don Quixote* finally arrived at the Palais Garnier in 1981, this time with costumes and decor by Nicholas Georgiadis, and very lovely they were too, perhaps more in keeping with the Palais Garnier.

"We worked on the costumes together," Georgiadis told me several years ago. "Rudolf wanted everything picturesque, and we were very inspired by Goya's happy period, by paintings such as 'El Pelele', and 'Le Jeu de colin-mallaird', where the Spanish painter's works were full of life, echoing the sentiments of his ballet. And although Cervantes lived in the 16th century, we set it very firmly in the 18th century. Above all, Rudolf insisted that the Kingdom of the Dryads had to be absolutely magical. We conceived a sort of Southern Spain with Russian sauce," he explained.

The story, as such, remains the same as in Nureyev's earlier versions, with Don Quixote, the redresser of wrongs, bringing about a happy ending to the thwarted love between Basilio the barber and Kitri the innkeeper's daughter. Danced by the French company, the ballet is totally irresistible. In each performance I have seen, and with every cast, the dancers' joie de vivre is communicated directly to the audience as they whizz and whirl through the evening in a feast of dancing. No danger of skidding on a squashed tomato here!

In 2002, however, well after Nureyev's death, Georgiadis' stylish designs were replaced by those of Alexandre Beliaev and Elena Rivkina, deemed more suitable, one supposes, for the larger Bastille stage. They, too, were inspired by Goya's paintings, but in designs reminiscent of the 1870s, which is when *Don Quixote* was created. Unfortunately, many of the costumes, particularly in the first act are ornate, heavy and over-fussy. It was also disconcerting in *Don Quixote*'s 'vision scene' to find the dryads in what can only be described as a disenchanted garden, bedecked as they were in crude shades of turquoise and lilac. Nevertheless, if some of the magic is missing, the choreography and dancing is such that seats are instantly sold out immediately after the ballet is programmed.

Ivry Gitlis

The end of 1972 brought me back to Paris, where, in great part due to the French/Israeli violinist Ivry Gitlis, and his companion, Sabine Glaser, one of my closest friends, I got to know Nureyev on a more personal basis.

Ivry, whom I had known for several years, would gather his kids and mine together on everyone's birthday for an impromptu concert at his home in Andrésy, some twenty miles outside Paris, or more often outside in the Corsican maquis where we both had houses. He was not only one of the 20th century's greatest violinists, but like Nureyev, was a man who radiated charisma. A rebel, he had had problems with the rigidity of the Conservatoire of Music in Paris just as surely as Nureyev had courted disaster with what was said to be his unconventional behaviour at the Vaganova Institute, the famous St Petersburg ballet school.

Both artists were giants in their own sphere; wildly unique and impossible to 'tame'. They spoke the same language both literally and artistically, and it was inevitable that there would be an immediate affinity between them despite the gap of years, Gitlis being born in 1922 and Nureyev in 1938. Both were Russian-speaking having been born to Russian parents, and they shared the same urgency to play the violin and to dance wherever, whenever and as often as they possibly could. Both were incapable of saying no.

Just as Nureyev 'popularised' dance, bringing people who had never seen a ballet before into the theatres where he appeared, so Gitlis seduced the masses, bringing classical music into the lives of people who otherwise had little knowledge of who Brahms, Bartok or Beethoven were. He created festivals of music wherever he could, just as Nureyev created his 'Nureyev and Friends', the small groups of young dancers who were given the opportunity to interpret solo roles otherwise unavailable to them in the Paris company. Until Rudolf came along, dancers didn't organise small touring groups; he set a precedent where they could have access to the great masterpieces of the repertoire. Now, such groups have become common.

In the early 1970s, the pair got together at the Théâtre des Champs Elysées, practically a second home for both of them, to present an extraordinary evening of music and dance. It was to Bela Bartok's second concerto for violin that Rudolf, clad solely in a pair of white tights, stalked regally onstage and paused on demi-pointe before launching into a mesmerising improvisation to Bartok's music. His every movement responded to each note Gitlis played, as if Bartok himself were there and speaking to him. Each gesture of his body was a reply to the composer, and as Gitlis later said, "His movements echoed the tone of each phrase of the music; he responded to Bartok, holding a conversation with him both musically and physically."

I had never really appreciated the music of the Hungarian composer before, but Nureyev did not simply dance in time to the music. By some mysterious alchemy, he illuminated the score in such a way as to enable one to see, or more accurately to feel, the meaning behind each passage. Many dancers and choreographers use music to display their own skills, as did, for example, Maurice Béjart, whereas Nureyev enhanced it. His unique musicality to bring the notes to life has stayed with me over the years. It was an extraordinary experience, one that was only intensified by meeting him after the performance.

We all met up together in Rudolf's dressing room after the show, and it was the first time that I actually stood next to the half-naked dancer. I was truly bowled over by the impact of his sheer physical beauty, a beauty that has never been fully captured neither in films nor in photographs. Peeking at him surreptitiously from the corner of my eye, for I knew how much he hated being stared at offstage, I saw his body was absolute perfection, a more slender version of Michelangelo's magnificent sculpture of 'David' in Florence. He was taller than I remembered, slender waisted and slim hipped. Fair skinned, his body gleamed silver with the lightest sheen of sweat on the patina of fine blonde hairs smattering his smooth-muscled chest, his skin flushed and almost translucent in the light. But above all, it was his enchanting smile that lit up his entire face as he greeted us that captivated me most of all.

Of all the many meetings and conversations with Ivry – whose personal joke was to refer to me as 'the old woman who lived in a shoe', after the birth of my twins – I recorded just one, in English, where he talks to me about Nureyev, or Rudi, as he called him. I now include it in its entirety, exactly as it was spoken.

"Nureyev's was an extravagant beauty," declared Gitlis. "He was so blatantly a diamond that everyone wanted to possess. But they could not because it was too radiant, it wasn't possible to touch it. It was meant to be looked at and so sometimes created antagonistic feelings, envy almost. It polluted the negativeness of the people around him who found it difficult to accept as one does the sun or the moon, just like the beautiful ray of sunshine coming into the room where we're sitting now. The leaves are falling gently and it's so beautiful and there's nothing you can do about it but be grateful. That's God's creation. And that was Rudi; he didn't even know it himself.

"You know, I can talk about him very objectively because I didn't have a love affair with him, I didn't sleep with him, I wasn't a dancer. I was just an artist in my own right.

"There was a childlike kaleidoscope in him and he wasn't in control of all the elements. He was born in Ufa, a very poor part of Russia, a long way from everywhere, and then suddenly he was catapulted here into this enormous world. It was as if he was his own cannon and his own bullet too. He played with life as a child would play with a football in his playroom and that's what people didn't understand. People saw his behaviour as provocation, but if it was, it was just as much towards himself, like when you walk and are unsure whether you're dreaming or it's real, so you pinch yourself.

"There are a lot of wonderful dancers, but not one remotely like him. Rudi was like an elf from the legends of the forest. He was so alive, so full of life. How many extraordinary people are there on this planet? Of course you can't look at him and say everything was wonderful, but that's the beauty of it all. In Greek mythology there's Zeus, Leda and Aphrodite; they have all been written about so they've been made almost human; well, Zeus used to fuck, so did Aphrodite, so did Apollo and Alexander the Great. Nureyev too. Why make such a song and dance about it, eh?

"Rudi was a person of very many facets," Ivry said, "and he was so very kind. He was a whole play of mirrors by himself, mirrors which project you to the next one, and so on, reflecting and deflecting. There was one occasion when I was given my own television show and could invite my own guests. For once, I wasn't in Tokyo and Rudi in New York, and so I could ask him to join me. Although he had had an important gala at the Opera the night before and hadn't got to bed until after four in the morning, he still came and danced a Tchaikovsky pas de deux to a big violin solo. He'd have been paid a fortune for that in the US, but he came and did it for me for nothing.

"He was so much more than a dancer. Some have a wonderful technique, like him. Some are poets, like him, but he was something else. And he gave. He gave, gave and gave. He gave so much pleasure, joy and happiness to the whole world. At his lowest, it was like what other people were at their highest, and you know, suns never die, because when they do, something in us dies too."

Lost in happy reminiscences, Ivry recalled visiting Nureyev in his house in La Turbie, not far from Nice, which he said, as did Jude and Georgiadis, was like the cave of Ali Baba. He recalled piles of objects stacked one on top of each other and above all, an enormous chandelier lit by candles. "He loved candlelight," he said. "He was from another age; he was like a prince from the *Arabian Nights* when he was there."

On the subject of houses, I remember clearly when Nureyev arrived in Andrésy one wet, windy and stormy evening. A small car pulled to a halt alongside the river Seine, opposite the small island where Ivry lived with his companion, Sabine. He climbed, or rather unrolled himself, from the car and, impervious to the howling wind, hopped down the steps of the embankment leading to where Sabine had tied up the little boat she used every day to cross to the mainland. He was undeterred by the fact that it was growing dark and was very wet and that the wooden bench we sat on was extremely slippery, while Sabine was scared to death Rudolf would slip and twist his ankle or worse while getting into the boat, already rocking dangerously in the swirling waters. Five or six minutes later, there was a repeat performance on the other side as he clambered perkily out onto the muddy bank.

Ivry had spoken of his home on the island, which was thickly wooded, mentioning that there was an old house for sale nearby. Nureyev, at the beginning of his search for a permanent base in Paris and loving forests, had been intrigued, and had come to see where it was himself. But possibly deterred by the fearful

Plaque at the doorway of Rudolf's apartment in Paris, 23 Quai Voltaire.

© Patricia Boccadoro

weather, by the fact that it was growing dark and above all by the dubious feat of having to regularly cross a stretch of treacherous water at sometimes four o'clock in the morning, he didn't follow up on this adventure. Several years later, an apartment on Quai Voltaire, within walking distance to both the Palais Garnier and the Opera Bastille proved to be a more practical if less attractive alternative.

The 'Bartok' evening at the Théâtre des Champs Elysées was the first of many such meetings, as each time Nureyev appeared there with his 'Nureyev and Friends', the group of dancers that he created in 1974, the three of us, Ivry, Sabine and I, would troop in, invariably late as Ivry had little notion of time, and so we would enter the theatre by the artists' entrance and end up backstage. Once inside, it was of course too late to find our seats.

On one such occasion in 1978, Rudolf was appearing with Murray Louis and company. Oblivious of events onstage, Ivry was chatting to everyone around him and I remember being stranded there, ill-at-ease and unsure of where to put myself. I was vainly trying to see Murray Louis performing onstage in the first half of the programme, when I was brought a chair, which was unfortunately plonked, I felt, in full view of the audience. So there I was sitting in the wings, feeling most uncomfortable and out of place, when someone else who had no such qualms came and deliberately put down a chair right next to mine. He then sat down, folded his arms across his chest and sat back with his legs stretched out, feet elegantly crossed in front of him, oblivious of those in the audience who could see us. I didn't need to look at the cloak he wrapped around himself to know it was Nureyev. "No one will bother you now," he seemed to say. "Sit back and enjoy the dancing." Which we did, watching Murray Louis perform together.

Louis was a dancer and choreographer who had performed with Alwin Nikolais before founding his own company in 1953, and Rudolf had long appreciated his playful works. The admiration was reciprocal.

After the interval, he gave us seats in his private box to enjoy the rest of the evening in which Rudolf himself interpreted two works Louis had created for him, *Moments* and *The Brighton Venus*, the latter which I remember very well, less for the steps and more for the amusing costume. He wore a sort of sleeveless white singlet, a striped bow tie, a funny little sun-hat, and, so it appeared, little else down below, though I can only suppose he wore flesh coloured tights.

Rudolf in Moments, a short piece created for him by Murray Louis in 1975. Photograph 1978.
© Francette Levieux/CNCS

One of the most interesting aspects of the 'Nureyev and Friends' performances was the fact that he brought a wider audience to modern dance by his inclusion of contemporary pieces coupled with the classics. On this particular occasion, spectators had crowded into the theatre to see him dance *Le Corsaire*, which had been programmed only after the staging of *Moments* followed by *The Brighton Venus*. Thus spectators who originally thought they only liked classical dance and had come primarily to see him dance *Le Corsaire* had their blinkers stripped away, so to speak, and were brought to experience and to enjoy contemporary works. It was also fascinating for an audience to watch him dance several different styles the same evening, which, of course, had been his intention all along.

He was a pioneer in bringing contemporary dance and classical ballet together, and in his encouragement of young choreographers such as the relatively unknown William Forsythe to work with classically trained dancers. Free rein was to be given to many modern choreographers, those who were already established names and those who were just arriving on the scene, shortly after he arrived at the Paris Opera Ballet a few years later. As far as dance was concerned, he could almost be considered as the first of the great 'crossover' artists, moving from the grand 19th-century classical roles to modern dance in the blink of an eye, as much as the great tenor Mario Lanza was to grand opera and popular songs in the 1950s.

On his arrival in the West, Nureyev wanted to dance everything. He went all over the world to see what was happening, eager to discover all the choreographers he'd heard of as well as those he hadn't. No matter how small the company, if they had something to offer him that he hadn't yet danced, then he was there!

Balanchine

The mid-1970s thus took Rudolf, and consequently me, into new territory. He had been hankering after new choreographers, new steps, and new ballets since his days in St Petersburg where the repertoire had been narrow and limited to the traditional classics. During these 'intervening years', before he took over the directorship of the Paris Opera Ballet, he was going to see everyone he admired, from Roland Petit, with whom he'd worked in London, to Jiri Kylian and the young William Forsythe, as well as the more obvious choices of Martha Graham, Merce Cunningham and Paul Taylor, the three giants of American modern dance. He was constantly in search of choreographers and ballets he had not performed.

However, his greatest dream had been to work with George Balanchine, a desire which, despite him leaving an indelible mark on several Balanchine masterpieces, remained basically unfulfilled as Nureyev was not simply a star, but a superstar for whom there was no place in Balanchine's New York City Ballet.

He worshipped Balanchine, his 1962 meeting with the legendary Russian master being a turning point in his life. He saw someone working in the same choreographic style as Petipa, and he always said that Balanchine was a genius because he knew how to translate music into movement. Balanchine would put steps and configurations onstage that corresponded precisely to Petipa's technique.

Despite Balanchine's brusque "Go away and dance your princes", Rudolf Nureyev performing George Balanchine's luminous *Apollo*, a landmark work in neoclassical ballet, remains forever one of the greatest interpretations of the piece I have seen. Whenever I hear Stravinsky's evocative score, created in 1928 for Diaghilev's Ballets Russes, it is always and forever marked by the image of Rudolf Nureyev.

Apollo

Unfortunately, I cannot say with any certainty just when I first saw Nureyev in *Apollo*, or more correctly *Apollon Musagète*, for George Balanchine did not change the title of his 1928 creation until 1978, when he removed his prologue, the act of the newly born god breaking free from his swaddling bands. However, it was probably around 1972 or 1973, at the Palais Garnier, with Noella Pontois as Terpsichore, the goddess of dance. Not only did Rudolf look like a Greek god, he was a Greek god. He was Apollo.

The ballet tells the story of Apollo's birth from the moment he struggles out of his baby wrappings and how, after his first, few stumbling steps and subsequent education with the three Greek muses, Terpsichore, Calliope, and Polyhymnia, the goddesses of poetry and music, he gradually emerges as a shining, radiant god as he ascends Mount Parnassus.

Apollon Musagète. Rudolf Nureyev at the Paris Opera in December 1972, with Noella Pontois, Wilfride Piollet and Nanon Thibon.
© Colette Masson/Roger Viollet

Rudolf in Balanchine's Apollo, Paris 1974.
© Francette Levieux/CNCS

Although I saw him interpret the role several times, including with the Ballet of Nancy and with his own group of 'Nureyev and Friends', I've chosen to write about an occasion some ten years later, when I saw him in *Apollo*, at the Palais Garnier where my memory is as clear as if I saw him dance a week ago.

I was sitting with Jacqueline Cochet, who had been the teacher of both Elisabeth Platel and Jean-Yves Lormeau, and we were expecting to see Elisabeth as Terpsichore, while I have since forgotten who was supposed to be dancing Apollo. No matter. At 19hr 30 precisely, the orchestra was in place, the audience expectant, but some five or six minutes later, nothing more had happened. People began coughing and shuffling in their seats, but before everyone got too restless, a slender figure, not wearing the elegant white costume of the Greek deity, but clad in the classic Balanchinian outfit of black tights and white T-shirt, bounded onstage at the same time as the orchestra launched into the first notes of Stravinsky's familiar score.

'Apollo' with the God-given features of Rudolf Nureyev had arrived and what more could we do but sit back and let ourselves be taken away to Mount Parnassus. Nureyev had not only the beauty, but also the artistry for the role, no matter what he wore. With his own 'star quality', Nureyev was the theatrical equivalent of a god, displaying the authority, radiance and power of an immortal. Did it really matter if, as he took his bow, that a latecomer might have thought there had been a programme change and that he'd just missed *The Four Temperaments*, Balanchine's 1946 work?

Obviously, whoever had been programmed to dance that night, had, by the grace of some other god as far as we were concerned, met with some kind of impediment, and Nureyev, in the wings, had stepped in at the last moment.

Polyakov

Genia Polyakov, the Russian dancer, choreographer and director, whom Nureyev brought to work alongside him in Paris as ballet master in 1983, once told me his favourite story of one of Nureyev's (mis)adventures with *Apollo*. He, Polyakov, was in New York, and had gone to see Rudolf dance the ballet on Broadway. Arriving at the last minute just as the curtain went up, he was puzzled to see Rudolf performing onstage decked out in his warm woolly bonnet and thick leg-warmers.

"Increasingly more astonished," he told me, "I headed off backstage to see him after the performance to get the explanation of such odd behaviour, and you'll never guess what he said; 'I was cold and the management refused to turn off the air-conditioning, so…'

"Anyway," Polyakov continued, "the audience didn't know that Nureyev hated air-conditioning, they'd probably not seen the ballet before, and they cheered and cheered their heads off at the end. I don't believe anyone else noticed. Still, it was pretty peculiar to see a Greek god clad in several pairs of woolly leg-warmers… and tatty old ones at that."

Portrait of Genia Polyakov, 1982.
Personal collection of Florence Clerc

Warming to his subject, he then recounted another anecdote that still amused him. "I don't recall exactly where we were this time, maybe Venice, but again it was absolutely freezing in the rehearsal room. There we were at the barre, gamely attempting our exercises, when the intense cold simply drove the dancers away. Only Rudolf, blue with cold but determined to set an example, carried on, wearing his cosy little bonnet and three pairs of woolly leg-warmers… but the following morning, guess who had over 40° temperature?"

La Sylphide

Thus the 1970s saw Nureyev reaching out to both neo-classical and modern choreographers, performing more frequently with young companies, where the level of dancing rose the moment he appeared. His presence not only fulfilled his constant need to dance, but also demonstrated the kind of stimulus a great artist can give to a troupe. I saw him appear with many small companies and he never, ever, dominated with his superstar status, but inspired the company to dance with a passion they hadn't known they possessed.

Such was the case with Scottish Ballet, a company founded in 1931, when I finally caught up with Nureyev's interpretation of James, the besotted young highlander in Bournonville's *La Sylphide*. The ballet, presented at the Palais-des-Sports in Paris in 1977 as part of a Nureyev Festival, was preceded by Nureyev dancing with the Ballet National du Canada in *Four Schumann Pieces*, a work by Hans van Manen.

But, truth be told, what I remember most about that evening was not his rendering of the neat, quick, light Bournonville's steps, nor his clean, high jumps, but rather the length of Rudolf's kilt, a blue one, ending way above the knee. Rather short as it swung out behind him with each of his spectacular leaps. Not having seen the ballet before, I thought little of it until some years later when I noticed that other interpreters of the role, including Mathieu Ganio and Emmanuel Thibault of the Paris Opera, wore their kilts at a much more decorous length.

La Sylphide, a ballet with choreography by Filippo Taglioni and created at the Paris Opera in 1832, where it was first danced by his daughter, the legendary Marie Taglioni, was the first of the truly Romantic ballets. The plot, inspired by the supernatural *Ballet of the Nuns*, which appeared as part of Meyerbeer's opera *Robert le Diable* the year before, tells the story of the impossible love between a human and a supernatural being. James is a young Scottish farmer whose thoughts are possessed by a beautiful Sylphide who comes to him in a vision. He thus runs off to be with her on the eve of his wedding to Effie, his childhood sweetheart.

In the Sylphide's realm, inhabited by winged creatures, he asks the evil Madge to help him keep the ethereal creature forever, but the witch tricks him with a poisoned shawl, telling him to wrap it around his Sylphide. Tragically, when he does so, her wings fall off and she dies.

As in many Romantic works, the hero pursues a dream and, in doing so, supposedly destroys his chances of happiness in the real world. However, I don't recall Nureyev's James as a particularly doomed lover; I felt his attraction for the little Sylphide, interpreted by Natalia Makarova, not his most favourite of partners, to be but a temporary infatuation, and suspected from witnessing his bouncy steps and lively manner that he would soon meet another Effie to console him.

However, what marked me more than his interpretation of James and his obvious delectation in performing Bournonville's light, quicksilver steps was how he managed and succeeded in presenting a festival of three different programmes with three different companies, dancing with three different partners, and with appearing himself in the works of Hans van Manen, Murray Louis, Glen Tetley, Maurice Béjart and Flemming Flindt, five vastly different choreographers. And of how he mastered the five very different styles… every night.

Returning to *La Sylphide*, the version which I saw Nureyev dance with Scottish Ballet was Bournonville's choreographed version of 1936, set to a score by Lovenskjold. He had been taught it by the Danish dancer Erik Bruhn, said by many to be the love of Nureyev's life, who had revived it for the National Ballet of Canada in 1964.

Some years later, mentioning the length of Rudolf's kilt in a casual conversation with the distinguished stage designer Nicholas Georgiadis, I was disconcerted by his huge guffaw of laughter. He enlightened me to the fact that Nureyev would only dance in costumes that not only threw light on the personality of the character he was interpreting, but also that he was intensely conscious of wearing costumes that flattered him. "As far as the kilt went, the shorter, the better, and finally, he also got rid of the sporran," he said, chuckling.

"From his early days at the Maryinsky," Georgiadis told me, "Rudolf would always reject costumes which were either ridiculous or unflattering, in all fairness, not only his own, but those of the other dancers too. Above all, he hated anything which would hamper his dancing. You must have heard about all the trouble he got himself into at the Kirov when he refused to go onstage in what he called a pair of baggy pants worn on top of his tights, in the middle of a performance of *Don Quixote*, I think it was.

"He'd seen performances in the West where male dancers wore tights which he considered suited him much better and they did." He smiled. "But that was one incident in which, for the moment, he didn't get his way and he was obliged, after an hour or so of arguments, to finish the performance wearing those hated baggy trousers."

Ghislaine Thesmar, the French principal dancer who taught at the Palais Garnier after partnering Nureyev on many occasions during her career, also related a story when Nureyev fumed against the costume he was given to wear in *Sleeping Beauty* with the Grand Ballet du Marquis de Cuevas back in 1961.

"I was in the corps de ballet at the time and I will never forget his dreadful white wig covered in little pink beads which he said made him look like a Christmas tree. Although it was a hot June evening, he thought he was taking part in a musical comedy and all the sequins and scintillating decorations were for Christmas. He really didn't want to dance decked out like a tree with its twinkling fairy lights."

A wig is something Nureyev always tried to avoid wearing. Indeed, I never saw him wear one, except perhaps once in his portrayal of the film producer in his 1986 creation of *Cinderella* at the Paris Opera when he appeared disguised as Groucho Marx complete with moustache and cigar.

Nureyev also performed frequently with the Ballet of Nancy, previously simply a solid 'provincial' company, which Rudolf raised to an international level with his numerous guest appearances. In 1982 I was fortunate enough to snap up a last-minute seat at the Theatre du Chatelet in Paris, where the company was giving a programme in honour of Diaghilev's Ballet Russes, including two legendary works, Fokine's *Petrushka* and Nijinsky's *L'Après-midi d'un Faune*. Nureyev was appearing in both of them, and the theatre was packed, anticipation high. His performance in *Petrushka*, which I'd previously seen back in 1969, was heart-rending, but this was the first occasion I'd had to see him in one of Nijinsky's works.

Nureyev, combining an animal sensuality with an understated elegance, gave a moving performance that remains unequalled to this day. He left an indelible mark as the solitary faun with his turned-in feet and turned-out palms, moving with stylised, odd-angled leg movements, so different from anything I'd seen him in before.

A one-act work set to a score by Debussy with beautiful decor and costumes by Leon Bakst, the ballet tells the story of a faun who is spying on a group of nymphs. When the one he desires goes down to bathe, he tries to snatch her, but only manages to seize the scarf she left behind in her flight. Lying down alone, stretched full-length on her scarf on top of his rock, he assuages his sexual desire with a pelvic thrust.

Charles Jude

The early 1970s also marked the beginning of Nureyev's lifelong friendship with dancer Charles Jude. Jude, whose father was a French judge and whose mother was Vietnamese, was born and spent his early childhood in Mytho, South Vietnam. When he was fourteen, the family moved to Eze, on the

French Riviera, close to La Turbie where Nureyev had his house. Jude began lessons at the Nice Conservatoire where his teacher was Alexandre Kalioujny, a friend of Nureyev's. Two years later, when Nureyev came to dance in Nice, he asked Kalioujny whether he had any promising pupils, and it happened that not only was Jude his best dancer, but he was the only boy.

A breathing space for Florence, Rudolf and Charles at Rudolf's house in Virginia, USA, 1986.
Personal collection of Florence Clerc

"It was August," Jude told me, "and I was lying on the beach when someone told me that Rudolf was looking for me and was at the beach cafe. Of course I'd heard of him, but I wasn't all that impressed because I wasn't thinking of becoming a dancer; I still thought it was only for girls. When I met him, I just said, bonjour monsieur, and we chatted for a few minutes and that was all. However, I gradually began to take dance more seriously and was accepted into the Paris Opera Ballet three years later. I then found myself in a bit of a hot spot when he came to dance with us in the Cour Carrée du Louvre, as I'd boasted to friends that I'd met him before and actually knew him more than I did.

"I can tell you, I was so relieved the following day during a rehearsal when he spotted me in the back row among the palace guards and he stopped dead in his tracks, pointing a finger in my direction with an imperious, 'You! Here! What are you doing?' After the rehearsal, he invited me out to dinner where we caught up with each other's news and became inseparable friends. Three years later, he chose me to dance Paul Taylor's *Aureole* with him at the Palais-des-Sports even though I was only in the corps de ballet, and soon after that, I became part of 'Nureyev and Friends', the small group of dancers that he formed to take on tour with him. And that was the start of my career.

"From then onwards, we were like brothers; he was certainly my closest friend, a friend who confided in me. He was my brother, my father, my friend and my mentor. We were in constant touch and he'd always ring me as soon as he arrived in Paris, interested in my life, my wife, Florence Clerc, and in everything we did, encouraging us to go to the theatre, to the cinema, to art exhibitions, to see other dancers, other choreographers, other companies and to read, read and read. All the things he loved doing; I never understood how he found the time to do so much. Anyone could ask him anything about literature, painting, opera. He was avid for knowledge, for culture. He instilled a love and respect for beauty in me, and perhaps it's because of him that I developed his love of antiques and carpets. He absolutely adored carpets and kilims."

Oriental carpets

"One Sunday afternoon, around 5pm, he telephoned me at home saying, 'Charlex, I need your help at the Opera,'" Jude said, recalling one of the many holidays they spent together in Europe and America, always at a moment's notice.

"I was very suspicious and rightly so because no one was there as there was an eight-day holiday at the Opera. Then I discovered that what he had in mind had nothing to do with work, but was more a pretext to ask if Florence, our two daughters and myself would join him for a week in Turkey the following day. Never one to waste time, he'd already bought the air tickets, but as the children couldn't go, he invited Marie-Suzanne Soubie, his secretary, to join us. The following day we found ourselves on a four-cabin boat with a two-man crew, and off we went on a cruise, his aim being to buy some more of the oriental carpets he so loved!

Rudolf and Charles Jude in the boat in Turkey, 1989.
Personal collection of Florence Clerc

"He disappeared the minute we anchored in Marmaris, going around all the shops there to hunt down his carpets without a word to anyone. Of course, all the merchants there knew him, and would run round after him, shouting, 'Nureyev, Nureyev.' But he bought nothing, knowing he'd be ripped off. Instead, he'd go into all the shops without saying a word, quietly choose the ones he wanted, then come back, sending me back there to bargain for the ones he liked because no one knew me. He'd give me a list and then pack me off to get the price of those he wanted! When I returned with the prices, he'd go carefully through the list, muttering, 'That's a bargain, that one too, but that's too expensive, while this one needs negotiating.' Then, naturally, I would go back and haggle, and when I'd got everything settled, he'd turn up to pay.

"But by the time we'd been to all the shops and bought everything he wanted, we had more than fifteen carpets, not easy to squish into the couple of extra suitcases we'd brought with us, so all the extra ones had to go in two plastic bags. We stored them carefully in the boat, but unfortunately when we finally arrived at Rhodes after a particularly rough crossing in the middle of a storm, the port was crowded. We weren't moored alongside the quay, but some three boats out. Now as luck would have it, we had to catch a very early flight the following day, so with all our luggage, plus the aforementioned plastic bags overflowing with large bulky carpets, there we were, hopping from boat to boat at five o'clock in the morning.

Rudolf and Florence Clerc on the boat in Turkey, chasing Kilims, 1987. Charles is holding a carpet up that we can't see... Rudolf's face says it all! Personal collection of Florence Clerc

"I was laden down with all the carpets and kilims, and arriving at the last boat in front of the quay, I missed my footing and slipped from the gangplank into the murky water below. So there I was, half drowning, trying to grab these two plastic bags of carpets bobbing alongside me and surrounded by floating bottles of Coca-Cola, cans of beer and all kinds of stinky garbage, when Rudolf dived in, no, not to save me, but to rescue all his precious carpets! The first thing he did on returning to Paris was to hang out all his carpets to dry around his apartment. That was some sight."

Jude continued by telling me that Rudolf must have possessed over fifty more of them, which he stuffed under his bed, hid under sofas, underneath the table and even in his cellar when there was no more space for them on the floor. Nureyev, he reminded me, adored beautiful objects and loved antiques as well as bronzes and paintings.

"Mind you," the dancer smiled, "I remember too well one occasion in Venice when we discovered there was a sale of paintings in one of the palaces. It was at a time when he was on the lookout for a very large painting to cover a wall of his New York apartment, so for once, it wasn't the subject matter which interested him, but more the size of the work. And believe me, he had all the measurements of his wall in his pocket. I saw him eyeing up this picture of a big horse with a lion lying on the ground which turned out to be that much too big. Nothing daunted, he blithely announced, 'Okay, we'll get it and just cut a piece of it off!'"

Rudolf relaxing in Turkey, 1986.
Personal collection of Florence Clerc

Back in Paris, Rudolf bought his third-floor apartment, number 23, Quai Voltaire in 1980, when he wanted a permanent home in the city.

"More correctly, I found it for him," Douce Francois told me, "because he simply had no time to look for one himself. He liked it because it was opposite the Louvre and just a block or two away from the Orsay museum. It was also next to all the antique shops he enjoyed dropping in on, and there was a magnificent view of the river Seine below."

She told me that her brother, an architect, had re-designed the interior while she herself had installed the kitchen, not that he did any cooking, she had added. "I remember having to take over all those practical details like the electrical and plumbing problems.

"I also found and bought much of the furniture," she said, "because, again, when would he have found the time to do so? I used to scour around the flea market here, hunting down all the things I knew he'd love, as well as visiting all the antique dealers in the area. As he already had many lovely pieces of furniture and had amassed many paintings on his travels, I mainly coordinated things as best as I could."

Two years after his death, on January 6, 1995, a commemorative plaque was put there by the Cercle des Amis de Rudolf Nureyev.

Song of the Wayfarer

While I never got the opportunity to see Charles Jude interpret Maurice Béjart's *Song of a Wayfarer* with Nureyev, which I would have liked, I finally managed to see it in 1983 with the Ballet of Nancy, when he was partnered by the young Patrick Armand. Each step, each gesture of the ballet remains imprinted in my mind. Set to the haunting lieders, *Lieder eines fahrenden Gesellen*, of Gustav Mahler, it became almost a signature work for the great Russian dancer. Even today, whenever I hear that music, it instantly brings back images of Rudolf Nureyev.

Song of a Wayfarer is a lyrical, highly intense duo, one of the French choreographer's finest works, which he created in 1971 for Rudolf and the Italian dancer Paolo Bortoluzzi, a star of Béjart's Ballet of the 20th Century.

The Wayfarer, Nureyev, with his hopes and fears, travels from town to town seeking work, but he is being shadowed by Destiny. As the ballet progresses, Nureyev, feline and tormented, gradually comes to understand the words to the lieders written by Mahler himself, and realises that only sadness and loneliness lie ahead. He has no future. The final image of Nureyev being dragged away into the darkness by Destiny, and of him twisting round while stretching out his arm in anguish in a final adieu to his audience, was heart-rending.

Although I was to see the ballet on several other occasions, including a later appearance with Patrick Dupond at the Palais Garnier, it was that performance in 1983 that marked me so deeply. Nureyev was at that time forty-five years old, and about to take up his position as Director of the Paris Opera. It seemed that this could have been a subconscious farewell

Nureyev with Paolo Bortoluzzi in Song of a Wayfarer,
created for them by Maurice Béjart in 1971.
© Francette Levieux/CNCS

to all those Russian princes. Since 1979, I had chosen to see Nureyev in contemporary works, including the valet in Cullberg's *Miss Julie* with Eva Evdokimova, or in character or demi-character roles such as the film producer in *Cinderella* in his own productions, where his superb artistry carried him through any potentially dangerous choreography.

Song of the Wayfarer was also a ballet he was able to continue to interpret towards the end of his life when the evolution of his illness made the great classics difficult, and consequently I was shocked when Douce Francois told me that Maurice Béjart had callously withdrawn the rights for Nureyev to interpret the work. She showed me the telegram the French choreographer had sent him, purporting that since Nureyev was no longer performing it according to how he, the choreographer, wished it to be danced, he was withdrawing Rudolf's right to appear in the work. I held the telegram with its few harsh words in my hand, finding it hard to understand such a heartless gesture, particularly when in the April of 1992, Roland Petit invited him to conduct the orchestra in Marseilles for *Coppélia*, Wayne Eagling, the director of the Dutch National Ballet, invited him to conduct *Petrushka*, and Nureyev was under intensive discussions with Charles Jude over a projected ballet, *Prince of the Pagodas*.

I was shocked by the fact that Maurice Béjart did not have the sensitivity nor the decency to at least discuss any problem with Rudolf face to face. It was such a mean thing to have done.

The Tempest

April 1982, the year before Rudolf was to take over the directorship of the Paris Opera Ballet, had me hot-footing it to London where *The Tempest*, his new full-length work, was being premièred at Covent Garden with Anthony Dowell as Prospero. I was fortunate to find two last-minute returns for a matinée performance. Knowing how much Rudolf admired Shakespeare, I wondered how he had dealt with such an intricate plot in a one-act, forty-five-minute work. Everything had to happen pretty quickly and certainly, if it was ever programmed in France where few people would be familiar with the play, there had to be some sort of strong storyline.

In brief, *The Tempest* is a tale of music, magic, betrayal and revenge, culminating in forgiveness and the triumph of true love. Prospero, the usurped Duke of Milan, is cast out to sea with his small daughter, Miranda, and lands on an island once ruled by the witch Sycorax. It's now inhabited by her son, the half human, grovelling Caliban, and the imprisoned spirit Ariel. For twelve years, Prospero has ruled the island and developed his magic arts, all the while plotting his revenge on his treacherous brother, Antonio.

The magician conjures up a storm in which his brother, together with his courtiers, the King of Naples, and his son Ferdinand, is shipwrecked. Ferdinand, separated from his comrades, meets Miranda and they fall in love, but Prospero tests the young man by setting him heavy tasks. Meanwhile, the villainous Stephano and his crony, Trinculo, meet up with Caliban but their plot to kill Prospero is thwarted by Ariel… and so forth. That is cutting a complicated story short. Tough going even for Nureyev. How was he to cram in so much in so short a time?

In this fascinating but over-crowded work, Nureyev presented the earthbound Caliban crawling on the ground on all fours, with Ariel, airborne, swinging on wires above his head, as the two facets of Prospero's own nature. Bravo to Nureyev, as this was a fact that, even though I'd seen performances of the play before and thought I knew the plot, simply hadn't occurred to me before.

While I cannot presume to write a precise account of Nureyev's ballet over thirty years after seeing it, I do remember that events moved along pretty smartly and that one had to have at least a fair idea of the story. The clearest memory I have is of the particularly lovely pas de deux he created for Ferdinand and Miranda where every movement seemed to flow naturally from Tchaikovsky's score, composed in 1873 specifically for Shakespeare's play. Nureyev's choreography led us to understand, through the beauty and sensitivity of each movement, that Miranda had never seen a young man before, and was both attracted to yet afraid of Ferdinand, who, by the tenderness of his dancing, conveyed his genuine love for her. This pas de deux alone gave an indication of what Nureyev's future choreography could be, once he was free in his mind to concentrate upon only that.

In stark contrast to the gentleness of their love duet was the pas de trois for Caliban, Trinculo and Stephano, who spent the greater part of their time rolling around on the floor. Far too much. Nureyev had read and so thoroughly digested Shakespeare's very words, that the poor Caliban, a creature of darkness, remained firmly entrenched on the ground throughout the entire ballet. I don't remember him being permitted to dance one step upright.

The role of Prospero was brilliantly interpreted by Dowell, a superb dancer at the peak of his form. It had been created for him, and from the moment he invoked the storm by commanding great golden stars to do his bidding, he dominated the stage. The costumes, Nicholas Georgiadis was later to tell me, were 17th century, but much of the more dramatic stage designs, the designer said, including that of the shipwreck, had been imagined by Nureyev himself.

My personal regret is that this highly theatrical work, which I would very much have liked to have seen again, has hardly ever been performed. It was taken to the Paris Opera the following year where it was poorly received, in great part because the French were probably flummoxed by the complicated storyline, and so only a few performances were given before it disappeared from the repertoire.

Mademoiselle Julie

In February the following year, Nureyev appeared at the Théâtre des Champs Elysées in a role diametrically opposed to anything I'd seen him in before.

Unused to seeing him cast as the villain, or more correctly the anti-hero, of a ballet, and a callous one at that, I found it fascinating to watch him take on the traits of the cynical valet, Jean, in Birgit Cullberg's dramatic *Mademoiselle Julie*. Cullberg, a leading figure of modern Swedish dance, created her 1950 work on Strindberg's social tragedy, setting it to a score by Ture Rangström.

The ballet opens at a servants' party where they are celebrating the Eve of St John. The aristocratic Julie, having brutally rejected her father's choice of fiancé, joins in the festivities, and being physically attracted to the valet, Jean, deliberately sets out to seduce him. Unfortunately, her plan backfires and she herself becomes dominated by the opportunist valet, who, at first startled, is then out for what he can get, both materially and sexually.

She spends the night with him, where we presume he cold-heartedly gets his way with her, but the following morning, unable to accept her humiliation at the hands of her father's servant, she takes her own life to save her family's honour. The vicious touch that sent shivers down my spine was when she pushed the hilt of the knife into the valet's hand, wrapped his fingers around it, and plunged the knife into her heart.

Nureyev gave a magistral performance as the heartless, ambiguous Jean in this cruel social drama, a conflict both of class and of the sexes. Eva Evdokimova, the American ballerina, was superb as the wanton, foolish young aristocrat unable to accept her degradation by a servant. But it was also strange to witness Nureyev in a role so alien to his nature, displaying no emotion, no pity, but total disinterest in the drama unfolding around him. There was no lingering around after this performance; I was too thankful to be leaving the creepy Jean behind.

Part III

The Paris Opera Ballet
1970–1983

It is perhaps important to understand what was happening at the Paris Opera before Nureyev arrived to take charge in 1983, and above all, to know a little of the history of the oldest and most famous company in the world whose roots go back to King Louis XIV.

After I first saw the French company in 1969, I went to the Palais Garnier several times over the next few years, each performance being more disappointing than the one before. I found the dancers to be stilted and technically poor. Fresh from what is now referred to as the Golden Years of the Royal Ballet, and knowing I had been extremely privileged to have seen the partnership of Fonteyn and Nureyev on so many occasions, it came as quite a shock when I saw *Sleeping Beauty* performed by the Paris Opera Ballet at the Palais-des-Congrès, a difficult setting for dance at the best of times.

Staged in 1982, it was a new production by Rosella Hightower, modelled on that of her old company, the Grand Ballet du Marquis de Cuevas, but all the dancers, the King, Queen, courtiers and princesses seemed to be kitted out as birds. The costumes were too gaudy; one might have been at the Folies Bergère and so from the beginning, the choice of what one could only call a second-rate designer was disconcerting. It was a bad start.

Obviously, the most important aspect was, or should have been, the dancing, but the corps de ballet was undisciplined and messy. Although I saw no one giggling as in a previous incursion to the Palais Garnier, when two of the swans in *Swan Lake* spent their time smirking at each other, the technical level of many was poor.

Things might not have been so disappointing if the performance of the two principal dancers had been good, but it wasn't. Not that it was their fault. Not every dancer can, nor should be expected to be able to dance everything, and this was one of the times they were simply miscast. Paris principal dancer Françoise Legrée had been given the role of Princess Aurora, but while she certainly looked the part, it was beyond her capabilities to dance it. She didn't possess the necessary technique. Legrée was indeed very pretty, but her dancing in one of the most difficult roles in the classical repertoire was worse than weak. In other less demanding ballets, she later proved lovely to watch, but she should never have been cast as Aurora. The poor girl was obliged to modify the choreography and to watch her wobbling on pointe as she greeted her princes had me quaking in fear for her. I was too anxious to enjoy the performance.

In contrast, her prince, étoile Patrice Bart, had no problem with the choreography and accomplished all the complicated steps in addition to being a solid partner, but having seen Rudolf Nureyev, with his unmatched grace and power, sail through the air in the last act, what is there to say? All dancers are unique, some being more unique than others. Patrice Bart was not a virtuoso dancer, being rather a fine character dancer who later left his mark when cast as Nureyev's Rothbart. He came into his own when he proved to be an excellent ballet master, working with Nureyev to transform the Paris corps de ballet into one of the finest in the world.

The Paris Opera Ballet, the oldest company in the world, traces its beginnings back to Louis XIV, who adored dancing, and who had appeared in his first court ballet at the age of twelve. Two years later, he was dancing his favourite role, that of the Sun in *Le Ballet de la Nuit*. He engaged the Italian musician Jean-Baptiste Lully to take charge of productions at court and Lully, in turn, hired Pierre Beauchamp, the man generally credited with the invention of the five positions of the feet, as ballet master, although it's more probable that he only began organising them. And then in 1661, Louis XIV founded the Académie Royale de Danse, which was renamed the Académie Royale de Musique in 1672, the forerunner of the Paris Opera.

Professional dancers were needed to perform in what now became a professional theatre, and by 1681 technique began to be codified and girls were able to make a career onstage; it was the beginning of ballet as we know it today. But unfortunately during 'La Belle Epoque', it was not infrequent for dance and opera goers to stroll around the Main Foyer or the Foyer de la Dance while the corps de ballet took over the stage to give the ballerinas a rest between appearances. Dance as such was little more than an excuse to meet one's friends and spend an amusing and pleasant evening.

Serge Lifar

By a quirk of fate, Serge Lifar (1905–1986), the smoothly handsome danseur étoile, was appointed artistic director of the Paris Opera Ballet on December 31st, 1929, instead of George Balanchine, as had originally been planned. Balanchine, fresh from his triumphs with Diaghilev, was laid low with flu and unable to take up the post. How the history of dance would have been changed!

Consequently, Lifar it was who, upon his appointment, was horrified to discover that instead of inheriting a company, there was only a raggedy group of young people. There was no troupe, no audience, and no living tradition worth speaking of. Attractive young women would trip gracefully around the stage, while men were required to simply set off the charm and beauty of their partners. Few would deny that an outing to the opera was the occasion to parade in the newest fashion and catch up with the latest scandal. Naturally, all the lights would be left blazing so no one would miss an unexpected arrival and no elderly gentleman would trip on his way to the Foyer de la Danse to waylay young dancers. Lifar consequently set to work on a series of reforms that were to lay the basic groundwork for Nureyev half a century later.

He began the work of transformation by dimming the great chandelier with its 400 twinkling lights as soon as a performance began, thus preventing spectators from moving around to greet acquaintances and obliging them to concentrate on events onstage instead. Moreover, once the show had begun, no one was allowed to enter the theatre, a rule which still holds true today. After 7.30pm precisely, latecomers must wait for an interval to claim their seats.

Up until the arrival of Lifar, no full evening of dance had ever been shown; ballet was used as light entertainment between well-known operatic arias, but the enormous success of *Salade* in 1934, set to a score by Milhaud and decor by Derain, enabled him to install a complete evening of ballet every Wednesday in July that year.

On a more practical level, holes in tights, elastic on shoes and all personal jewellery were banned, and since an Albrecht sporting a moustache was considered unacceptable, male dancers had to shave. Stage make-up was introduced, Lifar himself teaching his dancers the technique for professional appearances. And one of his hardest tasks was to insist that ballerinas should dance on pointe instead of demi-pointe, which they had grown used to.

Once Lifar had begun this initial period of cleaning up, he was free to concentrate on the real work of training dancers who could ally a faultless technique to their other qualities, and in 1932 he created a 'classe d'adage' which he taught himself. Male dancers began to have a little more to do despite protests from some of the older, established ballerinas, including the famous Olga Spessivtseva. He considered the teaching of Carlotta Zambelli to be "limited and somewhat torpid", and so the most promising students from the Opera school were sent off to study with the great Russian dancers who had settled in France after having been driven from their homeland by the Revolution.

Kchessinska and Preobrajenska, two of the greatest teachers of all, as well as Trefilova and Volinine had opened private schools in Paris. They formed dancers including Toumanova, Baronova, Darsonval and Yvette Chauviré, the most famous of the French étoiles who partnered Nureyev before her retirement, after which, with his encouragement, she began to coach dancers at the Paris Opera.

Simultaneously, a correct working atmosphere was established at the Palais Garnier when the exquisite Foyer de la Dance was closed to unwelcome visitors, those ageing Paris rakes or 'abonnés', lascivious gentlemen who assumed that their financial aid to the company also entitled them to other dubious privileges. Lifar would rapidly sweep his dancers away, arranging rehearsals as soon as he saw them arrive. Talent and hard work were rewarded with promotion at the same time as he restructured the undisciplined corps de ballet, laying the groundwork for Patrice Bart when Nureyev appointed him Maître de Ballet many years later. With the arrival of Bart, the era of giggling girls in the corps de ballet came to an abrupt end.

However, all this was far from easy, for the Paris Opera was only partly subsidised by the state, and early on Lifar had to face the anger of the 'abonnés' who believed they had the right to promote their personal favourites. Complaints poured in, calling Lifar a "young barbarian" who was a threat to the future of dance in France.

But Lifar possessed influential friends in Picasso, Max Ernst, Stravinsky and Prokofiev, the painters and artists whom he had known in the Ballets Russes. The famous French poet Jean Cocteau wrote *Phèdre* for him, while Chagall painted the decor for *Daphnis and Chloe* in 1958, and so, undeterred, the ballet director did his best to abolish favouritism, which resulted in a great improvement in the corps de ballet once they saw they were getting a fair deal. Happily, the situation was further helped by an increase in state funding.

Lifar gave great importance to the harmony between dance, music and painting in his works, drawing inspiration from sculptures and other works of art, history, mythology and biblical sources. A new, serious public was brought to dance. Having seen the expressionist style in Germany, and being aware, as was Nureyev, that dance was in perpetual motion, Lifar introduced new steps and new positions; the sixth and seventh position of the feet became his trademark. He invented arabesques penchées, arabesques portées, and arabesques en seconde, giving the French dancers a style of their own, best seen in his plotless ballet *Suite en Blanc*.

Consequently, as well as laying the base for the future, Serge Lifar lives on as a creator of over 100 ballets, although most of them have now disappeared. However, three of his finer works were eventually revived and brought back into the repertoire by Nureyev, who programmed an evening of ballets including Lifar's *Suite en Blanc*, *Mirages*, and *Icare*.

From George Skibine to Rosella Hightower

George Skibine took over in 1958, his greatest achievement being to guide and form many remarkable dancers, Christiane Vaussard and Attilio Labis amongst them, who became extraordinary teachers themselves.

However, Michel Descombey, artistic director from 1962, was far from inspired. "He was ambitious and wanted to be ballet master and director, but he used the company for his own ballets, which were not very good," Patrice Bart told me.

"There was a breeding ground of excellent young dancers, including Noella Pontois, Claire Motte and Wilfride Piollet, but it was the standard of productions that was poor. There were just too many second-rate creations from Descombey, who was finally asked to leave in the turmoil of 1968 when John Taras took over for one year, rapidly followed by Claude Bessy the year after. Being an étoile herself, she tended to stage ballets just for the principal dancers and consequently, little was done for the corps de ballet." But then Bart shrugged his shoulders. "What can anyone do in one year?"

"Raymond Franchetti came next, from 1972 to 1977. He was a tremendous teacher, but neither a great dancer nor choreographer, and I think he remained too involved with his own school in Paris as well, so everyone was a little bit lost. There were, however, one or two good moments," Bart continued, "such as when Roland Petit was invited to stage his *Notre Dame de Paris* here, and Maurice Béjart came with *The Firebird*. But generally speaking, it was rather dull and things didn't really work out with Carolyn Carlson either when she came in 1974. Rolf Liebermann nominated her 'choreographer étoile', but she was never really accepted because she worked in a very different way.

"In 1977, the artistic direction was taken over by étoile Violette Verdy until 1980, followed by Rosella Hightower from 1980 to 1983. While Rosella Hightower, who frequently partnered Nureyev, was a wonderful ballerina and an excellent teacher, she, like Franchetti, spent too much time running her school in Cannes. Neither was she able to fight against the General Administrator. The artistic director of a ballet company has to be able to resist the general administration," Bart explained.

"There was nothing basically wrong with Georges Hirsch either, but, in the same way as Pierre Bergé, he wanted to be all-powerful and had his own ideas. As did Bergé, Hirsch wanted to be involved with everything, even ballets. Hightower would give into him time and again, and do what he wanted, not necessarily what was the best for the company. She mounted her own production of *Sleeping Beauty*, which was not very well received.

"Both ladies were very sweet and very nice," Bart continued, "but neither had any idea how to run the company. There were 153 people here, and it was unwieldy. We needed someone very tough to deal with us, particularly as we were virtually two companies.

"There was a smaller troupe at Salle Favart that had their own repertory," he reminded me. "They performed their own bits and pieces but their level wasn't nearly as high as at Garnier, so trouble was inevitable when we merged. There were fat dancers, thin dancers, ageing dancers, short dancers as well as some really tall ones, and when one added to that those who totally lacked musicality, well, the situation was dramatic. And, by law, all of them had to stay until they retired at forty or forty-five. It was not at all conducive to a homogenous corps de ballet. It was catastrophic!

"And don't forget the famous French temperament," he added. "Although we work very hard, we're an unruly lot. It doesn't do any good to be too kind."

Claude Bessy

If the fortunes of the company were declining, and very much so, quite the reverse was happening in the school. The energetic and forceful Claude Bessy, directrice from 1972 to 2004, had succeeded Geneviève Guillot and had proceeded with a series of reforms. "Nothing had changed since I'd been a pupil here myself," she told me. "Apart from the fact that the full history of the school's teaching includes 300 years of famous names, it was static and time for a change."

Before her arrival, enrolment was limited to about sixty pupils from Paris and the nearby suburbs as there were no facilities for boarders. With the help of Rolf Liebermann, the general director, Bessy obtained the money to rent three large flats in Paris, enabling her to extend her selection to all of France and beyond. At the same time, she hired more teachers and pianists. She'd travelled a lot and seen what went on elsewhere, and so she tried, and succeeded, to get the best of all worlds.

Academic schooling was piecemeal and so she harassed the ministry of education to review the curriculum which had long been neglected. Mime, folk dancing, contemporary dance and adage were added to the classical dance lessons, while problems of getting up before dawn to share two small rehearsal studios with the opera dancers were solved when a beautiful, new, spacious school was opened in Nanterre in 1987. Now the children had no fewer than twelve rehearsal rooms to themselves plus a 300-seat auditorium just a fifteen-minute metro ride from the Palais Garnier.

Claude Bessy, who invited choreographers like Béjart and Petit to adapt ballets for her pupils, told me that she had a certain idea of her art. "I've a good vision of people. I know what I want and I choose the right teachers, most of whom led brilliant careers in the company. I'm present from morning to night and my life is dedicated to the company, the same as Rudolf Nureyev.

Dancers here," she continued, "have security of employment now and if someone doesn't shake them up they get lazy."

Elisabeth Platel explained that all the teachers at the school were from the company. "It's a transmission from generation to generation," she said. "All the teachers I worked with always spoke to me of the teachers they themselves had. Christiane Vaussard spoke to me about Carlotta Zambelli, and Franchetti of Gustave Ricaux, one of the most important pedagogues of his time. Raymond Franchetti's lessons were directly influenced by Ricaux's teaching, both in the company and the school, crucial because the pupils of today will not only be the dancers of tomorrow, but also the teachers of the future."

Agnès Letestu, a pure product of the Paris Opera school, spoke to me of the highly selective admission criteria. "At first," she said, "pupils are chosen for their perfect physique, for their suppleness, arched feet, elevation and straight spine and musicality. Then there is a stringent medical test, and after that, one has to compete with over a thousand other applicants for only thirty places."

The level of young dancers joining the company was very high; the scene was set. All that was needed was for Rudolf Nureyev to arrive.

I talked to Patrice Bart, himself trained at the opera school and who had joined the company at the age of fourteen and a half, rising through the ranks to principal dancer in 1972. With the encouragement of Nureyev, he began teaching after his retirement, becoming Ballet Master in 1987 before being given the title of 'Ballet Master Associé à la direction de la danse' in 1990. I asked him to explain exactly what had gone wrong in the period up to Nureyev's arrival as artistic director in 1983 and to describe the actual situation Rudolf was confronted with.

"The Paris Opera dancers had the ability but their technique was poor. I'd been dancing with the then London Festival Ballet from 1970 to 1981 and seen all the productions at Covent Garden. When I made the comparison with Paris, it wasn't too good at all. We fell far short and something had to be done but we didn't know where to turn. No one seemed capable of directing us. Dominique Khalfouni had just left us for Roland Petit's company, but in 1983, we still had some outstanding étoiles including Charles Jude, Patrick

Dupond, Elisabeth Platel, Florence Clerc and the recently nominated Monique Loudières, plus some lovely soloists. Moreover, the corps de ballet was improving because the Opera school was starting to become very, very good, but if the best dancers in the world are not used properly, there's nothing you can do. We could only dance what we were given.

"That's where we were when Nureyev arrived. We needed a forceful director capable of directing the company, someone not only with the artistic requirements for the job, but someone with the political support behind them in order to obtain the money we require. We get a large subsidy from the state but to get it, you have to be strong enough to fight the unions and the Ministry of Finance."

Nureyev thus inherited a company with a whole galaxy of potential young stars waiting, including Sylvie Guillem, Isabelle Guérin, Elisabeth Maurin, Manuel Legris and Laurent Hilaire. However, one problem that he faced was, as he remarked himself, that while all the current étoiles were beautiful dancers, there were several young soloists more beautiful than some of the étoiles. By law, the étoiles had to be cast in priority. If not, revolution lay ahead!

Part IV

Nureyev in Paris
1983–1993

In 1982, in spite of opposition from the Soviet authorities but with the approval of President Mitterrand, Jack Lang, the far-sighted French Minister of Culture, offered the post of artistic director at the Paris Opera Ballet to Rudolf Nureyev. I heard the news as I was having lunch with a dancer friend in the top-floor restaurant of the Parisian store Galeries Lafayette, overlooking the rooftops of the Palais Garnier. Upon hearing he'd agreed, I was torn between anxiety for him, knowing what an undisciplined lot many of the dancers were, and excitement over the drastic changes he was sure to make despite the heavy bureaucracy he would surely come up against. I can honestly say that my fears were more for him than for the dancers, and they proved to be not completely unfounded.

Already in 1971, Rolf Liebermann, administrator of the French company, had suggested bringing in Nureyev as artistic director, but at that moment in time, the dancer's demands proved a little excessive. At thirty-three and at the height of his career, not only did he want to dance everything himself, but he wished to bring half of the British corps de ballet along with him, a fact unacceptable to the French administration, though perhaps not to the public!

Twelve years later, grown more reasonable and after having appeared regularly as guest artist at the Palais Garnier, as well as the Palais-des-Congrès, the Palais-des-Sports, and the Cour Carrée du Louvre, Nureyev was forty-five years old and ready to take on the challenge of directing a large company. He'd come to a turning point in his career and his virtuoso days were coming to an end, although he had a whole new range of roles he wanted to dance. His early hopes of directing the Royal Ballet of London had gone nowhere, but he knew the French company; he knew the dancers and was fully aware of the enormous potential there. He felt certain that it was a company that he could leave his mark on. He'd seen Sergeyev, Nijinska, Ulanova, as well as Erik Bruhn; he'd copied and absorbed their gestures and now he was ready to adopt the French company and pass on his knowledge.

"If I can make them understand everything I have learned, then I shall be perfectly happy" were his first words upon accepting the appointment.

"*Vouloir c'est pouvoir*," declared Nureyev as he took up his post in September the following year. What happened then has been described by Brigitte Lefèvre, assistant director at the time, as "a series of electro shocks".

The first thing he did, which was also a condition for him accepting the position, was to pressurise Jack Lang into creating three large studios on the top floor of the Palais Garnier where the dancers could rehearse three different programmes simultaneously. This would also enable him to invite guest choreographers more easily, and he didn't hesitate to invite people like Robert Wilson, William Forsythe, and Maguy Marin as well as Jerome Robbins, Roland Petit, and Maurice Béjart amongst many others.

Strong, positive and knowing exactly what he wanted and how to get it done, Nureyev's direction of the Paris Opera Ballet ranks amongst his greatest achievements. No other director in any other company ever achieved so much in so short a time when taking charge of an established troupe.

"I had to be authoritative," Rudolf told me in conversation a year or so later, "simply because it was impossible to direct such a large company of over 150 dancers in a democratic way. They had the talent and I wanted to give them the enthusiasm and the precision."

I asked principal dancer Florence Clerc just how authoritative Nureyev actually was. "Well," she replied," authoritative and demanding he might have been, but above all, he had endless patience with all those dancers who genuinely wanted to work.

"I'd met him before he took over the company, when I was only just in the corps de ballet, but what struck me most was his extreme kindness. It was the way that he cared so deeply about the dancers. Each and every one of us. He'd spend his time explaining not only how to do each step, but why, and if we didn't quite grasp what he meant, he'd start all over again. He made us understand the meaning behind each step. Nothing was ever too much trouble for him.

"I was only nineteen, and couldn't understand how someone like him could waste so much time with me; my admiration had no limits."

Rudolf rehearsing Sleeping Beauty with Florence Clerc.
© Francette Levieux/CNCS

Charles Jude, the danseur étoile who met Nureyev in 1969 and who became his closest friend, described to me what it was like when Rudolf arrived.

"At first everyone was petrified of him because he was such an enormous star, but it was quickly obvious that he loved the dancers here and we found it extraordinary to work with him because we were being taken in charge by someone who really knew what he was doing because he'd taken the time and trouble to get to know us.

"At the beginning, we all looked up to him as the legendary superstar; everyone wanted to dance like him, to have his aura and his magnetism, even his special way of walking onstage and wearing a cloak, but he never forced himself on us. He didn't influence us to dance as he did, not wanting us to copy the way he danced at all! What he did give us was the passion to dance, the desire to be onstage, and, not least, a desire to please him.

"He would tell us to start dancing and then stop us, suggesting we try the step differently," Jude said. "When he saw how we danced, he would suggest a way of changing it which would suit our own style. How a step was done depended on the dancer he was talking to. We were all different, and he knew instinctively how to bring out the best in each of us. This was patently obvious in the way he created very balanced dance partnerships; he'd put two dancers together who drew out the best of each other in any given role. He asked me, for example, to dance *Cinderella* with Sylvie Guillem, while Laurent Hilaire danced my role with Elisabeth Platel, Elisabeth and I being the dancers with the experience to bring our partners towards us.

"By working like that," he continued, "Rudolf enabled each dancer to create the role he was interpreting around his own personality. He had the generosity and the intelligence to recognise our differences. He had worked at the Opera before and loved the theatre and the dancers; he knew their potential and what to do with them. He was very happy to be here. He'd often said he wanted to settle in France, saying, 'France is my wife and Italy my mistress.'

"He danced with the company because he needed to show the dancers what he was still capable of doing at forty-six, and if he could do it, so could they. That was what gave him the right to be exacting with us. He never changed the choreography, preferring falling over or getting it wrong rather than doing what he called cheating. He'd prefer the public to see him dance badly instead of short-cutting and taking the easy way out, and he never did anything that he didn't want the dancers to do later."

Charles Jude told me how Nureyev's generosity extended to everyone as he tried to pass on and share what he himself loved. He wanted to make them all understand that there was a discipline to be respected in dance, stressing that classical dance had to be hard as it was the only way to ensure the future. He'd seen botched-up and messed-up versions of great works such as *Sleeping Beauty* and *Swan Lake*, which were no longer faithful to their Kirov origins and betrayed Petipa. His insistence on certain positions and movements was his way of keeping the ballets intact.

Wilfried Romoli, who entered the company three years before Nureyev's arrival, spoke to me of the new director's tremendous ideas and of his superb theatrical conception of dance.

"What was fantastic for the company was how open he was to new steps, new choreographers and new ideas. He pushed us to look outside and to do other things, because although his great love was Petipa, he brought people like Maguy Marin and Dominique Bagouet here. And while I wasn't an étoile or even a 'premier danseur', but only part of the corps de ballet, he still had all the time in the world for me. It took me ages to realise that for him, it wasn't the technical exploit that counted, it was the manner in which it was done."

Francis Malovik, who became ballet master at the National Ballet of Bordeaux after his retirement, spoke of when he was a long-standing member of the corps de ballet in Paris. He told me practically the same thing.

"I was a nobody, way down in the hierarchy," he said, "yet Nureyev had time for me. I remember, before one of those concours for promotion, when he just came up to me and asked whether I'd like him to teach me the variation from *Le Corsaire* for the competition. I was so taken aback by his thoughtfulness and encouragement and the amount of time he spent with me. I was really happy working with him and his patience was endless, and then, after seeing my disappointment when after all the effort I wasn't promoted, he made a point of coming up to me in the Opera courtyard, saying that I had danced very well, and telling me the most important thing was that I had had a great time, and the only thing that mattered was that I was dancing.

"I was truly overwhelmed when he gave me the role of the Grand Braham for the première of *The Bayadère*. It was a consecration; I was only a coryphée, near the very bottom of the hierarchy."

Étoile Agnès Letestu recalled how he would come not only to rehearsals, but also to lessons. "He was never a teacher as such, but would watch us all carefully in class. And then he'd give someone some advice and it was always exactly right and just what was needed. He always saw what the trouble was immediately… and his solutions were so simple; he was so quick! He'd tell you what to do about it and how to correct it, whether it was a leg or arm movement, and the problem would be solved. He was so interested and concerned.

"And while it's acknowledged that he completely changed dance for male soloists, he also obliged the public to take notice of the men in the corps de ballet too.

"When he arrived here, it seemed to me as though he was a magician. He wanted to give us all his enormous talent; it's crazy, but I'd never seen anything like it. When I was onstage, in the corps de ballet, I watched him guide Sylvie Guillem with a look. She'd stay suspended in the air for him. I'll never forget the look of pride on his face. All his partners understood what he wanted them to do as if by magic. He helped us offstage, he helped us onstage. Guillem could always stay 'en équilibre' longer for him.

"When he was there, something very special happened."

Étoile Monique Loudières echoed Letestu's words, adding, "When Rudolf gave me the role of Kitri in his *Don Quixote*, I said I could never do it, but he'd push me, insisting, yes, yes, yes, you can. And I could.

"He would encourage us all; he was so different from anyone else, so attentive and caring. Progress for him had never finished, and perfection was always out of reach. He'd tell you how to correct steps we had problems with, and all we had to do was follow what he said. He gave me the confidence in myself that I needed."

Each of these words were repeated by danseur étoile Hervé Moreau, who, he said, spoke for all of the dancers at the Paris Opera. "Nureyev's versions gave meaning to the great classics. He revolutionised these ballets, so much so, that when the dancers guest elsewhere with other versions, we actually find them boring. For myself, my one regret is that I only saw him dance on video."

I did try to find some 'embittered' dancers, some of those older grumblers who objected to the way Rudolf expected them to work and were only too ready to cause trouble. The handsome danseur étoile Jean-Yves Lormeau was one of them. He had been a pupil of my close friend Jacqueline Cochet, and one evening in December, after Jean-Yves' performance as Siegfried in Nureyev's production of *Swan Lake*, the three of us went out to dinner.

"Jean-Yves doesn't like Nureyev," asserted Jacqueline. "I asked him to tell you why." At first, the danseur étoile merely shrugged his shoulders, pulled a face, and looked everywhere except at us. Finally, he condescended to speak.

"It's not that I dislike him," he explained, "but more that I resent him. He's a better dancer than me, he's better looking than me, he's more intelligent than me, he knows more about everything than me… and I just can't take his attitude any more, even though I know he's right. That's the problem, he's always right! He's just too much!

"It's not just that he expects us to dance with passion and explodes in temper when we don't, but more that he won't give up until we do dance with passion! His entire life is dance; all that matters to him is dance, dance and dance!

"And he's done it all by himself, while me, I was just lucky. I arrived here at the right time, I'm tall, not bad-looking, and I fit the image of the French 'danseur noble'."

Patricia Ruanne

Patricia Ruanne, the English ballerina who had created Nureyev's first Juliet in 1974 and who had come to the Paris Opera from Covent Garden at his invitation to take over the post of ballet mistress, said immediately that Rudolf had taught the dancers to be disciplined and to rehearse intelligently and constructively.

"He was someone with an extremely open mind and was the last person to put himself into any category. He had no limits, never had blinkers on and his horizons were always widening. Did you know that he spoke five or six languages? Well, perhaps not all perfectly… He always used to say that he needed to learn more and that he learned when he taught.

"He visited art galleries, training his mind to see all aspects, every element of everything, pushing others to do the same. Art, music, theatre; he never rested on his laurels, opening doors to show the dancers here what they were capable of doing and helping them to understand something they hadn't realised before," she explained. "They are all better artists because of an incisive comment here and an acute observation there. He constantly challenged what the dancers thought to be impossible. Dance for him was a vibrant, living art, expressing emotion."

Ruanne had left England, her family, her friends, even her own language as she spoke little French, arriving in Paris with her husband, Frédéric Jahn, who had created the role of Tybalt in Rudolf's 1974 production.

"It was a big step to leave England," she told me one evening in the attractive apartment in Montmartre that Nureyev himself had found for them. "But with everything he'd given me, it would have been churlish to refuse the only thing he'd ever asked of me.

"He arrived at a time in my life when I was most receptive and at the right stage in my career when I could accept what he offered. He gave me enormous confidence in my ability to interpret and accomplish a role for which I'm eternally grateful. Certain people touch you at certain moments in your life and Rudolf came along at exactly the right moment for me to absorb all he had to offer. Then he did the same for all the dancers at the Paris Opera.

Nureyev with Patricia Ruanne at the Palais Garnier surrounded by dancers from left to right, Manuel Legris, Elisabeth Maurin, Kader Belarbi, José Martinez, Frédéric Jahn, Wilfried Romoli, Nicolas Le Riche and Agnès Letestu.

© Jacques Moatti

"Also," she added, "despite the fact that he was so demanding, I'd always enjoyed working with him regardless of having to burn the midnight oil. Anyway, I'm here and that's self-explanatory.

"Before Rudolf arrived, ballet was nothing, a minor art, but he excited people's interest. He was simply amazing. If your son wanted to be a ballet dancer, then, because of Rudolf he could become one as dancing became a respectable profession, and boys weren't afraid to say they were dancers any more. It's too obvious to say that when he arrived at the head of the Paris company he knocked the socks off everybody, but it's true. And in doing so, he enhanced all our lives. Nureyev's contribution is everywhere and can't be measured, individually and collectively. Words alone are too banal to describe the importance and range of what he accomplished.

"He desired to bring new life to the classics, to re-see them, making better use of today's techniques, and in doing so, shook everybody up. He turned them all around," she told me. "And it was a very bumpy ride for him as well as all the dancers.

"Certainly, one of the biggest shake-ups I witnessed," Ruanne continued, "was when he broke through the system of hierarchy. All of a sudden, young dancers from the lower ranks were interpreting roles usually given to more experienced, that is, older, dancers. He had tried his hardest to transform the company into three categories, that of corps de ballet, soloists and étoiles, but unable to achieve this, began to simply cast the dancers with potential from the lower ranks regardless."

The hierarchy

As is generally known within the dance world, the Paris Opera ballet has a very rigid hierarchy and until Rudolf's arrival, chances to interpret main roles or even solos lower down the ranks were few. Since the system of exams for promotion had been installed in 1860, a 'quadrille', the most junior grade in the company, could only apply for the post of 'coryphée', the next rank up, should one be available that year, following it up by promotion to 'sujet', a rank that is still part of the corps de ballet, but not quite soloist in its own right, which was again dependent on whether a position was available the following year. The top of the ladder is the rank of première danseuse/danseur, excluding nominations to étoile, a title normally given to exceptional dancers and directly awarded by the artistic director and general director. Places are limited and highly coveted and competition is fierce.

The contest actually begins well beforehand as ten out of a possible thirty points given are also awarded for performances during the previous season, which was fair enough if you had been given the opportunity to dance! It wasn't always the case. Assiduity in attending classes can lose or gain you extra points, but most of all, the qualities that the judges are looking for differ. Some are looking for personality and temperament whereas others demand impeccable technique and presentation. Worst of all, certain judges, many of whom were from the company, could be biased if friends of theirs were competing. Favouritism was rife.

Principal roles when Nureyev arrived on the scene were strictly reserved for the étoiles, the fifth and highest rank, and one of the problems Nureyev faced was that not all the étoiles were to his liking. Nor to mine, I should add. Women were obliged to retire at forty, while male dancers, inexplicably, as their careers tend to be shorter, were stuck there until the age of forty-five, no matter what their ability, and woe betide the unfortunate spectator if the tubby monsieur given the role of the prince had long outstayed his welcome.

Fortunately the law has since been changed to make it obligatory for all dancers to retire at forty-two and a half.

Patricia Ruanne explained to me that the foundations of the Paris Opera were built on hierarchy and passing exams, but that Rudolf broke through that system because he was determined to guarantee that great talent visible in very young dancers should not be left to stagnate and wither.

"Of course these youngsters had doubts, I had doubts, but he helped us all to realise that doubts never knock down your ability if you are disciplined and rehearse intelligently and constructively. Your body gets into the habit of accomplishing the steps the right way, so once onstage, it leaves you free to interpret the role.

"There's a right moment and he encouraged them and gave them their chance, regardless of whether they'd passed exams or not. Rudolf showed the young that where they want to go is their own responsibility. You can help, advise, be a pair of eyes, but they are the ones who have to do it. He gave them room for their desire to go somewhere; there's little point in desiring something desperately if you're blocked for the next twelve years.

"His contract might have stated that he was to spend six months in Paris, but quite frankly, he was here, he stayed here and the contact with him was never lost as he would be in constant touch via his daily phone calls, wherever he was. You always knew exactly where he was."

Thus it was, in December 1983, I saw dancers from the lower ranks I'd never seen before take over important roles in Nureyev's *Raymonda*, discovering Laurent Hilaire and Manuel Legris, aged twenty-one and nineteen respectively, both young members of the corps de ballet, who were sensational as Béranger and Bernard, two important, technically difficult secondary roles. Hilaire later told me that he had first met Rudolf when he was seventeen, taking lessons with Alexandre Kalioujny, when the Russian dancer had also joined in the class.

"And then," he said, "I had just gained the rank of sujet at the Opera when Nureyev arrived to take over and yet he gave me the role of Franz in *Coppélia*. It was an enormous opportunity and a huge risk for him to take, and then shortly after he nominated me étoile directly, even though I was not yet premier danseur."

Teaching

Charles Jude emphasised that the director was in class every morning and that they not only saw him dance, but also were able to watch him at the barre.

"The teacher would give the lesson, but it was Rudolf who corrected every dancer. Each time there was a step that someone couldn't do, or wasn't doing it correctly, he'd call a halt and show the dancer what to do. 'It's done like this,' he'd explain, and he'd demonstrate the step himself.

"He showed us how to do things we hadn't been accustomed to doing; we hadn't got that kind of technique, but he wanted to pass all his incredible knowledge on to us."

Patrice Bart

"Rudolf would always go to different classes in order to see everybody," Patrice Bart, Nureyev's associate from 1983 to 1989, told me. "He knew everything about ballet, both classical and modern, the French school, the English school, the Danish school, and he brought us, first and foremost, the pure classical beauty and rigour of the Kirov school. If Russian princes in the grand Kirov tradition originate in St Petersburg, then Rudolf knew how to allay that technique with the noblesse and elegance of the French school to create something different. He took the best of everything and gave us our own way of dancing."

From the beginning, Nureyev captured everyone's interest because what he was doing was very special and completely new. "There he'd be, first thing in the morning," said Bart, "telling the teachers how to teach, and some of them didn't take too kindly to that at all, but the next day, he'd go to another class and start all over again. So he drew everyone into his net; the teachers had no choice. Patricia Ruanne, Eugène Polyakov and myself were all working in the same direction and something wonderful was happening. The corps de ballet became the finest in the world.

"Even so," Bart continued, "he not only created the role of Rothbart around me when my career as a dancer was nearing its end, but he encouraged me

Rudolf with French choreographer Roland Petit at a rehearsal of Notre Dame de Paris at the Palais Garnier in November 1988. Ballet master Patrice Bart is standing behind.

© Colette Masson/Roger Viollet

to stage my own productions in Berlin, Helsinki, Milan, Munich and Paris. I worked very closely with him, learning everything from him, even to working with the lighting technicians.

"Rudolf would never give up," the ballet master said, "until he'd got something right. He was a perfectionist, exacting with himself, which gave him the right to be exacting with us.

"He had so much warmth, so much kindness and generosity. He could explode at any moment and hurl his thermos flask of tea across the room, but it was always because someone was not giving their best. He taught us never to take a short-cut, but to keep working at certain combinations of steps even if we fell, as he did. You just got up and did it again. We were never allowed to take the easy way out. Don't cheat, he'd say, don't lie. And when you finally managed to do it, well, you could dance. He was, however, merciless with the mediocre and with those who gave up with his fine run of Anglo-Saxon adjectives! He had no time for lazy dancers. But everyone respected him."

"We followed Rudolf blindly," Charles Jude told me. "He mesmerised everyone and the progress that he accomplished within the company was phenomenal. I myself began working with him before he took over the post at the Opera, back in 1974 when he picked me out of the corps de ballet here to dance *Aureole* with him, and from then on I danced with him all the time. Everything I know about dance came from Rudolf.

"He taught me all the roles in the repertory and the different ways of dancing. He came here to create a dynamism in ballet and to make the company understand that the more they danced different roles, the more easily they would acquire the technique necessary to progress."

But Nureyev did not only change the dancers' approach and break through the hierarchy; he widened their horizons with a whole new repertoire. His own range was enormous, including all the classics as well as contemporary works, and at the same time that he brought new life to the classics with his productions, he commissioned new works and invited a constant stream of contemporary and often controversial modern choreographers to work with the company.

He'd already given the example, appearing himself with such people as Murray Louis, Paul Taylor and Martha Graham and he planned to break down the barriers between modern dance and classical ballet.

He presented 17th- and 18th-century reconstructions by Francine Lancelot, *Bach Suite* and *Quelques pas graves de Baptiste*, which he took great pleasure in dancing himself, as well as Ivo Cramer's *Harlequin, magician of love* and *Dansomanie*, French baroque ballet that had been totally forgotten. In doing so, he kept the traditions of Louis XIV alive. He programmed a whole range of classical favourites, the base of the company's repertoire, but he also embraced all the masters of the 20th century, from Balanchine and Harold Lander to Antony Tudor, whom the Paris Opera had never seen before.

Genia Polyakov – "Bonjour la danse!"

But Nureyev didn't accomplish all this single-handedly, for shortly after he accepted the post of director, he asked his compatriot, Evgeny Polyakov, a man of great sweetness, to join him in Paris.

Genia, as he was affectionately known to everyone, was born in Moscow on April 27th, 1943. He joined the Bolshoi Ballet School at the age of ten, and regularly spent his holidays in Saint Petersburg where, in 1958 at the age of fifteen, he first met Rudolf Nureyev at a meeting of all the dance schools throughout the Soviet Union.

Dark-haired, slight and of medium height with a gentle, expressive face, he became a principal dancer with the company of Novosibirsk in Siberia where he danced all the great classics from *Swan Lake* to *Sleeping Beauty*, and where he began to choreograph and mount his own ballets. A pedagogue of limitless patience, he accepted a post at the Bolshoi school from 1970 to 1976, before leaving to

Eugene Polyakov relaxing at home, 1982.
Personal collection of Florence Clerc

settle in Italy to become ballet master at the Theatre de la Fenice in Venice where he created his version of *Giselle* for Nureyev.

"It was not so much that I was friends with Rudolf, which of course I was," Polyakov told me one day over coffee in a favourite bar of his near the Palais Garnier. "It was more that he looked after me and advised me what to do. I'd just arrived in Western Europe and things were not easy. Rudolf went out of his way to help me. He was so very, very kind. Kindness," he added, "is perhaps the most important attribute in any human being. It's everything.

"You know, it's not surprising he had so many friends, really true friends, not just people he knew. Each of them corresponded to a certain aspect of his character, touching a different part of his heart. There were those he spoke to of literature, others shared his love of art and paintings, while he had so much time for those whose vision of the world coincided with his own.

"And then," he added, "we shared the same tastes, had similar ideas, and I do think Rudolf was happy to have me with him in Paris as we were, after all, both from Russia."

It was also in Venice that Genia met Patrice Bart, who was at the time a principal dancer in Paris, and with whom a wonderful working relationship was to develop some ten years later when, together, they created their own version of *Giselle* in 1991, on the occasion of the 150th anniversary of the ballet's creation.

As director of dance at the Teatro Comunale in Florence where he stayed for five years, Polyakov had invited Florence Clerc and Charles Jude to dance his versions of *Coppélia* and *La Dame aux Camélias*, before accepting Nureyev's invitation in 1983 to join him in Paris as senior ballet master, but where he was so much more, virtually Nureyev's assistant. Although he was not officially a teacher, he, like Rudolf, was an outstanding pedagogue, knowing intuitively what was right for each dancer.

"We'd meet over dinner and discuss together the work to be done," he said, "and then in his absence, I'd work alongside Claire Motte."

The dancers were his passion, he told me, and his life was devoted to helping, guiding and supporting them, particularly the younger ones.

"Everyone wanted to work with Genia," said Florence Clerc. "Wherever he went, everyone loved and respected him; he didn't have an enemy in the world. His work in Paris was extraordinary, and in his private life he was a wonderful person. He would always go out of his way to help any small company who needed him, and then rush back to Paris if someone wanted him here. I was very fortunate to have such a special relationship with him, a result of having danced in many of his creations in Florence as well as in all of Rudolf's ballets in Paris which he helped stage."

Agnès Letestu explained how he would come to her before a performance to check over her hair, her costume, and her make-up. "I had to be luminous and radiant; he'd tell me I had the technique and the bravura but I was not to dance like a 'bourgeoise'!

"Genia loved everything 'avant-garde,'" she continued. "He loved his work, and he loved life. He'd always find the time to dash off to Venice if there was a special exhibition there and he wouldn't hesitate to show his special collection of rare books on Anna Pavlova to promising ballerinas.

"He'd point to photographs which particularly illustrated the line of her neck or the beautiful poise of her head. I also remember him making time to go to London to see Matthew Bourne's all-male *Swan Lake*.

"He had such a weakness for attractive women, admiring any new outfits we were wearing and commenting to us all, eyes twinkling, 'What are all these top models doing at the Opera?' He himself loved fashion too, often sporting a favourite ruby-red shirt he was particularly fond of.

"He was so joyous, such fun to be with, and he and Rudolf were so close. Like Rudolf, he was also a man of immense generosity who never spoke about himself. The two of them were irreplaceable."

Elisabeth Platel

Elisabeth Platel, the dark-haired young ballerina who was to create the main roles in almost all of Nureyev's productions, recalled the atmosphere at the Paris Opera when Polyakov and Nureyev began working together on *Raymonda*, a great, grand traditional 'Russian' ballet, in September 1983. She was just twenty-four at the time, having entered the Paris Opera School for one year after winning first prize at the Conservatoire of Paris. She had joined the company when she was seventeen, rising swiftly through the ranks to the post of danseuse étoile in 1981.

"Rudolf's arrival certainly shook us all up," she told me. "He made me dance everything, and within a few years, I created not only *Raymonda*, but his *Swan Lake*, and his *Sleeping Beauty* too. I was taking class with Alexandre Kalioujny, also a wonderful teacher, an étoile here himself in 1947, and then rehearsing with Rudolf and Genia Polyakov in the afternoons.

"The 'shock', Nureyev, Polyakov and Kalioujny was incredible; they were all three in tune with each other. They were truly the three great pillars of the Opera. There was Charles Jude, Monique Loudières, and me, the three confirmed 'stars' and an incredibly talented new generation, including Isabelle Guérin, Sylvie Guillem, Laurent Hilaire and Manuel Legris. He formed us, and then left us free to interpret roles in our own way, once he had ensured we had the structure.

"It was quite amazing to see *Swan Lake* danced on different occasions by Isabelle, by Sylvie and by me; we were all dancing the same choreography, but all interpreting the role in our different ways.

"Nureyev came from the Kirov and Polyakov from the Bolshoi and it was so exciting, a totally magical time from the very beginning," she said. "Nureyev was everywhere, and he and Genia were constantly vying with each other, one surpassing the other. If someone wasn't working properly and not giving their best, Rudolf would hurl insults at them in Russian in his fury before storming off, and Genia would be left to 'translate' and smooth things over. A stream of colourful epithets in Russian, not very pretty ones, would be smoothed over and translated as… he said you weren't working very well, in the most contrite tone.

"Rudolf, as is well-known, was without pity for lazy dancers who took short-cuts and for whom he also had a fine run of Anglo-Saxon adjectives! Neither could he tolerate any interference with his work. It was nevertheless a magical time, full of laughter and packed with the most fantastic memories," she recalled with nostalgia.

"Rudolf insisted upon everything being done as he wanted for the first two years, and then left us free to develop our own personalities and interpret the role in our own way. He formed the dancer I became, and although I frequently argued with him at the time, absolutely everything he said and did for us was right. For example, he refused to let me dance Juliet… '*Romeo and Juliet* not your job,' he'd growl. 'I'm better Juliet'… He saw me as a princess, and so I was Gamzatti in his *Bayadère*.

"What he taught me, and, I think, all the dancers here, is that technique was at the service of the role and should not be used to astonish the spectators. Now that I'm older, I understand what he meant. I do remember being so taken aback when I learned that some people, critics or otherwise, actually counted my pirouettes as the Black Swan, to check whether I'd accomplished all thirty-two of them…"

For two young soloists, Laurent Hilaire and Manuel Legris, who danced Bernard and Béranger, two of Raymonda's friends in the ballet of that name, it was essentially a tremendous time. "Rudolf was very happy, very concentrated and extremely motivated. He expected a lot from us and he gave us so much," Laurent Hilaire told me. "Everything was precise, everything extremely Slav, which made *Raymonda* into something so unique.

"He would demonstrate the steps to us," Hilaire continued, "and we were just overcome with admiration because he had such style and nothing was ever showy or ostentatious. Moreover we partnered Monique Loudières and Claude de Vulpian, who were both principal dancers, and that in itself was most unusual. Principal dancers just didn't dance with mere members of the corps de ballet."

Raymonda

"Don't talk, work!" were Rudolf Nureyev's opening words to the dancers of the Paris Opera Ballet on his arrival there in September 1983. The result was the staging of his sumptuous version of *Raymonda* two months later. It was important, not only because it was his first big production as director of the French company, but also because of the personal links he established with the dancers via his choreography, teaching and direction.

Nureyev knew that it was essential to win over the company by creating a good working atmosphere from the beginning, and while the three large studios he had requested were being built on the top floor of the Palais Garnier, he used a vast studio in the Rue Berthier in the Paris suburbs to begin work on *Raymonda*. Familiar as he was with the work of Petipa, he quickly made it known that the legendary French-born choreographer had never wished for his ballets to remain untouched, just for his name to be remembered. He thus revitalised *Raymonda*, dusting it down to make better use of the dancers he had who possessed greater facilities than those of over

100 years before.

"Rudolf completely reworked Petipa's masterpiece, a three-act ballet created for the Maryinsky Theatre in 1898," Patrice Bart explained. "He reorganised the steps to give everything a reason and a logic, developing all the characters in order to make sense of the libretto and eliminating everything that had become superfluous over the last century."

After an early commission to reconstruct the work from memory for the Royal Ballet's touring company, which was performed in Spoleto in 1964, Nureyev created a version for the Australian Ballet the following year, and one for Zurich Ballet in 1972, followed by a further reworking for the American Ballet Theatre, whittling the story down to its bare essentials. His ultimate, carefully thought out version in 1983 was tailor-made to suit the French dancers.

Set in the time of the Crusades, the ballet tells the story of Raymonda, a beautiful girl who is engaged to marry the nobleman Jean de Brienne, despite the fact she's never met him, and who, moreover, is away fighting the infidels. During his absence, she is captured and carried off by the wicked but seductive Saracen prince, Abderam, but Brienne returns in the nick of time to rescue her and all supposedly ends happily ever after.

To begin with, Nureyev replaced all the mimed scenes with dance and developed the personality of Jean de Brienne, previously a relatively colourless character, by adding some spectacular variations for him. He also created some superb choreography, a combination of classical and colourful oriental steps for Abderam, whose original role had been purely mime. The Saracen prince thus took on greater importance and became a worthy rival both in Raymonda's eyes as well as with the audience. Rudolf reckoned, correctly, that the plot had not made much sense before.

"But unfortunately," Bart recalled, "what happened here was that all the male dancers, as far as I know, wanted to dance the role of the glamorous Saracen knight rather than that of the conventional hero!"

However, the weak storyline was merely an excuse for a glorious explosion of pure dance, leaving the spectators as breathless as the dancers, which was precisely Nureyev's intention. There could hardly have been a ballet better suited to enhance the brilliance and fine schooling of the Paris troupe.

"When I arrived here," Nureyev told me, "I wanted to make everyone dance. I wanted roles for everyone. Make them dance, fill house!" His avowed aim was to ensure that every seat in the opera was sold, which it was and still is to this day, for all of his productions. Effectively, the level of the company rose to exceptional heights, and it was after the production of *Raymonda* that the company's supremacy in the world began to be recognised.

True to his word, Nureyev gave importance to many of what had been considered minor roles, distributing them to large numbers of the younger dancers. And *Raymonda*, programmed at the Opera a few months after his arrival, remains one of his most spectacular works, with dancing for the whole company. He had worked closely with his set designer, Nicholas Georgiadis, and the first act opens in a great hall hung with lamps, where oriental tapestries recalling chivalrous deeds jostle with mediaeval manuscripts and ornate paintings, all set against an opulent background of red, black and gold. There was a sumptuous setting before the dancing even began.

Besides the three main roles with their lyrical pas de deux, the dramatic sword fights, and the 'vision' scenes, there are glittering solos for over a dozen more dancers and some outstanding ensembles including lavish Hungarian dances, an exuberant Spanish dance, a magnificent polonaise as well as a scintillating pas de quatre and pas de six! The lively traditional folk-dances and lovely adage were given the rigour and discipline the dancers had lacked since the departure of Serge Lifar in 1958.

With choreography by both Petipa and Nureyev, music by Glazunov, and with the decor and costumes inspired by mediaeval paintings and tapestries by Georgiadis, the famous Greek set designer, the ballet was an overwhelming success despite the unconvincing storyline.

Nicholas Georgiadis

"*Raymonda* was the first work we staged for the Paris Opera," Nicholas Georgiadis told me one sunny afternoon in his beautiful apartment in the Marais area of Paris. I liked the designer immensely from the first moment I met him.

Gentle and softly spoken, his initial words when I first met him, to put me at ease, were to compliment me on the attractive skirt I was wearing. True, it had taken me considerable thought to dress to meet one of the world's greatest costume designers. I have also kept that pale navy linen skirt, oversewn with white, diagonal thread, as a souvenir of that early encounter.

Distinguished and gracious, Georgiadis was what one would call the perfect gentleman. Touched with genius, it was no surprise that he had such a long and fruitful collaboration with Nureyev.

Born in Athens in 1923, he had begun studying design in his hometown before moving to continue his studies in New York in 1952. He then won a scholarship to the Slade School of Fine Art in London where he was quickly noticed by Dame Ninette de Valois, the founder of British ballet, who brought him to the notice of the choreographer Kenneth MacMillan. Thus he became the designer of both the set and costumes for MacMillan's *Romeo and Juliet*... which Rudolf would dance in 1965.

From this early contact, a close partnership with Nureyev developed and he went on to create the set and costumes for Rudolf's own production of *Swan Lake* for the Ballet of Vienna in 1964, when, he recalled with a smile, the ballet received eighty-nine curtain calls, a record that went into *The Guinness Book of Records*. The ballet was filmed two years later.

Nureyev turned to him again for many of his further works, including the 1981 *Don Quixote, Manfred, Washington Square, The Nutcracker, Sleeping Beauty, The Tempest*, and, unsurprisingly, *Raymonda*, his first, sumptuous production for the Paris Opera in 1983 after his appointment as artistic director there.

"We had already worked together on *Raymonda* in Switzerland in 1972," the designer recalled, "but this time, I wanted to design something new because the stage here in Paris is much bigger than the one in Zurich. What I had in mind was something inspired by the work of Diaghilev and the Ballets Russes, and I love creating very atmospheric sets, very Byzantine.

"We had an extremely close collaboration," he continued, "and I find it extraordinary now when choreographers and designers just go ahead and do something without having real discussions together. Why does a director allow that?

"With Rudolf, there wasn't one thing that he would not examine, then re-examine, and then re-examine again. Sometimes he was impatient, but I learned not to change things until we were sure. For example, the masks in *The Nutcracker*, those huge monster-like heads, well, the first day the dancers put them on they were all moaning and complaining, yet they didn't have to wear them for very long. But the problem was that Rudolf wanted the dancers to be happy!

"Nevertheless, I insisted that they would get used to them very quickly. I learned to not follow him automatically, but to give him time to get used to an idea. I had to use a bit of psychology and be careful of how to introduce new ideas and technology. But it wasn't always easy for me to come up with exactly what he wanted because there was this contradiction between the fact that he was basically very classical at odds with his desire to have highly theatrical designs.

"Often," Georgiadis told me, "the things he found awful at first became quite acceptable when he'd grown used to them. I remember one example being the costume of the ballerina in the 'vision scene' of *Don Quixote* because he found that costume awful in Zurich, but when we staged the production in Paris, he declared it 'best costume... why do you want to change it?' were his very words. It was the same thing for the scenery too." He laughed. "Because that, too, had become 'best scene'. Often with Rudolf, it was really funny how things he first found dreadful became 'best' later on.

"I also enjoyed designing the costumes for his *Tempest*, a ballet where we were completely on the same wavelength. It was just a bit long in parts but otherwise very good and it worked very well in London. I don't understand why it was such a total flop in Paris.

"What amused me though," he added, "was when Rudolf decided that he had better lengthen his own solo to ten minutes, the excuse being that he wanted to ensure that the French audience understood what Shakespeare meant. He'd convinced himself that Parisian audiences wouldn't know Shakespeare, and I think he was proved right. Anyway, although the role of Prospero had been created for Anthony Dowell, Rudolf planned to dance it himself on alternate performances, so wanted it longer…

"Well, I said, Rudolf, your solo is already ten minutes long (although I knew he meant twenty). Yes, he replied, but I really want to make sure that they understand what it's all about. I told him, no, for heaven's sake, no, but he did it all the same… He knew his weaknesses but just wanted to be onstage for another ten minutes. All he wanted to do was dance and any excuse would do.

"He had a lot of very theatrical ideas which helped enormously in developing the set of *Raymonda*," Georgiadis continued. "The idea of Abderam's magnificent silken tent in shades of gold, bronze and yellow in the centre of the stage was his.

"He had a tremendous sense of the theatre, and would really exhaust himself to explain to the dancer what he wanted. All he wanted was to give his gift to others and I remember watching him rehearsing with one dancer in Spoleto for *Raymonda*. He was so patiently explaining to her how she should dance and was saying: 'Imagine that you ate a lot of wonderful food, and drank a lot of wonderful wine, and now you are terribly, terribly happy'… He was really killing himself to explain to her what it was all about and was going on and on and on… but to no avail. The poor girl got it all wrong anyway. At the end, she clapped her hands like a little mouse. One had to laugh! Rudolf had all the time and patience in the world for the most insignificant person when he saw that they were doing their utmost.

"He came to the West bringing with him a great tradition that was so precious if one was bright enough to pick it up. He himself was one of the most intelligent people I ever met. Any time there was a problem, it was because the dancer was too slow or was simply lazy. I saw him dismiss dancers who hadn't done their homework in favour of younger ones from the corps de ballet. He seized every opportunity to bring the gifted dancers forward. His conception of things was very clear.

"Of course it's true that there would be explosions of anger when someone wasn't giving of their best, but what has rarely been said is that afterwards, it was quickly forgotten and there Rudolf would be, pulling faces with his back to the audience.

"I do recall his Soviet paranoia, with the KGB and all these conspiracy theories in Russia, there in his past, today and no doubt in the future," Georgiadis reminisced. "It made him very suspicious, and this would come out in many acute observations, always, I found, absolutely accurate. He rarely trusted people because he was brought up in an atmosphere where you couldn't trust anyone.

"It also took him a long time to rid himself of many preconceptions, like his resentment of coat-tails. There had been such terrible scenes with Cecil Beaton over the costumes for Ashton's *Marguerite and Armand*, when he said that everyone would think he was a waiter.

"And then, as with the monster heads in *Nutcracker*, Rudolf just wasn't able to accept anything he thought ugly. Once, I made a kind of curtain out of rags on one side of the stage, and he kept eyeing it with great suspicion, even when it was necessary to have something frightening onstage. He'd look at it with such resentment. He almost thought ugliness was a sign of evil; whether that's true or not, I don't know, but that's what I felt.

"Rudolf so loved beauty," he told me, "which of course extended to the costumes in his ballets, and wherever he went, he bought wonderful ancient fabrics, each one more stunning than the next, often from the 18th century. Some of them were terribly expensive and he kept them all under his bed in Quai Voltaire, bringing them out each time one went to his home. It was like being in the cave of Ali Baba. 'Look,' he'd say to me. 'Look what I bought in Constantinople!' He'd exhibit them to me, often, I realised, to inspire me.

"He was such a great hoarder with his enormous collections, which really did demonstrate his fascination with beautiful things and tradition; he also adored antiques and I believe he had an agent hunting down kilims for him. He also had a splendid collection of costumes, which he kept all over the place. Many were here in Paris, but others were kept at Victoria Road in London, at the home of Maude and Nigel Gosling, others in his New York apartment and yet more at his house near Monte Carlo. He loved them all in an almost sensuous way.

"Nureyev was also a man of immense culture," the designer added. "He devoured books, visited art galleries and exhibitions, attended concerts and plays and operas. He even sang many roles himself. Where did he find the time to do all that?"

Modestly, Georgiadis did not talk much about the contribution made by his own designs, sumptuous but never heavy which infallibly drew gasps of delight from audiences. He told me that they were frequently a mix of fantasy and history.

"In retrospect," he recalled, "although we both spoke English, I think there was a sort of language barrier between us sometimes, as I wasn't always sure of what he was saying, what he really meant, and I was afraid of not understanding what he wanted. But then the problem certainly never stopped us working together again, on *The Nutcracker* in 1985, a ballet conceived by Marius Petipa in 1891/2, and taken from *The Story of a Nutcracker* by Alexandre Dumas, itself inspired by a tale by E.T.A. Hoffmann.

"I received so many different vibrations from him, particularly when we revived his 1968 version which we had staged for Covent Garden. Then," Georgiadis continued, "oh yes, we had a lot of problems because he had all these preconceived ideas. He was so upset because I didn't want to do the early Empire costumes as in the London production.

"I really did not want to do exactly the same thing again. I just plain refused, and so we had a long fight before he finally accepted my suggestion which was centred around setting the ballet in 1905. But after listening to me, he was so worried that he told me he couldn't sleep at night because he still thought it should be set in the usual early Empire period!

"Anyway, he finally agreed to my proposal, but then again rebelled against the set and costumes, which of course were no longer in 1810. Fashions had changed, had they not, in the course of 100 years! He was so upset and had such difficulty in accepting my designs, even for the snowflake scene, which I set in the Imperial Palace in St Petersburg, which was the Russian touch I wanted to bring in for him. He was actually more upset that it all looked like a scene out of a Chekov play instead of *The Nutcracker*, and he was, in fact, quite right, because it did."

The Greek designer repeated that Rudolf had this fixed idea that he had brought from Russia where only waiters wore coat-tails, and as with Cecil

Nureyev's 1985 production of The Nutcracker, Scene of the Driades, with the decor and costumes of Nicholas Georgiadis.
© Sébastien Mathé

Beaton, Georgiadis had the male dancers wearing a sort of mini coat-tail, which Rudolf had objected to, saying that it wasn't elegant.

"You see," Nicholas Georgiadis explained, "no one has ever analysed the difference in peoples' vision whether in Russia or here. What wasn't accepted there was accepted here, and what was accepted there wasn't accepted here! It was a real problem for him. It was a constant clash between wanting everything classical yet dramatic at the same time.

"Rudolf was basically so traditional," he said, "yet at the same time, intrigued by new developments and ideas."

Nutcracker

Nureyev had first remounted *Nutcracker* for the National Ballet of Sweden in 1967, then for both the Royal Ballet and La Scala of Milan the following year, with a further production for the Theatre Colon of Buenos-Aires in 1971, but it was the Paris Opera who benefited from his final, psychological production at Christmas in 1985 with Georgiadis' glorious scenery and costumes.

Nureyev himself had first taken part in the ballet while still a student at the Leningrad Ballet School in 1958, but after dancing in the children's group, he had subsequently interpreted the role of the prince in Vainonen's light-hearted full-length production there aimed primarily at children. It's very possible that he was aware of the weak libretto and lack of strong dramatic action, and maybe it was then that the seeds were sown for his own first production for the Swedish National Ballet.

What Georgiadis pointed out was that Rudolf wanted to rid the work of the cloying Sugar Plum Fairy and develop the role of Clara. He wanted to do away with the ballet's saccharine, syrupy side in order to bring out the underlying tension in parts of the score often passed over in the fun of the Christmas celebrations. The designer told me that Nureyev adored Tchaikovsky's music, which he considered had previously been dealt with too superficially. This was also true in his approach to *Swan Lake*, when he was very much guided by the music.

In his final version for the Paris Opera Ballet, étoile Monique Loudières interpreted Clara, the young girl ready to leave her childhood behind to become a teenager, with Laurent Hilaire in the dual role of Drosselmeyer and the Prince, representing the two sides of her ideal man.

However, the first time I saw the ballet was at a matinée performance when, knowing the work was the projection of an adolescent girl's confused dreams of love coloured by fear, I took my two teenage daughters along to see what they would make of it, and we saw Fabienne Cerruti, a young dancer whom Rudolf liked, in the role of Clara.

It is certainly hard to imagine a greater crowd-pleaser than Rudolf Nureyev's sparkling Russian-style production, particularly over the Christmas holidays. My daughters adored it. Born for the seasonal festivities in Imperial Russia in 1892, this two-act ballet, libretto by Petipa, choreography by Ivanov, has been pounced upon by countless choreographers both great and small, not only because of Tchaikovsky's ravishing score, but also because it was considered wholesome entertainment for the family.

Set at the turn of the century as Georgiadis has described, Nureyev's production is a ballet that has something for everyone, from the charm of Tchaikovsky's hauntingly evocative music to the glittering Christmas tree and party with games for the children. There is the excitement of the arrival of Clara's godfather, Drosselmeyer, his arms piled high with presents, who, in a dramatic turn of events, is subsequently transformed into the Prince in order to protect her from the family and friends who menace her uneventful childhood. The toy soldiers and rats, which become bats with human heads, are figments of Clara's imagination, as is the Nutcracker doll, a sort of white knight who chases them off before being transformed into the handsome fairy-tale prince. He then takes her around the world and she sees Chinese, Arab, Spanish and Russian dances performed, but all the faces of the dancers are familiar; they are the guests around the Christmas tree.

The big ensemble numbers are in grand style, not least the magical Snowflakes Waltz, set in a beautiful winter garden reminiscent of a St Petersburg Palace, which, Georgiadis added, was where Nureyev's heart was. It was also at this moment, watching the perfect, crystalline geometry of the corps de ballet, that I fully realised the magnificence of Rudolf's vision of the choreography, albeit after Petipa and Ivanov. The exquisite Waltz of the Flowers, which followed shortly after, culminated in one of the prettiest pas de deux created by Rudolf for Clara and her prince.

Nureyev discarded the notion of the work being merely for children, and in order to draw in all audiences he developed the story that is seen through the eyes of a child rather than those of kindly, well-meaning adults. He thus transformed Clara's role into one for a true ballerina, who passes from being an innocent child in Act I to becoming the aristocratic woman of Act II, as well as giving the prince the double role of interpreting Drosselmeyer at the beginning and end of the ballet. He originally created the part of the fairy-tale prince for himself, and the role is one that demands an aristocratic style together with a total mastery of technique as well as a sense of fun.

"Enchantment" was the word used by the young Rudolf Nureyev to describe his first visit to a ballet in the late 1940s. In his own autobiography, he recalls the soft lights, velvet seats and that special atmosphere when the curtain rose on a magical fairy story, far from his dull, poverty-stricken background. Thus we often find that the heroes and heroines of his productions frequently escape from their humdrum lives by way of a dream. It is not for nothing that audiences will stand and queue for hours to see one of his productions, knowing that they will emerge happy and uplifted. His version of *Nutcracker*, which takes place on Christmas Eve and is conceived as a young girl's dream, is no exception.

Elisabeth Maurin, the young ballerina who danced the role of Clara in the 1988 film (NVC Arts TELDEC classics International), with Laurent Hilaire as her Prince, spoke to me of the joy as well as the challenge of interpreting the heroine as a child, as an adolescent, and then as a woman, adding that Nureyev's version of the ballet was by far her favourite one.

"Rudolf modernised it so that other productions now seem old-fashioned," she said. "The traditional Sugar Plum Fairy disappears to become the adult Clara, which gives greater depth to the character. The whole ballet goes so much further than just dancing in the Kingdom of Sweets. I've interpreted other versions, and when I simply remained the childlike Clara, it left me feeling very frustrated.

"The entire time the ballet was being filmed, I felt as though I was living out a dream," recalled Maurin. "I can still see it all now… the sheer joy of being directed by Nureyev, and my happiness when he nominated me principal dancer the day before filming was completed."

Journalists

Sometime after having seen *The Nutcracker*, I was approached by a journalist from one of the top British newspapers to ask whether I could arrange an interview with Nureyev to talk about his work with the French company and his forthcoming *Cinderella* for him. One Wednesday morning, I rang Rudolf's secretary, Marie-Suzanne Soubie, the lovely lady who dealt with all the administrative aspects of his work, to see when this would be possible. There was no messing about as was the case later on with director Benjamin Millepied, when I had no reply whatsoever, as shortly after my call, Nureyev enquired if it would be possible for me to see him the following day. He asked whether 14h30 would be okay. Of course it was.

Nor was this the only occasion when I would ask him if he could spare the time to help. When a young dancer, Iouri Borodin, arrived from St Petersburg, asking whether I could arrange for him to talk over his future with Nureyev, he wasted no time in contacting the dancer, who had been a principal with the Kirov Ballet, and giving him solid advice about his future. Iouri subsequently took over the position of principal dancer with the Ballet de Nancy, before accepting a position with the Berlin Opera, a company with a repertoire that suited him admirably.

So, returning to the journalist in question, promptly the next afternoon we met Rudolf in what was called his office, a tiny room no bigger than a cupboard, on the top floor of the Palais Garnier under the eaves. There was scarcely room for the small wooden desk and two wooden chairs that were there, but out he went to get a chair for me and the three of us crammed in together. Informal it certainly was. His 'office' was where the dancers were. Frankly, I don't believe that Nureyev ever had what one would call an office, contrary to his successor, Patrick Dupond, who, for the short time he was there, chose one of the most beautiful airy rooms in the building, a gorgeous room overlooking Boulevard Haussmann, lit by a magnificent crystal chandelier. There, the enormous desk he had served as a highly convenient footrest.

The interview with Rudolf, in English, started out well enough with references to his creation of *Cinderella*, but then the journalist in question seemed more interested in what the legendary director was doing when he wasn't at the Opera since his contract stipulated that he had to be there only six months of the year. Despite the fact that the reporter had said the interview was about Rudolf's work with the French dancers, he was very insistent on demanding why, at nearing fifty, Nureyev was shortly going to appear as the Prince in *Swan Lake* in Manchester. It should be added, too, that while Nureyev's youthful phenomenal beauty had faded, he was still an immensely attractive man, probably more 'princelike' than many…

Rudolf, however, neatly avoided the trap, replying that Frederick Ashton had once told him that he'd give up all the ballets that he ever created for five minutes of dance. "I'd willingly do the same," he added firmly. "I'm first and foremost a dancer, then a choreographer, and after, a company director. I'm going there to dance."

Recalling that I myself had gone to see the sublime Maya Plisetskaya dance in *Phèdre* at the age of fifty-one, with Iouri Borodin, the young dancer from the Kirov, and had felt tremendously privileged to have done so, I nevertheless feared the conversation was heading in the wrong direction. Rudolf's joy of dancing, at no matter what age, to audiences only too happy to see their superstar for real, was not the subject of this interview.

At that moment, to avoid the conversation revolving around his guest appearances abroad, I leaned forward to say how much I had enjoyed seeing Fabienne Cerruti, a young 'sujet', as Clara in his *Nutcracker*, a role normally danced by an étoile. Sujet is an indeterminate ranking for dancers who remain part of the corps de ballet, and yet are not quite soloists in their own right.

"Ah." Rudolf smiled, pleased to talk about his work. "When I see quality in a dancer, I give them their chance. I don't show them the top, but I show them where the top is and then I make them work for it. I make each member of the corps de ballet work onstage; that's how étoiles are made, and the younger they are nominated, the better.

"There was a drain of good dancers in the 70s," he continued, "because potentially gifted dancers need recognition, which is what I intend to give them. I take lessons with the company and watch how they work; I encourage the good elements and tell them that where they want to go is their responsibility because they are the ones who must do it.

"I have to break through the system of hierarchy here as there is a right moment to give young dancers their chance, because otherwise, they would be near retirement age before they became étoiles… with the right to dance main roles. I cast dancers regardless of whether they have passed exams or not. There are many beautiful étoiles here, but also others more beautiful still.

"You know," he continued, "I'm not even sure if the French realise that classical dance was born here with artists such as Auguste Vestris and then it was exported to Russia with Marius Petipa. Dance moves around and finds different capitals; there's always been a centre for dance. It was Paris, then

Russia, it moved to Copenhagen, then London, and now I've brought it back to Paris again. In time," he added, "it will move on again, but I hope it stays here for a while as I want to open up the company to different forms of dance and change their approach."

He spoke of classical dance being the base of the company's repertoire, but that he wanted to widen their range and bring in people like Merce Cunningham, Martha Graham, Rudi van Dantzig, Glen Tetley, Lucinda Childs, Karole Armitage, Robert Wilson, Nils Christie and the relatively unknown William Forsythe. His hope was that he would be remembered as the link between classical dance and contemporary.

"Classical and modern dance have to merge," he said. "They have to borrow and learn from each other. Every art is influenced by the next and dance is Dance; the different forms, whether classical, neoclassical, tap, contemporary, modern, street dancing, call it what you will, they can't be broken down and separated.

"I always wanted to have a company and to have my own theatre," he continued. "It's better to work with a company one can transform rather than one that is already in a good shape. You don't find dancers of this potential anywhere else, but they lack style; they don't dance enough. The Paris Opera isn't Covent Garden, but it's a company I can leave my mark on."

We asked if there really was a difference of style between companies, and the answer was a definite yes. In Russia, he stated, the accent was on style, whereas in the US Balanchine moved very fast, and had eliminated all the heavy, pompous style, making dance much lighter.

Even temperamentally, companies in other countries were different; he explained, "With English dancers you can have a row and they'll go away and sulk and then come back after a cup of tea. Here French dancers have so much character that they are just as likely to stamp off, slam the door, and go and work by themselves until they have corrected their mistake."

As the interview drew to a close, the journalist, whom I gradually realised had probably never seen a ballet in his life, grabbed his bag and quickly scurried off down the corridor to regain his office, no doubt to write his piece.

The tension dropped and Rudolf and I slowly gathered our things and left the 'office' together. I thanked him for his time as he left to go where he belonged, which was with the dancers, but not before talking about Margot Fonteyn. As soon as I mentioned her name, his behaviour changed, his whole face lit up and he announced happily that he was having dinner with her in London the following evening. As we spoke of his work in London, he told me how lucky he had been to have had those London years with her. "She taught me to be professional, to get out and do it. Do it! she used to say." He laughed. "She is a very, very great friend of mine, my family. I adore her." From the look on his face, that was practically an understatement!

Although I had seen him dance with almost all of the greatest ballerinas in the world, never had I seen a partnership like the one he formed with Fonteyn. She was great, he was great, and together they formed something even greater than the two parts. Seeing how happy he was when we went our separate ways, I knew that that legendary partnership, if not a conventional love affair, had led to the most beautiful and lasting of relationships. My personal belief is that he never came to terms with her death in February 1991, coming as it did barely a couple of years before his own.

Returning to our meeting, I was less than happy when I read the resulting article after publication, which, little did I know at the time, was going to change the direction of my life. Neither Nureyev nor I had had the forethought to ask to see the piece before publication, and upon reading it, I went hot and cold in embarrassment. It was not only because of the cynical, snidey tone of the piece but mainly for its fatuous content. It was hardly surprising that Nureyev was wary of journalists.

The article was not that bad, and nothing was particularly incorrect, except that much of what Nureyev had talked about was simply omitted. What on earth did the clothes that Rudolf wore have to do with his work? What was this ridiculous paragraph devoted to his "unflattering woollen bonnet and rather dull baggy clothes"?

I squirmed to read of Rudolf "intending to star upfront till he dropped", of him being described as a "master manipulator, a "controversial choreographer", that his dancing might "depress" audiences and then hinting that many critics thought he had come to Paris "as part of an easy pre-retirement plan". Worst of all, perhaps, was to quote his fabulous production of *Raymonda* as… "laughable", which was shameful. Had this journalist actually been to see it? I asked him later to find out that, no, he hadn't.

Meeting up with Rudolf some time later, I hung my head in shame as he studied me slowly through half closed eyes before enquiring sardonically as to whether I was still writing for *The Sun*… the British popular tabloid. My stammered apologies that I had had nothing to do with the finished article were halted when a sudden, imperious finger jutted out at me with a "You! You write!"

Those words, together with the encouragement I had had from my close friend Jacqueline Cochet, the teacher of both étoiles Elisabeth Platel and Jean-Yves Lormeau, who had introduced me to many of the dancers in the company, were the final push I needed, and on arriving home, I sent a letter to Mary Clarke, editor of the prestigious, London-based *Dancing Times* magazine. My writing career has never looked back.

Maurice Béjart

As bad luck would have it, one of my first pieces for Mary was based on a trip to Lausanne, to interview Maurice Béjart, a man I had never taken to. Arrogant and puffed up with self-importance, Béjart, the French/Belgian/Swiss choreographer (choose whichever nationality you please), had recently clashed violently and disagreeably with Rudolf.

As Director of the Paris company, Nureyev had commissioned Béjart to create a ballet for the dancers, programmed in March 1986. It was a work pretentiously entitled *Arépo*, supposedly a tribute to the Paris Opera Ballet. Even the title, Opera in reverse, irritated me, and as for the show itself, despite the dancing of Manuel Legris, Eric Vu-An, and Elisabeth Maurin, three dancers I loved, I remember little as there was nothing to recommend it apart from some effective scenery. I thought it was a confused mess. As, to my knowledge, the full-length work was never programmed again, my judgement was probably not incorrect.

However, at the end of the performance, onto the stage struts Maurice Béjart, a visiting choreographer, who had the effrontery to nominate both Legris and Vu-An to the coveted rank of étoile in front of a packed audience. For those who know little of the Paris Opera's policy, it's been the case from the beginning that étoiles can only be nominated by the company's artistic director, in this case, Nureyev, after the approval of the General Director. Béjart, who had attempted to take over the Paris troupe as artistic director on more than one occasion, had vastly overstepped the mark.

As the two dancers came offstage, Nureyev quickly de-dramatised the whole event, with a laconic, "April Fool". With Rudolf having the complete backing of the administration and of all the dancers, Béjart had no option but to back down and accept defeat, but not without creating a turmoil in the press vaunting his wishes.

Washington Square

Washington Square, programmed later that year, is unfortunately the ballet pounced upon by Rudolf's detractors to proclaim his mediocrity as a choreographer. I remember sitting through it in dismay, but, like Manfred some years before, it was a 'one-off', part of his growth period. He made his own judgement and didn't intend to programme it again nor keep it in the repertoire. Many great choreographers created unsuccessful works; even Petipa had several hundred unsung ballets. Who amongst us has ever heard of *Un Mariage sous la Régence*, created in 1858, or *Le Roi Candaule*, ten years later? And as far as *Roxane, la belle Albanese* is concerned, the work that followed on after *La Bayadère*, perhaps the less said, the better. Several ballets by Roland Petit and Maurice Béjart, two famous French choreographers, have rarely seen the light of day since their creation. Does anyone remember Petit's *Puss in Boots*? And Béjart created a whole series of ballets that were picked to pieces by the British press. *Washington Square* was an experiment that didn't work. One is allowed not to get it right some of the time.

And yet it was a ballet that could have worked, and which was in fact created for a tour to the US in 1986, to please American audiences on the company's first visit to New York since 1948.

Based on Henry James' book *Washington Square*, with a libretto by the talented French writer and translator Jean-Claude Carrière, and set to a score by Charles Ives, it was, as Georgiadis told me, Rudolf's fantasy of America. Moreover, the orchestra was conducted by Michael Tilson Thomas. Everything was in place for a resounding success. But it wasn't. It was not even saved by Georgiadis' colourful scenery and costumes. Despite having lived two years in the US, I had no idea of what was going on, and not having read the book, I found events, such as they were, mystifying. We in France remained bewildered by the succession of cowboys, a July 4th parade, dancers decked out as pioneers and even Ku Klux Klan figures crossing the stage.

What Georgiadis remembers about it, he told me, was when in the middle of the performance, a spectator at the Palais Garnier shouted out, "Is this a ballet for the Opera or for half the Opera?", because they couldn't see what was happening.

"Rudolf hadn't given me very precise instructions and I'd designed a wall, which did effectively block many people's view."

Fortunately, at the same time it was taken on tour, so was Rudolf's superb, symbol-laden version of *Swan Lake*, which was a huge success. The American public were captivated by the idea that the ballet was but a long dream by a prince brought up on romantic novels as Jude has pointed out, and who imagines the lake and the swans as an escape route from his duties and responsibilities. In his mind, it becomes the 'other place' he yearns for.

But most of all, they were enthralled by the dancers, by Sylvie Guillem and Charles Jude, and by the plethora of brilliant young artists they saw, including Elisabeth Platel, Isabelle Guérin, Monique Loudières, Laurent Hilaire, and Patrick Dupond. It was such an overwhelming success that they were invited back the following year with Nureyev's *Cinderella*, and again in 1988 performing Forsythe's *In the Middle*, and Béjart's *Chant du Compagnon Errant*, together with again *Cinderella* and *Swan Lake*. Five performances of *Nutcracker* were also given.

Nor were the American tours, which gave the troupe international status, the only ones Nureyev organised. As well as appearing in many cities throughout France, the company danced in Geneva, Vienna, Japan, Denmark, China, Rome, Athens and Bangkok, appearances that added to the company's international fame. Younger dancers were also encouraged to accept the growing number of invitations from outside France when Rudolf would frequently telephone London, Milan or Vienna to promote them himself.

Cinderella

In contrast to the disappointing reception given to *Washington Square*, Rudolf's next production for the company, an original fun-packed version of *Cinderella* set in the US to a lively score by Prokofiev, and programmed shortly after, was no less than a 'smash hit' with both audiences and dancers alike! Inevitably, disparaging reviews by certain opinionated critics crept into a couple of biographies, books which in turn were mined by other biographers, giving credence to a false idea that Rudolf's ballet was poorly received. It was not. Time and time again, and I have seen the ballet performed with many differing casts, on each occasion, the audience goes wild with delight. Not only is it visually pleasing for spectators, with Petrika Ionesco's eye-catching stage designs and Hanae Mori's gorgeous costumes, but it is enormous fun to dance and the company loves it. The dancers' enjoyment sweeps over the floodlights and orchestra pit to the public and everybody leaves the theatre happy.

With its larger-than-life decor, and numerous secondary roles including Polynesian dancers and a towering King Kong, it is packed with action and is a showcase for the talents of as many of the French dancers as Nureyev could find roles for, as well as being a tribute to American pop culture at the same time. Maybe the one criticism to be made is that the more burlesque parts of it could possibly have been pruned down, as seeing members of the splendid male corps de ballet decked out as ballerinas didn't really appeal to me.

Nevertheless, ballet master Patrice Bart told me with a smile that the entire company loved *Cinderella*.

"There is a great clarity in the construction, in the ballroom scene, and in the design as a whole. If it were filmed from above, you could see how elaborate it was, and also, the fact that the male dancers were used as much as the girls resulted in the increasingly high level of all the company."

The steps for the ugly sisters, technically very difficult and initially created for two principal dancers, are particularly inventive as well as being highly complicated. Not only are they hugely enjoyable to dance, members of the company have told me, but they are also extremely entertaining to watch and suit the style of the Paris Opera dancers to perfection. They have since been performed with malicious glee by a variety of casts, several of the danseuses étoiles pleading to dance the ugly sisters in preference to the heroine.

Rudolf and designer Ionesco chose to transpose Perrault's fairy tale into America during the post-Depression period. It was an extremely clever idea to take Cinderella to the film studios of Hollywood, the dream-factory par excellence, and the work, a mixture of pure classical dance and musical comedy, has only improved with the passage of time.

The basic story, which hasn't changed, takes place in the 1930s and 40s.

Cinderella, who lives with her alcoholic father, shrewish step-mother, and two bitchy step-sisters, dreams of escape and freedom via Hollywood. Her wish seems to be coming true when she is 'discovered' by a film producer/fairy godmother figure, who is on the lookout for young talent, a role in gold for Rudolf to play himself, which he did. She's then whisked off to the film studios in a sumptuous pumpkin/limousine and makes a more than promising debut, winning the heart of her glamorous leading man/prince along the way.

The story develops with Cinders dreading growing old and losing her beauty, and reminded of the relentless march of time, she's filled with doubts, fearing the collapse of her dream. It's all too wonderful to last, and afraid that her newfound happiness will tumble like a pack of cards, she flees from the ballroom, losing her slipper in her hurry. Her lover, a famous film-star and handsome to boot, then moves heaven and earth to find her.

There is a fascinating sequence where Nureyev creates a combination of classical and contemporary steps for the choreography of the Hours, show-casing twelve young men from the corps de ballet, but I was more enthralled by everything in the ballet that could be traced back to Nureyev's early training at the Kirov. He created two beautiful solos for the young étoile Sylvie Guillem, who opened the ballet with gentleness and grace, unforgettable in her simple grey dress, albeit haute couture. Nureyev had created the choreography with her pure, glorious line in mind, and she was equally at ease in the classical pas de deux as waltzing around the immense stage in her high-heeled glittering shoes and the softest of peach-pink chiffon dresses in a show-stopping piece reminiscent of the young long-legged Cyd Charisse.

The outstanding pas de deux at the end, amongst Rudolf's most beautiful, is also a direct product of his Kirov years, while the moment Cinders' film-star boyfriend arrives at the house to find the owner of the shoe is touched with genius. When she appears and shyly shows him the matching slipper, which she had hidden up the chimney, there's no pantomime of trying any matching slipper on. No fool, he simply takes one look at her, his heart in his eyes, scoops her up in his arms and carries her off for eternity. Audiences adore every minute of the work.

Charles Jude

While the work was created around Sylvie Guillem, it was no surprise to find the handsome Charles Jude cast as the hero. I spoke to him some time after the production.

"Rudolf had always been fascinated by musical comedy and he particularly admired Fred Astaire, whom he had met shortly after his arrival in the West. He dreamed of dancing like him, with the same airy lightness. Dance was movement; Fred Astaire was movement plus grace.

"And so when he began working on *Cinderella*, he recreated this style of dancing, setting it to classical steps. His heroine is shown dancing first like Charlie Chaplin and then like Fred Astaire. He'd have loved to have been dancing it himself… much like he enjoyed doing a soft shoe shuffle in the style of Astaire in the second half of Jim Henson's *Muppet Show*, which can easily be found on the internet.

"After *Washington Square*, Rudolf learned to simplify many steps but remained obsessed by what he called 'giving the dancers plenty to eat' in case they were bored. But the dancers still got indigestion because as a

Rudolf enjoying himself with Kermit the Frog (Miss Piggy not far behind), on Jim Henson's The Muppet Show, 1977.
© courtesy Ronald Grant archive/Mary Evans

choreographer, Rudolf knew too much after working with all the world's greatest choreographers, from Martha Graham, Cunningham, Balanchine, Robbins and Roland Petit," Jude continued. "He'd absorbed too many steps with the result that in his early works, there was just too much. It was often too elaborate and he was accused of being over-fussy. There were also complaints that it was too difficult to dance… but," said Jude, "*Cinderella* marked a significant step in his career. He began to have an idea of the whole piece and to realise that he no longer had to set a step to each note to achieve what he really wanted."

With amusement, the dancer recalled Rudolf arriving at the Opera with a book for him one day. "He knew full well I preferred red wine while he only drank white, but nonetheless, he gave me this book, telling me to choose a castle in it! He informed me that there were a lot of castles for sale in France, adding, 'So, Charlex,' which was what he called me, 'choose the one you like best, and we'll all go and live there.'

"But, Rudolf, I said, if I pick a castle, I'd choose one in Bordeaux where I'd drink red wine. Fine, he replied, if you see one you like, we'll buy it and we'll go and live there, both of us, Florence, the children and the dogs. I laughed; it was a dream, but Rudolf was quite serious, for as professional as he was when working, there was another side to him that was very childlike, always wanting a family around him.

"He was like a father to me," Charles said. "He was very protective, anxious to ensure that all was well in my future. Yet at the same time he was such fun to be with. On a professional level he taught me everything I know about dance. Most importantly, he showed me what he meant by the quality of dance.

"His vision was all towards the future, reminding us that we had to keep the essential from the 'living' past to give to younger dancers, but at the same time," Jude recalled with a smile, "he insisted that one must never look behind. "If you look behind, you fall over," he'd say.

"His house at La Turbie was situated high up in the mountain with magnificent views of the Alps behind and the sea and Monaco down below. But inside it was like the cave of Ali Baba. He hoarded his treasures and there they were, objects upon objects piled up, one on top of another under an enormous chandelier lit by candles. He loved candlelight.

"For me," Jude mused, "Rudolf was from another age because his choices were not of today. He'd have been the happiest person in the world if electricity hadn't been invented and yet, at the same time, he was avid for images.

"He adored going to the cinema and never missed a new film. He wanted all the different TV channels, yet he never had enough time to watch a complete programme. Afraid of missing something, he got great fun out of zapping to another channel, wanting always to know what was happening elsewhere. And then," Jude reminisced, "he was like a child with electronic gadgets. He didn't have a fax machine, and one day on tour all the dancers decided to get together and surprise him by giving him one for a present. He was thrilled to bits and rushed back to his hotel to start playing with it.

"That's the way he was; he got such great fun out of things. There were two facets to his nature; one that wanted to preserve the past and the other that charged headlong into the next century. Every six months he'd ask me, 'What's new?' He understood nothing of the technology because it didn't interest him. All he wanted was for everything to work, and work immediately!

"Gadgets were toys to him. He'd plug in whatever it was and then sit back

Relaxing in the ocean. This little gadget can pull me as well as the boat! 1987.
Personal collection of Florence Clerc

and enjoy it, like on one of our trips to Turkey when he bought some kind of mechanical thing that shot through the water and dragged our boat behind it.

"He was also, as you well know," continued Jude, "a man of immense culture, who devoured books, visited all the art exhibitions and galleries, attended concerts and rarely missed seeing current plays and operas. He'd sing many of the roles himself." The dancer smiled, confirming what Georgiadis had one day told me. "One could ask him anything about painting, literature, cinema and opera and he always knew the answer, and although he systematically read all the newspapers, his only politics was dance.

Brief holiday in the Seychelles, 1986.
Personal collection of Florence Clerc

"It seemed there wasn't a book he didn't know," the dancer said, "reading Shakespeare in English, and when working on his ballet *Manfred* I was astounded by the amount of research and background reading he did. Not only did he read everything written by Byron, one of England's greatest Romantic poets, but he also got his hands on all the works of his friends and contemporaries, particularly the poems of Shelley."

Manfred

Manfred, based on the poem of that name and created for the Paris Opera, which I saw in November 1979 at the Palais-des-Sports in Paris, was a rare occasion when I was truly disappointed with a Nureyev ballet. First of all, the immense Palais-des-Sports is not conducive to dance, and secondly, before any consideration of the ballet itself, Nureyev, who was programmed to dance the role of Manfred, the troubled hero, broke a bone in his foot and could not only not dance, but also had to conduct rehearsals with his foot in a plaster cast.

Instead, it was the Paris Opera étoile Jean Guizerix who appeared in the central role. With the best will in the world, Guizerix, a fine dancer, lacked the charisma and the stage presence that might have held the ballet together. He possessed the technique, but lacked the dramatic authority necessary. He was partnered by Wilfride Piollet; neither dancer was set to put the world on fire, and the ballet, quite simply, never took off.

Not knowing this particular poem, I was nonetheless a great admirer of Byron's other poems, having even gone to Tuscany to visit the house where he had lived. Since I'd read 'She Walks in Beauty', the handsome George Gordon Byron, who died from fever at the age of thirty-six while helping the Greeks in their fight for freedom from Turkish oppression, had always seemed the epitome of romanticism. It was doubtless that aspect that had fascinated Nureyev, plus the attraction of Tchaikovsky's *Manfred Symphony*.

Unfortunately, the lack of a coherent libretto, the vague theme being that of Byron's own loves and hates, made any relevant choreography for any other interpreter less gifted than Nureyev, well-nigh impossible. The programme, with its vague references to the poet's quest for wisdom and peace, in friendship, in love, as well as in patriotic fervour, was not much help either. All I could gather was that the hero spent the entire hour of the ballet searching for his half-sister, with whom he had supposedly had an incestuous affair, during which there were various pas de deux, pas de trois and pas de quatre.

When the ballet was restaged at the Palais Garnier in 1986, despite the fact there was Nureyev in the central role with Florence Clerc as his half-sister, I didn't go back to see it; maybe I should have.

Young choreographers

One of the most amazing things about Rudolf Nureyev was not how he found the time to do so much but the fact that he didn't hesitate to take enormous risks. He took risks not only when he danced and with his poorly received creations of *Manfred*, *The Tempest*, and *Washington Square* in 1979, 1982, and 1985 respectively, but also when he invited little-known contemporary choreographers to the Opera. They made terrific demands on the young dancers to whom their style was unknown, and on the audience who were forced to accept it.

I still remember the eruption of the young Sylvie Guillem onstage in William Forsythe's now acclaimed work *In The Middle, Somewhat Elevated*, back in 1987. Before the work even began, the ear-splitting, grating sounds of the Thom Willems' score nearly made spectators jump out of their seats,

Rudolf with American choreographer William Forsythe, during a rehearsal at the Opera Garnier in May 1987.
© Colette Masson/Roger Viollet

so alien were the sounds to what they were accustomed to hearing at the Palais Garnier.

Shortly after his appointment as director of the Paris Opera Ballet, Nureyev had invited the relatively unknown American choreographer to the Opéra Comique in Paris in order to create a work for the young 'sujets' of the company. *France Dance*, set to a compilation of Bach and Western 'cowboy' songs, was thus created for Sylvie Guillem, Manuel Legris, Laurent Hilaire, Fanny Gaida and Eric Vu-An.

Aware that the choreographer's work was firmly rooted in classical vocabulary, and intrigued by how it had become a base for his daring experimentation with abstract forms at increasingly faster rhythms, Rudolf subsequently commissioned Forsythe to create a second work for the Paris company, which was performed at the Palais Garnier.

This was followed by invitations to Karole Armitage, Dominique Bagouet, Lucinda Childs, Nils Christie, Maguy Marin, Robert Wilson, David Parsons, Michael Clark and Jiri Kylian to quote just a few, who all came because it was Nureyev who had invited them. They came for him.

During his years at the Paris Opera, Nureyev must have invited up to fifty different choreographers, who all familiarised the French dancers with their different techniques. The range was stupendous, helping him in his avowed aim: to break down the barriers between classical and modern dance, a process he had begun himself, interpreting works by Glen Tetley, Paul Taylor, and Murray Louis as well as by Graham, Cunningham and Balanchine.

One year with Rudolf, the dancers would work one way, and the next, another. Jean-Claude Gallotta came, more a man of the theatre than a choreographer, who brought together actors, musicians and designers as well as dancers onstage, alongside such monuments as Martha Graham and Merce Cunningham. Nureyev would test the young choreographers by inviting them to put on a short work such as Kylian's *Sinfonietta*, and asking them to make the dancers understand what their work was all about. His intention was to re-invite them to create a more important work if he thought they understood their style, and of course, if the choreographer was happy to work with the company.

He had a vision, several of the dancers told me, and he was always planning five, ten, and fifteen years ahead as in 1986, when he took the company on tour to New York, its first appearance in the US for more than thirty years.

Sleeping Beauty

I first saw *Sleeping Beauty* at Covent Garden long ago with Margot Fonteyn and David Blair and had not been particularly thrilled or moved by it, although I had adored watching Fonteyn herself. She was exquisite, but

Rudolf in The Sleeping Beauty, Paris early 1970s.
© Francette Levieux/CNCS

despite the fact that Blair was said to be one of the company's best dancers, I remember thinking that I could never have fallen in love with him. To my teenage eyes, he was far from being the prince of my dreams. I also recall my dislike of the two cats with their dreadful masks as well as a simpering Red Riding Hood with her pantomime wolf in Act III.

The version the Royal Ballet possessed was by Nicholas Sergeyev. Settling in London in 1934, he had produced the 1939 production of *Sleeping Beauty* there, when he had been instantly acknowledged as the only person outside Russia who could stage the classical ballets in their original Petipa/Ivanov form. But with disappointing memories of the work, believing the prince not to arrive until the last act, I therefore avoided the ballet until January 1976 when Rudolf Nureyev was appearing with the then London Festival Ballet at the Palais-des-Sports in Paris with his own production, after the original choreography of Marius Petipa.

Despite my aversion to the Palais-des-Sports, I couldn't resist going to see the work he had described as the "pinnacle of classical ballet", particularly as I knew he was dancing in it. He had already staged it for La Scala, Milan, in 1966, and then for the Ballet National of Canada in 1972. This time, he was partnering Eva Evdokimova with the British ballerina, Patricia Ruanne, dancing with him on alternate evenings.

The costumes and decor for this 1975 production, as for the two previous versions, were by Nicholas Georgiadis and were sumptuous. The brilliant Greek designer had created an 18th-century court reminiscent of Versailles with all its rituals and etiquette. The visual effect together with the lavish costumes, each a work of art, was dazzling. It was not for nothing that Rudolf had insisted on Georgiadis as his designer.

By 1989, Rudolf had pruned and polished this majestic version of the *Sleeping Beauty*, the most resplendent of Petipa's great 19th-century works, for the Paris Opera Ballet. Just months before his enforced departure as artistic director of the French company, he had smoothed away any minor imperfections of this shining "ballet of ballets" as he was wont to say, and with the collaboration of Georgiadis, a glittering setting for Aurora and her prince was made.

Nureyev's own story with the *Sleeping Beauty* in the West had begun shortly after his dramatic arrival in 1961 when he appeared as the prince with the Grand Ballet du Marquis de Cuevas in Paris.

"I was in the corps de ballet at the time," recalled Opera étoile and coach Ghislaine Thesmar, "and I will never forget seeing him dance for the first time. I was completely bowled over; he flew. I had never seen anything like it before! But on the practical side, he was so upset by that dreadful white wig covered in little pink beads he was obliged to wear. He really thought he was taking part in a musical comedy, and that he was the Christmas tree...

"Then several years later, I partnered him when we performed the work together at the Palais-des-Congrès here. He loved the fact that he was dancing it in France with a French girl because, written by Charles Perrault, a Frenchman, it's a French story, adapted into a ballet by Marius Petipa, a French choreographer.

"Dancing with him was like a dream, not only because he was such a wonderful partner, but also because it took me back in time, into the 17th century. I felt we were telling the fairy story to the very aristocratic world of the Czar of Russia and his family for whom it was created.

"Rudolf considered it as an exercise in style," Thesmar continued. "It had to be danced in the grand academic manner where each port de bras had to be performed in the classical manner, for he wanted us to show the postures and positions seen in the drawings of courtly dance during the reign of Louis XIV. Protocol had to be respected and you had to stand up very straight to wear the structured costumes with their corsets, hats and feathers. And Nicholas Georgiadis really went to town with all the feathers!

"So we had to learn how to wear a costume as much as how to dance the steps, and to respond to what he called the 'grandeur of the dream'. He really did have the soul of a child, and would relive the story each time he heard the music. He was very pure in that sense."

Nureyev's production of the ballet is an absolute feast of music, dance and beauty. Sadly, for a new production of the ballet in 1997 after Nureyev's death, the Greek designer's splendid decor and costumes were replaced with designs by Ezio Frigerio and his wife, Franca Squarciapino, which, Georgiadis told me, made him very upset.

I can still hear him shaking his head and saying, sadly, "Why did they do that?"

I had no answer, as I did not particularly like Frigerio's glinting, over-ornate scenery of the first act either, which had presumably been made to suit the huge Bastille stage, larger than at the Palais Garnier where it had been originally programmed with Georgiadis' decor and costumes. Now, one must simply accept the gold and green curtain, the gold and green pillars in the palace, the golden doors, golden decorations and gold on the costumes, all heavily massive and oppressive. The atmosphere of magic, woven by Georgiadis, had gone. Even the costumes, each one beautiful by itself, were too highly decorated and bejewelled, and vastly overdone when seen together.

However, nothing mars the beauty of the dancing. Petipa's choreography, in perfect harmony with the score, has been handed down virtually intact, including making the Lilac Fairy in her exquisite floor-length gown into a non-dancing role as dictated by Petipa in 1895. The scene as she takes the prince by boat over misty waters to Aurora's castle is sheer enchantment.

In opposition, instead of a crabby old hag, Carabosse, nastily malevolent, is transformed into a comely matron, albeit with sinister black snaky hair, and the two, representing the forces of darkness and light, are more evenly matched. The children's fairy tale gives place to the more realistic account of the opposing forces of good versus evil represented by the Lilac Fairy and Carabosse.

Nureyev merely did away with what he called the "bla-bla chi-chi poo", the unnecessary flourishes added over time. He kept the exquisite Rose Adagio and the grand pas de deux of the final act exactly as they were. But what roused the ire of the die-hard traditionalists used to the 'definitive' version brought by Sergeyev so many years earlier, and so quick to find fault, was his introduction of a seven-minute solo for the prince in Act II. Too much dancing for the prince, they grumbled, despite it being one of the most moving sequences of the ballet.

It's also both interesting and amusing to note that Nureyev, as he did in *Swan Lake*, incorporated several of his warming-up exercises into the prince's variation when he escapes from a hunting party in the forest prior to falling in love with Aurora, who is brought to him in a dream.

Aurora is one of the most difficult roles in the classical repertory. When the ballet opens, she's a vulnerable young girl, a fifteen-year-old princess who grows up into a woman in the second half where she has to dance with the panache of a great aristocrat.

"I'm working as Rudolf wanted," Ghislaine Thesmar, who worked as a coach for the soloists, said. "He was more concerned about how Aurora behaved than in the steps she accomplished. The style and atmosphere were of the greatest importance. It's no wishy-washy, airy-fairy staging," she underlined, "but a ballet in keeping with the Kirov tradition, which is where it was created. Nureyev used to constantly remind the dancers that many of the soloists in Russia, including the fairies, were mistresses of the Czar and were very strong-minded young ladies, full of spirit, speed and energy, qualities which also had to come out in Aurora's dancing. *The Sleeping Beauty* embodies one of Rudolf's greatest gifts to us in the wonderfully noble bearing he instilled in the company. He gave us," she added, "the classical excellence and precision to dance such works."

Part V

1989 to 1993

Towards the end of 1989, an enormous cloud was looming over the dance world in Paris. Nureyev's contract as artistic director had expired on August 31st and the General Director, Pierre Bergé, in one of the most foolish acts in recent French cultural history, had not renewed it when he normally should have. Consequently from September onwards, the company had no director and no one, neither the dancers, the administration nor Rudolf himself, knew what was happening.

As matters were dragging on, and exasperated by what he called a bizarre Dostoievskian situation, describing his time at the Opera as a love story with a bad ending, a betrayal, as in *The Bayadère*, Nureyev decided to go to Hartford, Connecticut, in October for three months. He'd always loved musical comedy, and he accepted an invitation to portray the King of Siam in the musical *The King and I*. He was still waiting for news from Paris, the question for him being whether or not he was wanted there and trusted to run the company, refusing to be simply the 'concierge', as he put it.

As everyone knew, Nureyev had made the Paris Opera Ballet the finest in the world in the six years he had been there and any decision to not renew his contract was mystifying to say the least. His wishes were very clear. He demanded total artistic freedom, directing the company the way he wanted and casting the dancers he chose, particularly in his own ballets, all the while continuing to spend six months a year in the French capital as was stipulated in his 1983 contract, one of the conditions upon which he had originally accepted the post. He was most certainly not prepared to take on a secondary role.

He was discovering yet again that inevitable clash between art and administration. Seemingly sharing in all the disarray, a swarm of bees who had made their home on the rooftops of the Palais Garnier during Rudolf's reign flew away at the same time he left. Honey as golden as Apollo's lyre had been collected from two beehives there and sold at Fauchon's luxury delicatessen nearby.

Jean-Albert Cartier had been appointed administrator general of the Opera, and, as such, had decided that his authority went beyond the recently opened Opera Bastille. He literally poked his nose into Rudolf's 'Palais de Danse' at Garnier, interfering both in casting and programming, particularly when Rudolf wasn't physically there. As far as Nureyev was concerned, the Palais Garnier was his domain; Cartier, a man he did not particularly appreciate nor trust, could rule at the Opera Bastille. What was the problem? The problem was that the government had not clearly defined the roles of either Nureyev or the administrator, Cartier, who took it upon himself to take decisions at the Garnier without consulting Nureyev under pretext that the latter wasn't there.

"But Rudolf was here," Patrice Bart asserted. "He was constantly here, and when he was away, it was as if he was still here… his contract might have stipulated his presence six months a year, but not a day went past without him telephoning at all hours of the day and night. His presence," he repeated, "was so strong it was as if he was never absent. Yes, there were dancers who complained because they didn't see him, and it's true that he wasn't here twenty-four hours out of twenty-four. It was more like twenty hours out of those twenty-four.

"Of course he fulfilled his contract, totally, totally, totally," Bart told me. "He had so much warmth, so much kindness and generosity. And those stories that he could explode at any moment and hurl his flask of tea across the studio, and which were invariably taken out of context, were always because someone wasn't giving their best."

Claude Bessy, the director of the Opera school at the time, told me that Nureyev's daily programme was so packed that she usually had to run after him to get instructions for rehearsals with the children from the school, adding to the image of effervescence and excitement already evoked by Patrice Bart and several of the dancers.

"He worked non-stop," Bessy told me. "I don't think people realised

Rudolf with pupils of the Paris Opera School in 1967.
© Colette Masson/Roger Viollet

that. When he arrived for his lesson, there would be four or five people already waiting to see him, and as I've said, I had to talk to him while he was changing to go to a rehearsal… he never had a minute's peace. It was impossible to see him for an hour, which is what I would have liked."

Rudolf loved working with children. He always brought the pupils from the opera school into his ballets when he could. They were there in force for *The Nutcracker*, and present in his sumptuous *Bayadère*, not only because the children were an integral part of the ballet, but also because he believed that a school had to be closely linked to the company.

Nureyev was fascinated by their spontaneity, spending time whenever he could with those of Florence Clerc and Charles Jude, with the three of Ivry Gitlis, those of the ballerina Linda Maybarduk, as well as children he encountered on vacation.

"We were spending a few days in Italy," Douce Francois told me, "and one morning he disappeared. I finally found him on the beach, giving a lesson to a small Italian girl in the sand. And there he was again the following day. He had all the patience in the world for her, and of course, she had no idea of who he was."

However, returning to the situation in Paris, another issue arose from the dancers themselves at the same time as Bergé's unreasonable demands. They were adamantly opposed to Nureyev's desire to hire Kenneth Greve, a tall, good-looking Danish dancer, as a principal.

Nureyev had spotted Greve while in New York. He was a dancer who had trained first at the Royal Danish Ballet School, continuing his studies at the School of American Ballet before joining New York City Ballet. At nineteen, blond and handsome, and over six foot four in height, Greve was not only an exceptional dancer, but was a perfect prince and would have been a welcome addition to the Paris company. Objectively, this should have been seen as an astute move beyond any personal favouritism, as he would have been an ideal partner for the younger, taller generation of ballerinas in the company as many of the best male elements there lacked the necessary inches to dance with them.

Since his arrival at the Opera, Nureyev had broken many rules, but his decision to bring in an attractive adolescent at étoile level was one too many. Étoile Elisabeth Platel just plain refused to be partnered by him, a boy nearly half her age. Despite being advised to first give the Danish dancer the rank of 'sujet', gradually working up to premier dancer before nominating him as étoile, which would have been more diplomatic, Rudolf refused. Rightly or wrongly, feeling their own positions in the company threatened by what they also saw as Rudolf's fascination for the young Dane, the dancers went on strike.

"It was hard to understand the dancers' reaction," Yann Bridard, a young member of the corps de ballet at the time, told me. "I saw Greve interpret Siegfried in Nureyev's *Swan Lake* at the Grand Palais," he continued, "and he was wonderful. He was exactly the sort of dancer we needed here, but his appointment as étoile did not correspond to the company's policy… I watched it all happening and, frankly, I believe it was a question of jealousy and resentment, where several dancers, not seeing beyond their own noses, rudely rejected Greve given his resemblance to the legendary Erik Bruhn, one of the purest classical dancers of his generation."

Undaunted by the rumpus, Greve went on to enjoy a brilliant career as principal dancer at the Royal Danish Ballet, combining it with two wives and three children. Paris's loss was Copenhagen's gain.

But as far as Rudolf was concerned, the damage was done.

I spoke at length to Charles Jude about the whole mess-up of Rudolf leaving his post of artistic director.

"Rudolf did not want to leave the Opera," Jude said. "He wanted to stay but there was a series of stupid misunderstandings. Pierre Bergé had been nominated General Director and realised that Rudolf's influence had been growing during the preceding six years. When someone has too much control, those in power 'above' them always try to limit it and, naturally, Rudolf refused to relinquish certain rights, beginning with the right of choosing his own casts for his own ballets as well as anything else he considered came under artistic directorship. The choice of making such decisions was his. He'd made us the best company in the world and he refused to have anyone else interfering with his work.

"It was at this very moment that *The King and I* was proposed in the US. He used it as a pretext and pretended to leave to do it. Part of him was attracted by the role as he'd always loved musical comedy, but it came at a time when, in early October, his position at the Opera was very insecure. He used it as a bargaining power, threatening that if he was not given his due rights, then he'd go.

"It is true that he'd been offered a million dollars, I believe, for accepting it, but it wouldn't have taken much for the Opera to have kept him. His terms were reasonable. He wanted to continue his work here with his dancers; he loved them very much and preferred to stay. And where did all that money go? Straight into his foundation for young dancers, providing funds for dance scholarships as well as for medical research, which he had set up in 1975.

"All he asked for in the US was a piano in his dressing room and in his hotel as he played a lot. He'd been given a portable telephone before he left with which he used to call me from his dressing room over there, seemingly reluctant to go onstage... never wanting me to hang up,

"'No, no, no,' he'd say. 'Don't go. I've got plenty of time yet.' All he wanted to know was what was happening here. He wanted news of the dancers, whether they were well, what they were dancing that night, what they were dancing next and how they were working. He wanted reassurance that they were working properly.

"He didn't want all the work he'd done with them to disappear. Each time he returned to Paris, his contract in the US being only for three months, he'd come straight to the Opera, reproaching anyone who kept away; they were still very much in awe of him despite the fact he would have done anything for them.

"Now, I think everyone here understands him better. They miss him. All the dancers are perfectly aware of what he did for each one of them; they aren't blind. He gave them an image, a world status. That won't happen again in a hurry."

Nureyev so much wanted to return to Paris that he finally accepted a post as chief choreographer for the company under the bemused eyes of the hapless Patrick Dupond. Appointed by the all-powerful Pierre Bergé in 1990, thirty-one-year-old Dupond took over the thankless task of artistic director, fresh from three years of directing the Ballet of Nancy, where the work I witnessed with the company had been far from memorable. He had been too tempted to programme personal friends, both dancers and choreographers, regardless of talent. A man of certain charm, who told me in his impressive office, lit by magnificent chandeliers, just how much he enjoyed his title of artistic director without quite understanding what he should do with it; he was just too 'nice', too ready to say yes to the last person who spoke to him.

Nevertheless, here he was, one of France's most outstanding dancers, languishing in the shadow of Nureyev, all the while attempting to run the company he should have been dancing in. Fortunately, Brigitte Lefèvre became the General Administrator of the Opera in the weeks before Nureyev died, was made Assistant Director in 1994, and took over the company formally in 1995, when Dupond was asked to leave.

Conducting

Meanwhile, well before Nureyev embarked upon *The Bayadère* in the July of 1992, he took up conducting an orchestra. Few people knew that Nureyev, who was also a pianist, had enrolled in the Juilliard School, had trained as a conductor in Vienna, and had led orchestras in Mahler, Mozart, and Haydn as well as in Tchaikovsky, Stravinsky and Prokofiev.

Douce Francois, who spoke to me at length about Rudolf's developing career as a conductor, told me it had been a long-time dream of his, since at least the 1960s. "He'd set his heart on it," she said. "He'd always loved music but had never had the time before. He had this exceptional understanding of music and began to work hard. It certainly was no sudden whim as has been suggested, but something he took very seriously. I remember him going to see Leonard Bernstein for advice. And similar encouragement was given by von Karajan. Rudolf's very first engagement was unsurprisingly with a 'Nureyev and Friends' tour in America when he conducted excerpts from *Sleeping Beauty* for Charles Jude."

"What he really wanted to do," Jude himself told me, "was to conduct all his own ballets, all those he had mounted, and all those turning around in his head.

"We gave four performances at the beginning of 1991," the dancer continued. "And as exacting as he was with me when I was dancing, wanting me to do everything right, as anxious he was that he himself shouldn't make any mistakes with the music. Even during rehearsals, he had been seeking reassurance from the orchestra about the way to conduct certain passages in the score. He was constantly asking me if what he was doing was not only okay, but right for me. He wanted to know whether he needed to conduct the orchestra more slowly, or take things faster, being so afraid of messing things up. In the end, I just told him to conduct the way he wanted and that I would simply follow him.

"He was incredibly good; his timing was perfect and the tempo exact. Even the way he held the baton was remarkable, conducting as though he was a gardener growing flowers. Everyone there was amazed."

Jude confirmed that Rudolf's ambition to become a conductor had indeed begun back in 1964 when he was encouraged by Papa Hubner, a Viennese violinist. The dancer said he believed the seeds had been laid soon after he arrived in Leningrad, when he used to collect every score he could find of Beethoven's *Heroic*.

"What he wanted," Jude emphasised, "was to conduct the dancers from the orchestra pit and frankly, speaking for myself, when he did so, it was one of the most extraordinary moments of my career.

"He conducted orchestras in Vienna, in Budapest, in Kazan and gave his last representation in May 1992 at the Metropolitan Opera in New York, for American Ballet Theatre, conducting MacMillan's version of *Romeo and Juliet* when the main roles were danced by Laurent Hilaire and Sylvie Guillem, two of his favourite dancers."

Back to Russia

At the same time as the confusion surrounding the renewal of his contract at the Opera, Nureyev was finally invited back to St Petersburg to dance at the Kirov, after an earlier two day visit in 1987 to visit his mother gravely ill, who died shortly after. Brejnev had repeatedly refused to give Rudolf permission to visit his mother until the very last moment when she barely recognised him.

Douce Francois accompanied him to St Petersburg in November 1989, where he appeared in *La Sylphide* at the Maryinsky Theatre with Zhanna Ayupova, dancing at last on the very stage where his career had begun, twenty-eight years after his defection. The magnificent turquoise, pale blue and gold amphitheatre was packed and excitement was high. He was by then fifty-one years old and far from well. Should he have accepted? Of course he should; his appearance there was as much symbolic as anything else and he was wildly ovationed the moment the curtain rose. Nobody watched to see how he danced; everyone knew it was too late for that. For years he had been classified as a traitor and dancers ordered to ignore him if they saw him on tour. Now he was back. It was all that was important.

He was also elated to be there, and welcomed the opportunity to see and talk to so many of his old friends and colleagues, including his first teacher, Anna Udeltsova, who came from Ufa especially to see him, and who was by then 100 years old.

During his stay of over a week, he renewed acquaintance with the delightful Ninel Kourgapkina, a former partner who had adored dancing with him, and who had interpreted Gamzatti to his Solor in *The Bayadère* amongst their many roles together. She would come to assist him to stage that same ballet a couple of years later.

"He was acclaimed for over half an hour," Douce Francois told me. "Nobody cared how he danced, they were just so happy he was finally there!"

And while there, aided and abetted by Douce, he managed to get hold of the original music for *The Bayadère* before leaving, which was nothing short of a miracle as no complete Minkus score was to be had in the West.

Minkus score

"It was folklorique," Douce told me from the safety of her Parisian apartment. "There were Rudolf and I surreptitiously photocopying the music for the *Bayadère* in the archives of the Kirov theatre in the middle of the night, petrified as to whether we would be caught or not. We couldn't do it quickly enough! And then the following day, we had to hurriedly smuggle the score, which we'd hidden in my knickers, out past the customs! I remember walking to the plane sort of sideways, holding my knees close together," she chuckled, "scared stiff in case the sheets of music slipped down. Luckily it was winter and very, very cold, so I was wearing this big, bulky coat."

Matters did not end there, however, when I spoke to Mario Bois, husband of the late Claire Motte and the director of a music publishing firm in Paris. He described the day in 1989 when Rudolf Nureyev arrived in his office announcing his intention to re-stage *The Bayadère* using the complete original score of Ludwig Minkus, the official ballet composer of both the Bolshoi and Kirov companies.

"When I reminded him that it was not available outside Russia, he simply gave a little smile, telling me not to worry because he'd see to it," Bois said. "The next thing I knew," he continued, "was when he staggered into my office with what appeared to be a whole score of several ballets. He had been to Russia at Gorbachev's invitation and amidst all his

Rudolf with Douce Francois at Karl Lagerfeld's Venetian fancy dress ball in Paris, 1978. She's dressed as Pierrot Lunaire while Rudolf appears as an Italian nobleman.
© Coruzzi Giovanni/Bridgeman Images

commitments with ceremonies, ballets and meetings, he'd managed to get hold of photocopies of Minkus' original score!

"Goodness knows how he found the time, but when I looked closely, I found that his photocopies had been made vertically instead of horizontally as the machine had evidently been too small for the large manuscript. Consequently, each page had been photocopied twice, but none of the sheets corresponded to the next. In his hurry, Rudolf hadn't worried about the order, and nothing had been numbered.

"It was like a jigsaw puzzle," he told me, "but after we got Act I together, we discovered that many other pages were barely legible as the machine had obviously been running out of ink… and that on others, Minkus had only written piano music. Worse, while there were only one or two notes on some sheets, it seemed complete pages were missing. The work of reconstruction was diabolical, for we had an ocean of pages almost impossible to read.

"The main problem was the orchestration, which Rudolf couldn't write. He wanted John Lanchbery, who was so happy to help him that he came almost immediately.

Rudolf's beloved double manual harpsichord in wood and ivory, c. 1627, Jan Ruckers.
© Christie's images/Bridgeman Images

"But that wasn't the end of the story," Bois recollected, "for the evening before Lanchbery's arrival with his own incomplete score, I suddenly realised that there was no piano in Rudolf's flat for them to work on.

"'No piano. Harpsichord,' stated Rudolf.

"I remember staring at him in amazement. Beautiful though his harpsichord was, it was 18th century and not properly tuned. I pointed out that it was hardly suited to work out a whole ballet score.

"'No piano. Harpsichord.'

"In despair, it occurred to me," continued Bois, "that

one of my children had a small electric organ; if Rudolf was adamantly against renting a piano, and it would have been very complicated, the electric organ was easily transportable and certainly more practical than an antique harpsichord, no matter what Rudolf wished!

"So that was what we did, and I arrived with Lanchbery the following day carrying my son's small electric organ. Listening to the pair of them reading the music together must have been rather like watching Petipa with Tchaikovsky," the music publisher commented, "for Rudolf started pouncing on certain melodies, identifying a pas de deux, then cutting things here, adding bars there, and wanting a woman's variation where there was none! John's contribution was to find linking material and ensure harmonisation with the barest of changes.

"Anyway," he concluded, "after they'd sorted out the piano music, they began with the orchestration, and, all the while remaining faithful to Minkus, put together a solid musical text in the six months before rehearsals began."

La Bayadère

Nureyev's story with *La Bayadère* began in St Petersburg in 1958 when he danced the role of Solor at the age of twenty, and had continued in Paris when his appearance as the Indian warrior with the Kirov in 1961 had caused a sensation. After his arrival in the West, it was his dream to mount it here, especially after his beautiful staging of the third act, *The Kingdom of the Shades*, in 1963 from memory, for the Royal Ballet in London. It was his first real effort at choreography.

So successful and so well received was the work that Nureyev had suggested to Ninette de Valois at the time that he should mount the complete ballet for them but it never happened. He had to wait until 1992 to finally stage a magnificent version of *La Bayadère*, the ballet he had been planning for so many years. It was his last, great gift to the Paris Opera.

Full of Russian soul and Russian excess, a melodrama rendered more moving as it was obviously Nureyev's last ballet, it was the perfect vehicle to demonstrate the astonishing and diversified talent of the company he had made the best in the world since his appointment as artistic director almost ten years earlier. Despite the fact that his energy was slowly slipping away because of his long fight against Aids, he adamantly refused to give up and stop working, and he staged his ballet with the help of Patrice Bart and

Rudolf in La Bayadere, Paris 1970s.
© Francette Levieux/CNCS

Patricia Ruanne. The presence and encouragement of Ninel Kourgapkina, with whom I later spent three days at the Kirov theatre and school in Rossi Street in St Petersburg, was invaluable.

Warm-hearted, spontaneous and utterly delightful, Kourgapkina didn't hesitate to come from Russia to help him. Prima ballerina at the Kirov, she had been his partner in many of the classical masterpieces over the three years they had danced together. She had also danced Gamzatti to Rudolf's Solor in St Petersburg. She was one of the last pupils of the great teacher Agrippina Vaganova and, upon her retirement as a dancer, had become the director of the Vaganova academy.

"I was dreadfully upset when Rudik defected," she told me when we met in St Petersburg in March 1994. "I'd lost a wonderful partner as well as a fantastic friend. I loved dancing with him so much; he was so very musical. He could feel the music, and we'd jump and always land together, and then we were so well suited; I was five feet three inches to his five foot nine inches, and he used to carry me way up in the air with one hand without any effort. And I used to ask him to do it again and again, I loved it so much, being up there!" She laughed.

"And did you know that, lucky for me, he was never a member of the corps de ballet, but came right in as a soloist? We used to go on tour together, and miraculously, even in the most remote places, everyone knew him! We had so much fun. And then," she looked at me and gave me her lovely smile, "I was not so easy in those days, but he was totally irresistible and so very handsome! I adored being with him, and I liked him so much that when he asked for my help with *Bayadère*, I didn't think twice! It was wonderful to be with him again, and we worked incredibly well together. After leaving the theatre, we used to talk for hours at night at his home in the Quai Voltaire."

The Bayadère, Rudolf Nureyev's last production for the Paris Opera Ballet, which delights and draws in the crowds, is a classical ballet set in India, based on the 5th-century masterpiece *Sakuntala*. Nureyev's magnificent production, premiered on the 8th of October 1992, contains one of the most beautiful 'white acts' in the history of dance, and a storyline that still hangs true today: the drama of a man who hesitates between his heart and his duty, and indirectly brings about the death of the one he loves. It tells of the tragedy of two women who stop at nothing to keep him and contains a whole range of human emotions: love, jealousy, weakness, betrayal, possessiveness, violence, as well as forgiveness. The moment the music begins, one is uplifted. It is a ballet where music, costumes, choreography and dancing blend into a sumptuous melodramatic whole. What more could one ask for?

It tells the story of the sacred temple dancer Nikiya, who is secretly in love with the noble warrior Solor. But unhappily, Solor, initially dismayed by his obligation to marry Princess Gamzatti, the Rajah's daughter, is subsequently seduced by the trappings of power and immense wealth offered to him. Agreeing to the engagement, he thus breaks his vow to Nikiya. But upon discovering his love for the beautiful bayadère, Gamzatti plots to kill her rival by planting a poisonous snake in the basket of flowers that is offered to her. To his shame, Solor does nothing to save the temple dancer until too late.

Wracked by guilt, and devastated by her death, the Indian warrior resorts to smoking opium and in his dream he meets Nikiya again in the famous *Kingdom of the Shades*, the Shades being the spirits of long-dead Hindu temple dancers. Thirty-two members of the company's matchless corps de ballet make a slow, hypnotic descent in arabesque from a ramp at the back of the stage, appearing as if from heaven, as in the original 1877 version. Wreathed in mystery, a second's hesitation from any one of them could break the spell. Contrary to certain beliefs, Nureyev changed not a step of Petipa's dreamlike White Act.

"At its creation, on October 8th, 1992, after the summer break, the Paris dancers had barely a month to rehearse and stage the work, accomplished under difficult conditions as Nureyev was so tired," Patrice Bart told me. "We had only danced the third act before, when Rudolf used to watch the very last member of the corps de ballet. They danced with their hearts because he treated them as individuals. He'd look at each one of them, even the very last girl at the back, and they all knew he was looking at them. He made them realise that what they were doing mattered just as much as the étoiles.

"Now," Bart said, "I tell them that they are all principal dancers, all Nikiyas descending from the heights of the Himalayas, all Bayadères, pure, limpid, and luminous. I tell them, as did Rudolf, that they must breathe the music, and be proud, strong and moving, reminding them constantly that they are also individual women and not an army of robots."

Bart likened the ballet, with its spectacular, vast proportions to a grand opera. "Maybe *Aida*," he mused, "created only six years earlier. With roles for the soprano, mezzo, tenor and baritone. After all, the dramatic element in both works is a love tangle. Aida is the Ethiopian slave loved by Radames, who, like Solor, is engaged to marry Amneris, a princess like Gamzatti."

The work, an absolute feast for the eyes, contains a tiger, an elephant, and even a palanquin, with countless opportunities for the dancers in the variations as well as the large ensemble sequences.

The ballet is not only rich in story and dance, but as Nureyev wished, it has been made unique by its decor and fabulous costumes. Rudolf, as he himself never tired of saying, wanted to stage "real productions", putting together all aspects of the theatre as did Diaghilev and Roland Petit before him. And although he chose Ezio Frigerio to create the decor and Franca Squarciapino to design the costumes, his own brilliant, flamboyant taste is evident in each rustle, swish and swirl onstage, illustrating his belief that every spectator who comes to a performance sees with his eyes, but needs to eat too.

"If he doesn't eat, he's hungry when he leaves the theatre," I heard him say on more than one occasion...

Above all, Nureyev had access to the Paris Opera's costume workshop, which was given what appeared to be a seemingly unlimited budget. The colours of the fabrics used simply take one's breath away. This was the Tartar giant's last work; people knew it and no expense was spared, although the scenery department at first argued that they had run out of money for his large, extremely lifelike jewelled elephant, which trundles on carrying Solor to his engagement celebrations. It was one of the last things he fought for, and got!

Squarciapino was inspired by Indian and Persian paintings as well as by what she termed 19th-century oriental influences, and the materials used for her costumes, many of which came from Bali and were chosen in collaboration with Nureyev, echo Frigerio's dream of the Orient inspired by the Taj Mahal. Nureyev himself had memories of the realistic but over-heavy traditional costume he was obliged to wear when he first danced Solor in Leningrad, which hindered his freedom to move, and which, with the cooperation of Simon Virsaladzé, the Kirov's designer at the time, he had greatly simplified. He was therefore anxious that all of the costumes should be 'danceable'.

However, both he and Squarciapino were aware of the difficulty of keeping a unity of style throughout the ballet, particularly when tutus were worn in the third act. While dancers wear exquisite dresses made from richly embroidered saris with pointe shoes in Act 1, they do not go on pointe, and if boleros, saris, exotic drapes and veils make their appearance in the mimed 'action' parts, then they are worn with low-heeled shoes. Tutus belong to the purely classical third act and to the formal appearance of Gamzatti with her handmaidens. All the traditional, magnificent costumes, which are weighed down with decorative materials, are worn by the 'extras' who have walk-on parts.

I spoke to Etienne Bretel, the person responsible for the production, who told me that many of the costumes were made from saris that came from India, but that the Opera team also worked with several Indian boutiques in Paris. Also, he added that they had a supplier in Germany who imported directly from India.

"We use the embroidered borders of all the saris, but the problem we have is that, being made of pure silk, many of the costumes are so fragile that they cannot be dry-cleaned too often."

Bretel showed me a sparkling new costume that had just been made to measure for étoile Nicholas Le Riche, pointing out that the delicate white material, shot through with metallic threads, was particularly vulnerable to oxidation from perspiration, which caused it to darken to an unsightly moss-green, and that new outfits frequently had to be made for each of the étoiles.

"At the creation," he said, "all the costumes are made to measure for each interpreter, while the simple tutu for the corps de ballet, with its body in white satin and lamé, is made in its entirety by one seamstress, who takes three days to complete it. On the other hand, those worn by the soloists, which are covered in gold and silver, take one person five days to finish. We sew some of the braid on by machine where possible, but all of the heavy embroidery has to be stitched on by hand. The bodices of the temple dancers in act three are so heavily encrusted that we then have to cover our handiwork by placing soft white organza under the arms so the girls don't hurt themselves on the metallic decorations.

"A tutu," Bretel said, "which was made out of approximately a dozen metres of tulle from suppliers in France, Germany and England, was approximately forty to forty-two centimetres in dimension and contained eleven or twelve flounces. Each layer was basted, each flounce being loosely hand-stitched to the one below separately, and starched, before being turned upside down to dry and stiffen. When being washed or dry-cleaned, they were completely pulled apart before being sewn together again by hand, usually being dried in a draught. The étoiles, however, were free to reduce the number of flounces if they preferred to carry less weight, and also to choose their own headdress and personalise their outfit as they pleased. One dancer, for example, asked for a different length necklace, while they all chose their own bracelets and necklaces. Each girl also had her own earrings to suit her face shape."

Several of the dancers I spoke to commented that none of the headdresses were heavy and that it had been exciting to try everything on. They spoke of their pleasure in wearing the scintillating costumes, particularly the delicate purple trousers, bolero, sari and diamond encrusted veil worn by Gamzatti for the mime scene of act one.

The costumes in act two are even more extravagant, with Gamzatti's four handmaidens wearing blue tutus decorated with large motifs of golden flowers painted on by hand by the department's gifted 'atelier de decoration'. Likewise, the men who arrive onstage bearing the princess, and who are not even mentioned in the programme, are all wearing hand-painted trousers, costumes which have to be repainted before each series of productions as the paint disappears when dry-cleaned.

Among the countless exotic, colourful outfits and dresses, the appearance of the Golden Idol is outstanding. The very costume, inspired by pictures of the Hindu gods, is a work of art in itself.

"It's made entirely by hand," explained Etienne Bretel. "Squarciapino worked from Hindu documents and the whole affair is excessively complicated with a great collar, arm bracelets, and short, gold, metallic skirt. It's absolutely magnificent and premier danseur Emmanuel Thibault, who interprets the role, came into our department to add some finishing touches to his headdress. He's unbelievable onstage, and that's before he begins to dance. His golden make-up is so extraordinary that one would think he was made from gold."

Thibault himself told me that it takes him three and a half hours to dress and make-up for the part, which lasts just two minutes. He added that all the elaborate jewellery he wears had been created by the department's atelier de decoration, as had all the diadems, necklaces, bracelets and earrings worn by the women. Stones and other elements from Hindu jewellers, which had been directly imported from India, have been used to create a collection that Cartier, Chaumet, Boucheron and Fred would be proud to possess.

For Rudolf Nureyev's *Bayadère*, that same workshop created all the extraordinary headdresses and hats in the production. All are handmade while each one is made to measure for each dancer. Those worn by the ten high priests who do not even dance are magnificent, while the Rajah's costume of billowing blue trousers threaded through with gold, a blue and gold tunic trimmed with red and gold, silken cape and a mind-boggling turban shimmering with jewels in intricately fashioned details is worthy of a place in any costume museum.

Everything has been carefully studied with all manner of fabulous exquisitely worked details, including the elephant, which is blue and gold, turquoise, silver and white, the very colours of the Kirov theatre.

The only part of the production that could not be worked out was the famous 'missing' fourth act, which Nureyev was said to desire so much. Through lack of time and his failing health, as by September 1992 Rudolf was beginning to be dreadfully ill, it couldn't be done.

He had initially hoped that Frigerio could reproduce the scenery for *Bayadère*'s lost ending, Petipa's fourth act having been abandoned early on. At the beginning, angered by the wedding of Solor with Gamzatti, the gods had exacted their revenge by destroying the temple where the wedding was taking place and crushing to death all inside. But by 1919 the destruction of the temple had proved to be impractical with all the danger from falling masonry, and the last act had consequently been dropped.

Monique Loudières

"*The Bayadère* is a ballet which has everything," Paris étoile Monique Loudières, who danced the role of Nikiya, alternating with Isabelle Guérin, in October 1992, told me. "It has the purely classical style of Act III, and at the same time, is so beautiful with exceptionally well-defined characters. Even the walk-on parts, the mime and the character roles are excellent.

"I went to the back of the Opera to watch it when I wasn't dancing, and I felt I was at the theatre. Rudolf is so theatrical and so dramatic. Everything was wonderful, from the decor, the costumes and the dancing. Usually," she added, "I watch only the dancing, but the production was so complete and the character dances so real, I scarcely knew where to look. Rudolf loves re-staging the ballets he danced at the Kirov, having an incredible memory and forgetting nothing. He knows and respects the spirit of these 19th-century masterpieces; it's part of him, and he brings it into today. That was one of his very great qualities. He gave himself, and gave of himself, to something originally created by someone else.

"All Rudolf's changes in the first part of the work were good because dance has evolved since Petipa wrote the ballet in 1877. Dance techniques are no longer the same and you can't just fill the music with a step, you must change it, all the while keeping the original logic of the story and the personality of the characters in it. And Rudolf, being so intensely musical, knew how to fill it.

"Rudolf was so different from anyone else I'd ever met," Loudières continued. "He was so very special; we all respected him so much, even those dancers who were supposed not to like him. Working with such an exceptional person was an enormous pleasure and privilege. Progress to him had never ended; perfection was always just out of reach and impossible to attain being so fugitive. One can never dance as one wants to dance.

"*The Bayadère* was extremely important to him. Solor was one of his favourite roles, but, you know, he was Solor; it was the first ballet he danced when he arrived here in 1961, and now, with this incredible production, it has come full circle."

Loudières then echoed the sentiments of many of the other dancers I spoke to, that finally it seemed only right that the ballet should end on a romantic 'high' with the Shades scene, with the haunting beauty of the Bayadères, and with the forgiveness of Solor after his thoughtless betrayal. But how extraordinary that it was a Russian who brought back to France what a Frenchman had given to Russia.

The illness

Nureyev had been diagnosed as HIV positive as early as 1984, but he wasn't unduly worried. He felt in good health and all he wanted to do was work. If the truth be told, he didn't become ill until the end of 1991. In one of my last meetings with him in 1989, he certainly wasn't ill at all.

He took every treatment that was available, believing a cure would be found, and amongst the reasons his illness wasn't made public was because he simply did not want to hear people talking about it. It wasn't important.

What was important were his artistic accomplishments and for him to continue working. Moreover, on a practical level, he knew contracts could well be cancelled, particularly in the US, where people with Aids, deemed sick, were refused entry.

First thing in the morning, he'd be sorting out administrative problems, castings and future programmes, then he'd go to the studio for a lesson before he went to rehearsals, working with the principal dancers. As soon as he could, he'd turn his attention to the corps de ballet. In the evening he'd be there to watch the performance and then go home to work on his choreography. I don't know when he would have found the time to go downing bottles of vodka with the international jet-set in all the fashionable nightclubs around the world that one reads about in certain biographies. If such occasions arose, then they were few and far between.

Life for him continued as it always had with his work at the Opera, and with his tours for the small groups of dancers where he'd also be making the necessary contacts and arrangements to take the whole company next time. As Charles Jude told me, when he first discovered he was ill, he simply brushed it aside.

"What mattered to him was to dance, to be the director, to demonstrate to the company that one could be ill, have a cold, whatever, the performance still came first. He'd fought against illness and injury all his life. He never ever complained," Jude said, "neither at the beginning nor during those last months when he really did become sick.

"We were always together on tour and he was invariably in class first thing in the morning, having a lesson to be on form. He never mentioned he wasn't feeling well; it was as though everything was perfectly normal. Even when I took him to the hospital for the last time, he never said that he didn't feel well. He resisted and fought against it constantly. It certainly didn't affect his work, always insisting steps were done correctly, and even when we were rehearsing the *Bayadère* in September 1992, he was meticulously checking the lighting and the decor. He never seriously thought he was going to die, but was planning to do a thousand other things; not for a moment did he think his life was over."

"Everybody danced the *Bayadère* for Rudolf," Patrice Bart told me. "He was present at every rehearsal, and sat in an arm-chair to direct us. Ninel Kourgapkina knew exactly what he wanted and was the strength and force behind the dancers."

Agnès Letestu

Agnès Letestu, who later became one of the company's most beautiful principal dancers, spoke of how Rudolf had always fascinated her, and went on to describe how he asked her to dance the Princess Gamzatti in *The Bayadère*, even though she was only part of the corps de ballet at the time.

"One day in the Opera courtyard," she said, "he crooked his finger, came up to me and asked me if I would dance Gamzatti. Just like that! I couldn't believe it as I wasn't even in the group supposed to dance *Bayadère*. I was with the group of dancers working on the *Giselle* of Mats Ek, but he was determined that I should dance Gamzatti and he argued and fought with whoever it was and weak though he might have been, he got me changed into the group dancing *Bayadère* and into one of the main roles!"

She recalled when she was sixteen and he took her out of a lesson with a loud, "Stop!"

"I was shivering in my shoes wondering what I'd done wrong when he gestured to the others, announcing loudly, 'Look! That's how it must be done!' It was because my line of pirouettes was alright.

"'Do it again! Do it again,' he commanded.

"When he was around, everything was so exciting; there was such a special atmosphere. He might not have been well, but he always found the strength to do what he wanted. I distinctly remember one occasion when he had just come out of hospital and he came straight to rehearsals here and directed everything. His life WAS the Opera.

"He would have been driven here, and he'd arrive all bent and tottering, with someone holding his arm, but once here, he'd fling his helpers away, sniff the air, throw back his shoulders, and puff out his chest as if to declare, Me! Rudolf Nureyev! He was no longer ill and needed no one, and this was near the end of 1992. He was so proud and wanted no assistance as he directed us from his arm-chair. There'd be lots of noise before he arrived, but the moment he appeared, there'd be total silence."

The company witnessed his titanic effort at rehearsals, but few spoke of his illness, honouring his wishes not to speak of it, as if by ignoring it, it didn't exist.

"Rudolf never spoke of feeling sick," stated Genia Polyakov. "And because he didn't, we didn't. It wasn't important; his focus was on his work.

Even when he was in hospital, he would spend hours chatting about his future projects on the phone. He was so full of life and gave so much."

On the night of the premiere, Rudolf watched the performance lying down in the box near the wings. At the end, he was helped onstage where he stood, supported by Laurent Hilaire and Isabelle Guérin, his two stars, in front of a tumultuous audience, many in tears, who knew they were seeing him for the last time. After the curtain fell, the French Minister of Culture honoured him with the title of Commander of Arts and Letters, the country's highest cultural honour.

St Barts

But that was far from the end, for after the last rehearsals for the ballet, Nureyev had asked, or more truthfully persuaded, his closest friends, Charles Jude and his wife, Florence, to accompany him to his beloved St Barts in the Caribbean, arguing he would feel much better there. So off they went, accompanied by Jeanette Etheridge and Soloria, his dog.

"He told me that he needed a rest after working on the ballet and asked

Rudolf on the rocks below his home in Saint-Barthelemy, March 1991
© Bridgeman Images

me to forget dancing in the *Bayadère*, which I was programmed to do, and go to his house with him for the next two weeks instead," Jude said.

"He was so happy when we got there despite the exhausting journey. It was a house all on one level we'd built together, little by little, and fairly rudimentary because all Rudolf wanted was either to be outside or, paradoxically, shut up in his room. Dancing in the US as often as we did, it was easy to get to, and he'd always arrange to have three or four days off. We used to go there to relax whenever we could before continuing with our tour.

"It's situated on the wild side of the island where gales blow in from the Atlantic and is perched on top of high rocks overlooking the sea with spectacular views. There's nothing and no one around. The climate there was wonderful. He so loved the sun and adored being on the beach. We'd take his big black dog, and go to Les Salines for swimming and long walks, returning via the little village to do our shopping.

"He knew exactly what he wanted to eat and was happy with chicken legs, usually 'en papillotes', or fresh salmon with a glass of white wine. I also made a lot of risottos, while in the morning, we'd usually have scrambled eggs and toast. I was put in charge of cooking as Rudolf hadn't a clue… He was also quite insistent on getting his favourite wine, Puligny Montrachet, which he'd spotted in a local shop.

"The first time we'd been there," Jude reminisced, "he'd been complaining that it wasn't close enough to the sea down below. So we'd crossed the terrace and garden, and after climbing down to the sea, I'd suggested that some ground could be dug away to build a couple of rooms directly facing the water. He could have his bedroom and private bathroom there and even construct a large wooden terrace out over the rocks where he could sit and contemplate the sea.

"Shortly afterwards," he continued, "he contacted an architect saying… Charles wants to know whether it's possible to build two rooms down there. He's in charge!

"Well, by the time we arrived in October, all the work had been completed, the terrace was finished, and Rudolf was planning what had to be done next. He was full of ideas. In fact, notwithstanding the videos of orchestra conductors, and working on new steps for the ballets he had in mind, we spent much of those fourteen days planning more house extensions as well as simply relaxing, idling around, eating and swimming.

"It was funny," he smiled, "because when we went swimming, he'd go into the water in his swimming trunks, and only take them off once no one could see him as he said they bothered him, and he was quite prudish about it. I do remember, in a documentary film that was made, that he was quite upset when they showed him swimming in the nude; they had promised not to do so."

Jude then said sadly that Nureyev had not wanted to leave St Barts and was reluctant to straighten things up and start packing. "He stated that he was fine there and did not want to go back. But we had to," said Jude. "Should he not be well, there was no adequate medical care for him there, and Florence and I had to get back to our children."

I also spoke to Florence Clerc about that last holiday in St Barts. She said that Nureyev had always needed music and that their days there were full of Bach and Mozart, and that when watching videos of conductors, he was transported into another world. She herself was fascinated by the enraptured expression on his face.

"We put music on all the time," she told me. "Bach in particular was his passion, which wasn't really surprising because he was constantly searching for the logic behind it. He was totally at peace there, so happy and smiling and joking with us. And it was such fun to watch him with Jeanette, a lifelong Russian friend of his. There the pair of them would be, telling each other their salacious jokes and cackling together in their corner. It was probably just as well that I didn't understand everything," she added. "But he was terribly funny and could make us laugh over nothing.

"My only regret is that our children weren't with us, as they adored him. His eyes would follow them everywhere, his expression so soft and gentle. His eyes, a dark blue grey when he was troubled, would become a sparkling green when he was happy. I called them laughing eyes, always so full of warmth and affection when he looked at our two daughters. He'd always loved children, just being with them as well as dancing with them. Their spontaneity fascinated him."

She spoke of the unique friendship and extraordinary complicity between her husband and Nureyev, of how Rudolf trusted Charles totally and how, when dancing together, they immediately understood what the other needed. She told me how Rudolf would often say that Charles was his favourite partner after Margot Fonteyn.

The family would often spend Sundays together and would join him on holidays somewhere, Greece or Turkey, usually at a moment's notice. She, too, related Charles' stories of him charging off to the local markets searching for kilims before their boat had scarcely docked... and then sending Charles off to buy them as he knew he himself would pay through the nose! The merchants knew Rudolf only too well.

"He so loved life," she added, "holding on to it until the very last moment."

Rudolf Nureyev died of cardiac complications at the Hospital of Notre-Dame-du-Perpétuel-Secours in Paris on January 6, 1993. I was at home, in my bedroom, and scarcely moved for the rest of the day after receiving that fatal call. The heart had left the Paris Opera. An epoch had ended.

La Bayadère – the film

In October the following year a moving film of *La Bayadère* was made. Patrice Bart told me that the film was their tribute to Nureyev. It was to say thank you to him for all he did for them, for the company. "He loved the Palais Garnier and the dancers here," he said, "so it was danced and filmed according to his wishes as a mark of our love and respect for him."

Laurent Hilaire, the danseur étoile who danced the role of Solor, both at the première in 1992 and in the film, was even more emphatic. "I did everything for Rudolf," he told me. "We all danced for him. I always thought nobody was irreplaceable until I met him. I'm replaceable, we all are, but he's not. Not Nureyev the dancer, not Nureyev the director, nor Nureyev the man who gave us so much. He was unique and I miss him so much."

The film's first showing, in a small amphitheatre at the Opera Bastille, was given to a small group of friends including Jerome Robbins, a man of few words, who sat next to me. Shaking his head, he spoke so sadly of the loss of the Russian giant, of his enormous admiration for him, before commenting on the excellence of the filming.

The director, Alexandre Tarta, had strictly followed the instructions Nureyev had given before he was taken to the hospital for the last time. He had clearly stated the cast he wanted, which was the same as at the première, with Isabelle Guérin as Nikiya, Elisabeth Platel as Gamzatti, Laurent Hilaire as Solor, and with Wilfried Romoli as the Golden Idol. The solos in the Shades scenes were to be danced by Clotilde Vayer, Nathalie Riqué and

Agnès Letestu, the young dancer Nureyev plucked from the corps de ballet to dance Gamzatti in another cast.

The film begins with the camera showing the blue and lilac poster of the ballet, and then swings to show the magnificent grand staircase, the ornate auditorium and Chagall's ceiling. Tarta has captured an atmosphere, intensified when a camera closed in on a portrait of Rudolf in an opened programme. He had already filmed three different performances the previous May, using five cameras, while for the last performance, a sixth camera was brought in so that the spectator had the unusual experience of sitting in five or six different seats, so seeing the ballet from several angles. He admitted to me that filming had been difficult, and that he had needed a further twelve days for the editing. That the film-maker loved the ballet was evident: the film is superb.

I later spoke to Elisabeth Platel, who said that the film, which had used several new techniques, had respected Nureyev's wishes throughout, opening as it did on the stage of the Opera. She commented that it made one feel like one was seeing a live performance. She spoke particularly of Act II, where the dancers' skin looked like porcelain and where the luminosity of the scene gave it an exceptional beauty, rarely attained in a live performance, adding that the whiteness of the floor made it even more ethereal.

"Possibly the greatest dramatic success for me personally was in the quarrel between Nikiya and Gamzatti, which was divinely filmed. Each gesture," Platel said, "each 'word', was filmed at the right moment. I wasn't betrayed in any way, and maybe it was even preferable for the audience to see us on film, as seated in the theatre you don't always see every movement. With the technique used, one notices details not normally seen in performance. The death of the temple dancer was also perfect. Tarta came to work with us, not just to film what he saw but to help us create a work of art. It was remarkable how he gave us complete freedom to dance; often, film-makers insist on us staying put on a small area of the stage.

"You know," she concluded, "when I dance, Rudolf is always there with me, with his compliments as well as his insults. He'll always be with us, not 'up top', but sitting quietly in the wings, ever present, watching us."

Inevitably, Nureyev's death brought about the publication of several hastily clobbered together biographies that were rushed out when he was no longer there to sue. Sensation sells. Salacious and titillating stories about the people he knew or was purported to have known, as well as stories of an armada of young men he was supposed to have slept with, abound in their pages. His list of potential lovers makes Don Giovanni pale into insignificance.

Where was Rudolf, the man I knew? Nowhere.

I even had problems with Julie Kavanagh's 'definitive' saga on Nureyev, a tome of almost 800 pages in which I only caught glimpses of him, since she, too, seemed unduly interested in the tumultuous love lives of people I'd never heard of. Her book abounds in stories of yachts, celebrities, bitchy remarks and, the first time I opened it and flipped through, I fell on the opinion of Lillian Carter, a former president's mother, concerning a nightclub she'd been to. All that idle gossip was to the detriment of Nureyev's astounding achievements, buried as they were in a morass of empty details. Unlike John Percival, the eminent British critic, I did not read it to the end.

What disturbed me most were not the inaccuracies Percival picked out, perhaps inevitable with the wealth of material in this authorised biography, but more the picture she painted of a most unattractive man. Who had she been listening to?

Had any of these people actually seen Rudolf dance in his early years? Had they seen him dance at all? Had any of these biographers with their sweeping statements, for the most part unfounded regarding his work, actually met and talked to him? Sadly, the worst of these books was, unbeknown to the dance world, used as the basis for a documentary film on his years in Paris.

The BBC film

I got myself involuntarily involved in a film to be produced by the BBC. I was asked to help, guide and support people who had, I later discovered, never met him, never seen him dance, never seen his ballets, but who had their own preconceived idea of what they wanted to do with their film, ostensibly about Nureyev's work in Paris. It was to cover the ten astonishing years he had spent there, and was initially entitled, 'Nureyev, the Paris Years'.

After lengthy discussions with Douce Francois and Charles Jude, it was decided to be worth the risk. It was a unique opportunity to demonstrate to a non-specialist audience just how Nureyev changed the dancers' approach, how he broke down the hierarchy to give young dancers their chance, and how he widened the whole range of their repertoire. In addition to his own splendid reconstructions of Petipa's great masterpieces, it could show how he commissioned historical revivals and invited a constant stream of little known as well as established choreographers to the Opera. His intention was that programmes would present both classical and contemporary works. And he did all this as well as taking the company on world tours, which were often combined with his own guest appearances throughout the world. It was a period of incredible productivity.

Initially full of misgivings, Douce Francois wondered whether I would be tough enough to deal with these film people and ensure they made a film worthy of Rudolf, which would indeed be about his work. For her, she said, it was a question of trust; she wanted to avoid the inclusion of what she called the "juicy bits" in anyone's life, included simply to make a film commercial.

Finally, aware of the positive side, and carried away by the project, she suggested offering her own amateur films of Rudolf rehearsing the dancers, and showed me her own collection of wonderful holiday snapshots she possessed. Indeed, some of the loveliest portraits of Rudolf I'd seen, with his hair blowing in the wind and huge smiles lighting up his face, hung on the walls of her pretty apartment, broken into, she told me with a frown, by a horrible 'sniffing' journalist. She had refused to see him, but undeterred, he had forced his way in all the same.

"Most days, after going to the Opera to take Rudolf his thermos of tea and bowl of rice," she told me, "I'd get out my camera, hide it under my clothes, I got good at hiding things with him," she laughed, "and make my way quietly to the back of the amphitheatre in the Palais Garnier. There, I surreptitiously filmed him rehearsing the dancers. I'd tried to do it publicly, but had been shooed away. I don't think they liked me very much at the Opera."

She was so ready to cooperate in every way she could and I agreed that if ever the film went off in the wrong direction, becoming heavily slanted on his illness rather than his work, I would instantly let her know.

Patricia Ruanne was much more suspicious. "Hummm," she said to me. "It might seem a worthy project, but I don't trust certain journalists or film people. They ask you questions and shove a microphone under your nose. Then, when you see yourself on television, they've taken their questions away, omitted half or more of what you said and twisted your words around, so that what you said comes out as being the complete opposite of what you meant!"

Nevertheless, with the whole-hearted cooperation of Mr Hugues Gall, the General Director of the Paris Opera, the enthusiasm of the dancers who welcomed the project with joy, free access to the Opera archives, and with the full support of the Nureyev Foundation, who offered unlimited access to films and videos not seen before illustrating his work at the Opera, there was a unique opportunity to make an exceptional film with all the people who knew him best. Their only requirement was that the film give a complete picture of Nureyev's accomplishments at the Opera over the ten years he was there, and not be concentrated on the last three months of his life.

Douce, a member of the Nureyev Foundation, went to meet the film crew and contacted many people on their behalf. My role was that of 'consultant', a word the dictionary defines as a specialist who gives expert professional advice. But there was no indication as to whether the advice would be followed, and in the case of this film, it was not.

I was filled with the worst misgivings fairly early on, on a visit to London to discuss the names of the people who would be in the film.

"Okey-dokey. Let's have 'em then" were the opening words of the producer.

"Charles Jude," I said.

"Ah, his lover, was he?" was the reply.

No, I said, he and his wife were Nureyev's closest friends.

"Patricia Ruanne," I volunteered.

"Who's she?" came the reply, unaware that she was one of Britain's most famous ballerinas.

"His ballet mistress," I said.

"Ah, his mistress, was she?"

"No," I said, "she was one of his partners who became a teacher and coach, and came to Paris to work with him."

"Do you know Margot Fonteyn? She's a dancer, isn't she? I want her in the film."

"No," I said, "she died two years ago…"

I fled, despairing. What kind of mess had we all landed ourselves in?

From the beginning, the one person nobody wanted in the film was his doctor, for obvious reasons. It was deemed that this monsieur, who arrived rather later than earlier in Rudolf's life, had nothing to do with Nureyev's work in Paris, yet, there he was, programmed to be filmed sitting in a box at the Palais Garnier. This, proving that these film people wished to concentrate on Rudolf's illness, was too much for Hugues Gall, who forbade them entry, and confirmed Douce Francois' worst fears that the film was trying to present an incomplete picture of Nureyev's time in Paris. She therefore warned her friends, including Jerome Robbins in New York, and all the people who had not already been filmed. The people who had the most interesting things to say withdrew their support, while those already filmed backed down.

Gitlis, who had been so pleased to talk about "Rudi", was horrified that a film crew intended to make a film about a man with Aids. "What?" he exclaimed. "They want to interview his doctor and make a film about his illness! Rudi wasn't the only genius to be sick," he said. "Chopin wrote some of his most beautiful music when he was dying, so did Schumann who committed suicide, and Schubert had syphilis, and so what? You don't make a film about that. Do they want to bury Nureyev twice?"

In fact, Nureyev had battled all his life against injury and sickness; he did not suddenly rush to 'get things done' as the film implied, because he had always done so, having limitless interests, projects and ambitions… orchestras to conduct and ballets to write and appear in. The whole theme of the film was misleading. Over and above all the personal objections made by those close to him was the overriding fact that the film-makers' idea, that of greatness diminished by disease, did not in any way apply to Nureyev. These film people were trying desperately to fit a flawed theme to the last ten years of his life, which was a period of incredible productivity. It was probably not the only occasion when certain elements of the media decided upon a story first, and then hunted down facts that they hoped would fit. A unique opportunity was missed.

"Nureyev was the symbol of life," said étoile Agnès Letestu. "You can't introduce a doctor and make a melodrama about him. He was too full of energy and he wasn't ill until the very end. Even when he came to rehearse us for *The Bayadère*, as soon as he entered the studio, his eyes would sparkle and he'd argue to the bitter end to get his way."

Memorial

It would be hard to imagine a more beautiful resting place than the peaceful little Russian Orthodox cemetery at Sainte-Geneviève-des-Bois, some fifteen miles from the centre of Paris, where Rudolf Nureyev was buried in January 1993. A gravel path along the 'Allée des Epicéas' leads past tall conifers, while yews, spruce and fir trees guard quiet alleys where deep blue pansies jostle with pink and white petunias, yellow daisies and purple violets. It differs from other cemeteries in that the friends and families of those who rest there don't simply leave cut flowers on their graves, but have planted growing vegetation.

The cemetery, originally designed for the burial of 'White' Russians who fled their country to live in France after the Bolshevik revolution in 1917, has a distinct 'Slav' atmosphere, enhanced by the small white church there with its pretty blue domes, a church modelled on those of the city of Novgorod in Russia.

The atmosphere on Monday, May 6th, 1996, differed from the heavy grief surrounding the actual interment three years earlier. There was a distinct sadness in the damp air as friends and admirers from around the world gathered in small groups, the crunching from the gravel path heralding new arrivals, their arms full of flowers. Roland Petit and Zizi Jeanmaire brought a gorgeous wreath of white lilies and roses from one of the most beautiful florists in Paris, while the deep red amaryllis in a pot that Genia Polyakov was carrying was almost as big as he was. People were murmuring quietly amongst themselves while waiting for Nureyev's tombstone to be unveiled.

In the months following his death, the Rudolf Nureyev Foundation had asked Ezio Frigerio, the Italian architect and designer who had worked on several of his last productions, to create a unique monument for him.

Douce Francois at the unveiling of Nureyev's tombstone in May 1996 in the Russian cemetery.
© Patricia Boccadoro

*Nureyev's memorial in Sainte-Geneviève-des-Bois,
surrounded by flowers and more flowers, on May 6th 1996.
© Patricia Boccadoro*

"None of us wanted a cold, marble slab with his name engraved on it, and certainly no cross. Rudolf was not religious, and so both Douce Francois and Jeanette Etheridge had the idea that since Rudolf so loved oriental carpets, then that was what he should have," Charles Jude told me.

As he unveiled the tombstone, one of the few non-orthodox monuments in the cemetery, Sir John Tooley, the administrator of the Royal Opera House from 1970 to 1988, and, at that time, President of the Nureyev Foundation, spoke movingly of the great dancer.

"He was one of the most extraordinary artists who ever hit this earth; we need to have something to remind us of him," he said. "Ezio Frigerio has created something quite remarkable, a tombstone which says everything there is to say about Rudolf, his Asiatic origins, his life of travel, and his taste; wherever he went, the contact with him brought something good. Rudolf dared, he was courageous and he went beyond everything. He will always be with us, and," he ad-libbed, looking up, "the sun has just come out to shine on us and on him."

Just as he spoke, the overhead clouds cleared and all of a sudden the sun blazed down upon a massive traveller's trunk, covered by a magnificent oriental carpet crafted entirely in mosaic and seemingly thrown carelessly over it, a copy of one of those so beloved by Nureyev. It was worked in jewel-like colours, ruby red, burnt orange, turquoise, blue, white and gold mosaic, bordered by a fringe of golden bronze, echoing that of the painted curtain of the Paris Opera. It was Nureyev's own final curtain. The carpet glowed and it was impossible to remain sad at such a wonderful sight. Those of us there had to smile.

The tombstone was made in the Paris Opera workshops, the mosaic by Akomena of Ravenna, and the bronze fringes by Blanchet and Landowsky of Paris. As Douce Francois commented, not only would the monument protect Rudolf for eternity, "But, look around at everyone's reaction," she said. "Their heartache has lessened and people have tears of joy in their eyes now as they remember what fun he was and how much this resembles him..."

After the short ceremony, Douce introduced me to Wallace Potts, a quiet, warm-hearted man I'd heard so much about and was pleased to finally meet.

Maude Gosling

Maude Gosling, standing somewhat apart under a tall tree, gave me a gentle smile. At an incredible eighty-four years old, she had lost little of her former beauty. Tall, slim and elegant in her calf-length black coat and matching hat, she was very lovely, with her pale, flawless skin and clear, cherry red lipstick.

Although born in South Africa, she had come to Britain to enrol in Marie Rambert's school, later becoming a principal dancer in Rambert's Ballet Club. Frederick Ashton and Antony Tudor had begun to work there and she gradually became Tudor's muse, creating many of his subtle, atmospheric works including *Jardin aux Lilas*, an Edwardian portrait of a woman entering into a marriage of convenience, and the psychological ballet *Dark Elegies*, both works that Nureyev brought into the repertoire of the Paris Opera Ballet.

Upon her marriage to the art and dance critic Nigel Gosling, she began to work with him under the pen name of Alexander Bland when they wrote reviews together for *The Observer*. The books they wrote on Rudolf still remain the best one can find.

They had first seen Nureyev dance with the Kirov company in Paris in June 1961, just before he defected, and then met him the following year when he came to dance at Margot Fonteyn's gala. She and her husband subsequently worked with him on his autobiography, *Nureyev: His Spectacular Early Years*.

They were initially asked to befriend him by Fonteyn; their friendship had grown, and he moved into their home whenever he was in London despite the fact he shortly had a house of his own in Richmond. There's little Maude Gosling doesn't know about him, the woman who considered him as her surrogate son, but as she would be the first to say, his private life was his private life. He, for his part, adored her.

She first apologised for not having been able to talk about him to me a few years previously, as she had signed an exclusive contract with the American writer Robert Gottlieb, which had excluded her from talking about Rudolf to anyone else, at least for a year. She had later regretted it, but then smiled at me, saying, "But I don't think I can tell you anything else about him that you don't already know. You know as well as I do that it was that courage of his, to take on every risk imaginable, which made him so exciting. And then, he was such a wonderful boy.

"Did you know that when Nigel died, he came to me immediately and moved in with me in London? His personal kindness had no limits because I really don't know what I would have done without his support. He also gave the same support to Margot when she fell ill. All the world knows about his dancing and choreography and things, but he was such a warm-hearted, kind and caring person, no matter he was a genius. I don't know why it's me standing here and not him. I was thirty years older and I always thought that he would be here to hold my hand. I never imagined it would be like this."

Part VI

Legacy

At the time Nureyev's monument was being unveiled, Brigitte Lefèvre had been the Directrice de la Dance at the Opera since July the previous year, although she had enjoyed close links with the company since the September before the opening night of Nureyev's legendary production of *The Bayadère*.

Appointed Inspector of Dance at the Ministry of Culture in 1985 and having become the first 'Déléguée de la Danse' in 1987 before her appointment as Administrateur General of the Paris company in 1992, she was well equipped to weave her way through the many intricacies and pitfalls peculiar to the French administration.

Brigitte Lefèvre

"The years I spent in Paris gave me the unique opportunity to work closely with Rudolf Nureyev during his directorship," Lefèvre told me, "and so upon my own appointment I only had one idea in mind: to continue and build upon the project he had begun over ten years before. He was more than a great personality; he was a myth. However," she added, "while he was like a blazing comet, I needed time to think things out and do them slowly in my own way.

"He gave us everything, and I hope to transmit his passion for perfection, and all those who worked with him must concentrate on instilling the spirit of each work being staged. He is our reference. We have his wonderful classical productions plus a whole new exciting repertoire which he kicked into the next century. Nothing can ever undermine his unique transmission of the classics, but we will also continue to move forward, building upon the legacy he left us.

"So I intend to do as he did, and take risks with new choreographers and combine our great traditions with what could be called the 'avant-garde'," she continued. "Thanks to Nureyev, who did so much to break down the barriers between classical and contemporary dance, we now have an extraordinarily vast repertoire, including works by Angelin Preljocaj, whom Rudolf contacted in 1989, and Dominique Bagouet, as well as works by Neumeier, Gallotta, Carlson, Bausch, and Kudelka, alongside so many of the American school Rudolf loved. And that's to name but a few.

Rudolf with the American choreographer John Neumeier during a press conference in Avignon in July 1987.
© Colette Masson/Roger Viollet

"Programming, as Nureyev demonstrated, is a combination of opportunity and intuition. He dramatically opened up the dance world when he presented William Forsythe's *In the Middle, Somewhat Elevated*, created for Sylvie Guillem in 1987, followed by the visionary staging of *Le Martyre de Saint Sébastien*, also with Guillem in the title role, with choreography, decor and lighting by Robert Wilson, the year after.

Rudolf," she added, "had the energy to move mountains; the mountains of conservatism."

She stressed that what was important was the sincerity behind a ballet, and not whether one liked it or not. She insisted that programmes should build upon the past and then go further, dancers and choreographers moving towards the future together.

Speaking to Lefèvre again some ten years later in her workmanlike office cum sitting-room on the top floor of the Palais Garnier, I found she was only too pleased at the opportunity to talk about Nureyev's legacy, announcing that she had never forgotten the raw passion coupled with what she now recognised as rigorous schooling the first time she had seen him dance.

"I was a pupil at the Opera school and we were all carried away by his sheer vitality and tremendous energy after seeing him dance the third act of *La Bayadère* in rehearsal," she told me. "I saw a tornado; he was absolutely incredible. It's that passion for dance combined with impeccable training that we strive to keep alive. It's not only the steps of the work which are important, but rather the way in which they are danced. He changed our whole way of thinking and brought in not only his wonderful re-readings of *Swan Lake* and *Sleeping Beauty*, far superior to what we had, but added *Raymonda*, *Don Quixote*, *The Nutcracker*, and *La Bayadère*, thus reinstating Petipa here, as well as adding his own *Romeo and Juliet* and *Cinderella*.

"His revised choreography for his productions after Petipa is extremely challenging, but when the dancers can tackle that, they can dance anything. As has so often been said, Rudolf made the dancers aware of something they hadn't known they possessed."

Lefèvre stressed that his ballets and very deep respect for the past were being passed on to the new generation of dancers, as they would be to future generations, adding that the Opera was certainly not a mausoleum any more than she was the museum's curator. She also pointed out that before Nureyev, there was a tradition at the Opera, but now there is his teaching. He knew full well that he was leaving behind people who would continue his work: Patricia Ruanne, Genia Polyakov and Patrice Bart, to begin with, from three entirely different schools, the British, the Russian and the French, three people who knew how Nureyev worked.

Manuel Legris

Manuel Legris, creator of Nureyev's Romeo in the filmed version of the ballet, to whom I spoke shortly after seeing him dance the role of Solor in *The Bayadère*, is another dancer who fully intends working in the direction indicated by the man he considers his mentor.

"I am what I am today because of Rudolf," Legris told me. "He made me work and nominated me étoile when I was just twenty-two. If I'd never met him, I'd have been nothing. Claude Bessy at the school trained us to be accomplished dancers and it's true to say that we were good instruments for him to work on, but he made us the artists we are today. So while I was certainly formed by the Opera school, everything I am now, even when I dance as guest artist elsewhere, is because of him. Without Rudolf's presence in my life I'd have stayed at home and done nothing!

"I remember him saying to me casually, oh, Manuel, you're going to La Scala to dance *Don Quixote* next week, and there I was, scarcely believing my ears. I'd never danced it before. Alone, I was incapable of doing anything, but with him behind me, I could do whatever he asked. And he was like that with us all… any one of us will tell you the same. Not a day goes by without me thinking of him, and when I'm tired, it gives me the strength to carry on.

"When I look back over the years he was here, there was not one negative thing, not even those outbursts of temper which were always justified, but often exaggerated and taken out of context. Everything he did was 100% positive, 150% positive, because what I imagined to be negative at the time, wasn't. Everything he said and did had a reason. When I look back as to how it was before his arrival, I shudder to think of how I resented his constant insistence that everything be done correctly. But I soon realised that he subconsciously instilled a discipline in me; while he wasn't strictly speaking a teacher at all, he was the most brilliant pedagogue I'd ever come across. He saw at a glance what our problem was and told us how to solve it. And every time, what he said became so obvious, and was exactly right.

"Working with Rudolf, a dancer can achieve anything if he sets his mind to it. Yes, he was demanding, but it was always for a reason. People today must understand that not one step should be changed, and when someone asks why, my reply is simply that each small detail gives a soul to the ballet; he made his productions come alive. Cutting out steps or simply taking short-cuts to make it easy gets me really angry!"

Legris spoke to me about how Rudolf's ballets, always very carefully worked out, were incredibly difficult to dance, but once mastered, everything else was easy.

Referring to the repertoire, the dancer commented that when Rudolf arrived, things moved. "He opened up the repertoire here, beginning by inviting people like Billy Forsythe, choreographers who had never put their noses inside the Opera before. They all came because he was such a big international star; they would do anything for him, and we were the ones who benefited from it all."

Legris explained how the French school, thanks to Nureyev, embraced the best of everything, becoming very pure and yet strong and harmonious.

"There's a distinctive style here, and when a dancer guests somewhere, one can immediately tell they are from the Paris Opera. Back in Russia," he added, "they haven't yet really moved on; they remain mannered and their make-up and wigs are so old-fashioned. When Rudolf came here, he not only gave another meaning to a prince in a ballet, but also pushed us to see what was happening elsewhere."

Upon his retirement from the company at the age of forty-two and six months as dictated by law, Manuel accepted the post of artistic director in Vienna, where I caught up with him two years later, in July 2011. Prior to his arrival, the same traditional 19th-century ballets were being staged year after year with little being made of the company's reserves of talent.

The general director, Dominique Meyer, told me that he had every confidence that Legris would direct the Vienna State Ballet in much the same way as Nureyev in Paris. "Moreover, thanks to Nureyev," Meyer said, "Manuel Legris has met all the most important choreographers in the world today, and because he knows them and has himself danced their works, he can readily obtain their ballets, thus opening up the repertoire here. Because they trusted Nureyev, they trust him. And like Rudolf, he is already giving chances to the younger dancers. He's working with the dancers here in exactly the same way as Rudolf at the Paris Opera. Nureyev's influence knows no bounds."

Following the example of the Russian master, and before his retirement from the Paris Opera, Legris had begun taking small groups of dancers from the company to Japan as early as 1996, and again, he told me, the fact that he'd worked alongside Nureyev showed him how to be attentive to the needs of individual dancers, each with their own personality, and of the importance of being in class with them and actually demonstrating the steps himself.

"Rudolf was always with us in class," Manuel explained, "in the studios and in rehearsals and I try to work as he did. His limitless generosity influences me in everything I do, particularly in his way of correcting us in class. I realise more and more that being in the studios with them, as Nureyev was with us, enables me to see the potential of everyone.

"All the dancers who knew him are only too aware of what he did for them. Every dressing room boasts either a huge poster or a laughing snapshot of him. They like to see his wicked smile and hear his ringing laughter. Nureyev, they will all tell you, gave them their intense desire to dance and the strength, force and opportunity to do so. They look at him, they tell me, each time they are called to dance onstage, and not a day goes by without his presence in their lives. When he was around, they say, they couldn't stand it because he pushed them to do things they really didn't think they could do, until they suddenly realised that they could.

"I can only hope that, in my turn, I will be able to give to the dancers here what he gave to me."

Differing somewhat from Legris' insistence that absolutely nothing should ever be changed in Rudolf's ballets, Elisabeth Platel and Isabelle Guérin got together to discuss how they would stage his ballets in the future should the occasion arise.

"Neither of us will be like the teachers at the Opera now who insist that there's only one way to dance his ballets. There isn't! I dance them one way, and Isabelle another." Platel smiled. "Rudolf's great gift here was to encourage us to interpret a role according to our own personality.

"Learn, learn, learn, he used to say to me… However, he always saw me as a princess, dancing the classics. He wouldn't cast me as Juliet, nor as Kitri in *Don Quixote*, telling me it was not for my temperament, and how I argued with him! But now I see how right he was."

Wilfried Romoli

Wilfried Romoli, premier danseur during Nureyev's directorship, strongly emphasised Legris' words, explaining once again just how Rudolf Nureyev's time in Paris turned a moribund French company into the best in the world in just a few short years.

"His ideas were simply fantastic," Romoli said. "His ballets, all of them, were never banal, they were theatrical and dramatic, while his conception of dance was just out of this world. His productions are a mixture of imagination and psychology, and when I danced the role of Rothbart in his version of *Swan Lake*, such a strange and ambiguous character, it was one of the most challenging of my career. He brought a new way of thinking to the classical system, including developing male dance. From having little to do, we, the male dancers, suddenly had a lot to do, and inevitably, both our enthusiasm and level rose.

"He instilled a passion in us," Romoli continued, "giving us roles that were almost too rich and too demanding. When I danced Romeo, which was all his own choreography, it was so exhausting that I was totally worn out, but he danced it too, and he wasn't!

"When he arrived here, he got things going and everything started happening; he wanted to do so much and all at once. He never stopped, not for one minute. He absolutely adored so many contemporary choreographers and was always open to new steps and new ideas… Rudolf was completely in love with movements, everything that one could do with the feet and legs."

The dancer listed all the choreographers Nureyev had brought to the Opera, adding that not only did he invite all the young generation of talented choreographers alongside such giants as Cunningham and Martha Graham, but he also knew how to surround himself with the right decorators.

"But don't forget… Nureyev always did what Nureyev wanted," Romoli pointed out. "He had a will of iron, and he'd always do what he believed in. When he had an idea, he'd carry it through to the bitter end, no matter what. Luckily," the dancer told me, "it was what audiences loved.

"Rudolf would do anything to ensure the dancers progressed and he had this habit of sometimes giving some of us a role for which we weren't really suited, pushing us to do something we didn't think we could do… because he believed it was like that one progressed. For me, that proved true and what was extraordinary but extremely disconcerting was that when I knew I'd done something badly, he'd simply say, fine, and walk away, but when it was okay, he'd say nothing!

"You know, one of the most surprising things about his time at the Opera was how those dancers who professed not to like him were always so pleased when he gave them the slightest word of praise. If he said it was good, they wouldn't forget it; it was enormous.

"For my part," Romoli continued, "when he truly praised me, I was very moved; he was so special and had such a way with him. He'd never give in or pander to anyone, not to us, not to the press and not to an audience; there was something so pure about him. He was an exceptional man."

Regarding Nureyev's teaching, Romoli reiterated what has already been said, that Nureyev never taught as such, but would correct everyone, and give advice to the teachers, who were only too pleased; those whose teachings he disapproved of had left long ago. He said that they all learned so much when he was there, adding that sometimes the dancers hoped he wouldn't appear because they felt too tired. But Nureyev was never too tired.

"I often wondered whether or not he was super-human with that incredibly sharp intelligence he had," Romoli mused. "I felt like opening him up to see what he was made of!

"It was such a very great privilege to have known him, and when one is fortunate enough to have had someone of his stature in one's life, it's impossible to ever forget them; he taught us all to dream and made so many dancers around the world the dancers they are today. He spent his first two years here forming, guiding and training us, and then he left us to interpret and dance roles according to our own personality. The way he liberated us is only one of the ways he made the company great. I find it amazing that each of us is able to interpret a role differently while all the time doing the same choreography. He gave us an incredibly sound structure, which is what I aim to do in my teaching; I try to work in the same way that he did."

Romoli has been teaching in the Paris Opera school since his retirement from the company in 2009.

Yann Bridard

Premier danseur Yann Bridard, who joined the company in 1988, told me how very, very fortunate he felt to have been there when Nureyev was the director, even though it was for such a relatively short time.

"The first time I met him was when he was walking down one of the corridors in the Opera school at Nanterre," he said. "I was twelve years old and we'd been taught to always say 'bonjour' to people we met, but when confronted with him, I was, for the first and only time in my life, completely tongue-tied. His very presence was overwhelming, especially when he looked at me so intensely. I felt that there was a magnetic aura around him.

"Later, in class, when I joined the company, Nureyev had his eye on everyone, and he'd be there behind me, correcting and telling me what to do," Bridard said. "I'd watch how he moved, and he'd come across to me, suggesting I try certain steps in a specific way. His advice and presence was inestimable. He was a man with a vision who brought so much beauty to so many people. Of course he flew into rages with certain dancers, and got exasperated when someone wasn't listening and not doing what he asked.

"Shortly after joining the company, I remember being very unsure of myself. I felt that I wasn't good enough and so I used to stay at the back of any group, remaining very much on the side, when one morning he came up to me, asking me quietly why I was sitting down. He was so kind, questioning as to why I wasn't dancing. He wanted everyone to go to the maximum of their capacities and beyond. He saw who I was in two seconds, understanding that I was 'marginal'. He asked the right questions at the right time, sensing my problem, and going straight to the point.

"Later, I heard that he'd wanted me to dance his Romeo. He didn't know my name, but asked for the 'tall boy with dark hair', a description that also fitted Nicolas Le Riche! And to be honest, Le Riche was a fantastic Romeo. It's one of his finest roles. But because a friend told me he originally thought of asking me, I realised he believed in me, and it gave me the courage to go to the dance competition of Varna in 1992 where I obtained the silver medal.

"The world today isn't as beautiful as when he was here. The Opera has lost its soul."

Florence Clerc

Florence Clerc repeated much of what Romoli and Bridard had said, telling me how dreadfully everyone missed Rudolf after he died. "We'd been so used to his presence; he was always there, for our work and in our everyday lives. Everyone really loved him, even when there was friction, because it was always compensated by moments of such sweetness."

Douce Francois had spoken to me of Rudolf's sensitivity, of how, she said, a feather stroked along his arm would have left a scar, and Florence Clerc also recalled how he took things very much to heart.

"He loved what he was doing with the dancers," Clerc said, "and wanted them to grasp what he was telling them so much that he'd quickly take offence if he thought we didn't agree with something. A problem only arose when people didn't react to his demands that the steps he was showing us had to be as close to perfection as possible. He was so much quicker than we were with his brilliant intelligence and passion for dance and he would get hurt so easily, when all the time, everything he was doing was for us.

"But if he got irritated quickly, then just as quickly he'd be sweet and gentle afterwards. It's true there were explosive scenes, but I know he never meant what he said."

One can question what is going to happen after so many productive years, when all those who worked with Nureyev leave, and when almost all of the new generation weren't even born when he died. Someone must obviously teach them as he did; he was in fact a teaching director and a leader as well as a guide. He changed all the old ways of teaching and coaching, telling the teachers in no uncertain terms exactly what he wanted, and making the dancers understand that a step had to be done in a certain way because it led on to the next.

Part of his legacy is now the responsibility of all the dancers he formed, all those who worked with him and who are now teaching and directing other companies elsewhere in the manner in which they themselves absorbed knowledge.

Charles Jude took over and brilliantly directed the Ballet du Grand Theatre de Bordeaux in 1996 until 2017, before opening his own school, the Jude Mikhalev Ballet Academy there.

Elisabeth Platel has been in charge of the Opera school since 2004, while Manuel Legris accepted the directorship of the Ballet of Vienna, bringing the company to international level, and only leaving after ten years to take over the Ballet of La Scala in 2020.

Charles Jude telephoning outside the Theatre du Chatelet in Paris before a performance of his Coppelia, created in 1999.

© Patricia Boccadoro

After inexplicably being passed over for the directorship of the Paris Opera Ballet, to the detriment of the French company, Laurent Hilaire was snapped up by the Ballet du Theatre Stanislavsky de Moscow, the most important company in Russia after the Kirov and the Bolshoi, but resigned after the declaration of war with Ukraine. On his return to France, the Staatsballett de Bavière in Munich lost no time in offering him the post of artistic director there.

Nureyev's last principal dancer, Kader Belarbi, took over the reins of the Ballet du Capitole de Toulouse in 2012. Meanwhile, Monique Loudières, Elisabeth Maurin, Wilfried Romoli as well as so very many other dancers are all working and teaching in the same direction as Rudolf. Florence Clerc not only coaches the dancers, but is also frequently invited to stage Nureyev's ballets for companies around the world.

Meanwhile, for the Paris Opera, the future lies in not only re-staging all his productions on a regular basis, but in bringing back choreographers who have already worked with the dancers as well as inviting new ones. People like Gallotta and Forsythe now have their place at the Opera, creating large productions for the company. Nureyev would invite people to create a short work, and then if he thought the dancers understood their style and if the choreographer was happy working with the company, then they would be invited back.

Since the departure of Brigitte Lefèvre in 2014, the company has lacked a director capable of inspiring them; the dancers are there, the teachers are there, the repertoire is there. All that is currently absent is a director to give them back the passion instilled by Nureyev, making them again one of the finest companies in the world.

Carnavalet

After his death, many moving and original exhibitions were held throughout Europe, not least at the Trussardi Art Centre of Milan, where a beautiful exhibition, 'L'Univers de Nureyev', was hosted preceding that shown at the Carnavalet Museum in Paris.

'Rudolf Nureyev, Une étoile à Paris', based on the collections belonging to the European branch of the Nureyev Foundation, an organisation he set up to give grants to promising young dancers and choreographers as well as financing medical research, opened at the Carnavalet Museum in April 1997.

The exhibition at the Carnavalet, a beautiful 17th-century mansion in the heart of the Marais, one of the oldest areas of Paris, evoked the life of the legendary dancer using a series of photographs, videos, posters and programmes as well as his own private collection of works of art. Films of him dancing were projected onto a large screen and included excerpts of *Sleeping Beauty*, Paris 1961, the pas de deux of *The Corsaire* with Margot Fonteyn, from *An Evening with the Royal Ballet*, 1964, and Roland Petit's *Le Jeune Homme et la Mort* with Zizi Jeanmaire, 1965, included as it was a particular wish of Nureyev to have this particular film in a documentary.

The curator, Jean-Marc Léri, told me that the exhibition had been assembled in Paris as a tribute to the exceptional man who had sought asylum here in 1961, and who had subsequently given so much to the city. He commented that Nureyev, whose love story with the French capital only ceased with his death when he chose to be buried in the small Russian cemetery at Sainte-Geneviève-des-Bois, was essentially very Parisian.

The young decorator Pascal Payeur gave a special atmosphere to the exhibition by using not only the dancer's stage costumes but also his personal possessions and the engravings, paintings and other memorabilia from his apartment in Quai Voltaire bought at public auctions by the Foundation.

"We have not tried to present a biography, but rather to evoke the image of Nureyev the dancer, the choreographer, art-lover and musician," said the curator.

Payeur added that he was also particularly pleased to be able to present the amazing collection of annotated scores Nureyev possessed, not only of dance works, but also of Bach, Brahms and Beethoven, alongside his own musical instruments. Rudolf was, as is now known, an accomplished musician, a fact which helps explain the perfection and outstanding musicality of his dancing as well as his ambition to conduct all his own ballets from the orchestra pit.

After the closure of the exhibition, a small part of these exhibits remained to form a permanent collection, but the rest of Nureyev's own films, personal archives, rare books, photographs and other documents went to the Bibliothèque Nationale and the National Centre for Dance at Pantin, on the outskirts of Paris. Other personal belongings as well as over 4,500 photographs are to be seen at the Centre-National-du-Costume-de-Scène, situated in Moulins.

Marc Richter, the secretary of the Zurich-based Foundation, commented that several countries had wanted to set up a permanent centre for Nureyev's work, but the Foundation had always thought Paris was the most associated with him, despite his acquisition of Austrian citizenship in January 1982 and his work with the Ballet of Vienna.

"We are anxious that there should be easy access to his unique collection of films on dance, as Nureyev," he said, "was very insistent on his work being available to others."

The only regret was voiced by André Larquié, President of the 'Cercle d'amis', who was at the origin of the project. He deplored the fact that the Foundation could not afford to buy more of Nureyev's possessions, especially his bronzes, and hoped that the collection would be enriched over the years by private donations.

Despite Rudolf's disparaging opinion of tributes held for people after death, remembering his laconic comment "Hommage… dommage" (A tribute, a pity!), countless conferences and exhibitions of every kind are nevertheless being held year after year. Evenings of specially conceived programmes of dance and gala performances are held throughout the world, some dedicated to his ballets, others to his roles.

The Nureyev Foundation gave many of his personal belongings, his furniture and paintings plus his stage costumes to the Centre-National-du-Costume-de-Scène. In 2009, a superb exhibition of over a hundred of his costumes that he wore in ballets such as *Nutcracker*, *Sleeping Beauty* or *Don Quixote* were displayed alongside films, maquettes and photographs for over a period of six months.

From time to time, a new book is published, films are made, documentaries are produced, while one has only to glance at the internet to discover the many thousands of photographs of him, whether onstage, offstage, with friends, with colleagues, with make-up, natural, on vacation, etc, etc. Some good, some bad, some without interest.

The late Ninette de Valois, founder of the Royal Ballet, has long spoken out about the important role Nureyev played in the development of English ballet, and an early tribute to him at the London Coliseum in 1994 brought together some of the greatest names in the dance world to celebrate his life and work.

Charles Jude programmed a magnificent tribute in Bordeaux in 2003, together with a beautiful souvenir album. No year goes by without an evening in his honour at the Paris Opera ballet, when his ballets are danced.

The Cercle des Amis de Rudolf Nureyev in Paris proposes meetings and conferences on a fairly regular basis, while in 2022, there was an exhibition hosted at the Saint Petersburg State Museum of Theatre and Music, 'Rudolf Nureyev. The Last Visit', where after twenty-eight years of absence, the Russian photographer Baranovsky chronicled Rudolf's final visit there in a series of unique, moving photographs. In September 2022, an important gala was given in his honour at the Drury Lane theatre in London, where he first appeared in Ashton's *Poème Tragique*.

Saint Petersburg

It was impossible for me to write about my memories of Rudolf without having visited Russia, perhaps not necessarily Ufa in the Bashkirian Republic where he grew up, but certainly Saint Petersburg, a hauntingly beautiful city. He spent five and a half years there, those formative years where his career began, and where, despite his love for Paris, a part of his heart always remained. Founded on the river Neva in 1703 by Peter the Great as his "window on the Western world", it is grandiose, magical, and unreal when covered with layers of glittering snow. It is the most theatrical of cities with its gorgeous churches, cathedrals, palaces, museums, fortresses and bridges.

Nureyev had also fallen in love with Paris, making friends with other dancers, strolling down the grand boulevards and visiting museums and art galleries, resulting in him being accused by the Russians of spending far too much time in the Louvre! However, the seeds of his love of art had probably been laid in St Petersburg, when as often as he could, he would surely have been found in the Hermitage Museum, where the paintings of the French Impressionists, including works by Matisse, Picasso, Pissarro, Gauguin, and Van Gogh jostle for space next to all the Rubens, Rembrandts, Titians and Raphaels, without mentioning the endless collection of Russian masterpieces.

The Hermitage itself, an extension of the Winter Palace, which is as romantic as its name suggests and was the official residence of the Russian tsars from 1732 until it was stormed in 1917, is a place of beauty in itself.

It was easy, too, to picture him on those long, interminable white nights, going for solitary walks around the city in the traces of Pushkin and Dostoievski, avid for poetry, literature, and art. Nor is it difficult to imagine him strolling around the sumptuous palaces open to the public, which border the numerous canals criss-crossing the city. When I myself wandered along them, it was March, and the canals were still frozen over, looking like something out of a child's storybook. As I turned in to the Nevsky Projekt, the views across the river Neva, still half frozen, were spectacular. The architecture of the city, part baroque, part neoclassical, is both harmonious and unique.

I went to the beautiful turquoise, ice-blue, gold and white Maryinsky theatre as the guest of Ninel Kourgapkina, where I spent three memorable days going to see performances as well as being invited to watch her giving class. I assisted at rehearsals in those very same studios where not only Nureyev had studied with Alexander Pushkin, but also Pavlova, Nijinsky, and Balanchine before him. In the theatre canteen over lunch, I sat next to Farukh Ruzimatov, a polite and thoughtful young man despite his ferocious good looks, and was also introduced to Diana Vishneva and Uliana Lopatkina after admiring them in class. It took only a small stretch of the imagination to visualise the youthful Nureyev there, working from 8am to 7pm. His studies, Kourgapkina told me, would also have included the history of dance as well as music and art.

However, a highlight of my trip was a visit to the famous Vaganova Academy founded by the Empress Anna Ivanova in 1738 but named after Agrippina Vaganova, the most famous teacher of them all. Situated on the elegant, colonnaded, Russian Empire style Rossi Street, I sat down on the very stone steps one sees in early photographs of Nureyev in Russia, published in books only available in the West.

In the Museum of the Vaganova School in Rossi Street.
© Yves Boccadoro

One of the numerous canals and bridges crossing the city.
© Yves Boccadoro

Once inside the attractive entrance hall, it was disconcerting to learn that after his defection, his name had been removed from the list of honour graduates and from all dance magazines published in the USSR, and that until recently, no photographs of him hung on the walls of the small museum there. Marina Vivien, the curator, explained to me how all mention of his name had been eradicated. Most people had never even

The famous steps leading into the Vaganova Institute in Rossi Street.
© Yves Boccadoro

The Mariinsky Theatre.
© Yves Boccadoro

heard of him, Rudolf Nureyev, one of the greatest dancers the school had ever produced, a boy who had arrived there at the age of seventeen, becoming the partner of Natalia Dudinskaya, the reigning prima ballerina there, by his 21st birthday.

"Rudik," Marina Vivien told me, "was put on trial in his absence, and sentenced to seven years imprisonment." However, she also revealed that a commemorative service had been held in his honour at the Cathedral of St Nicolas de l'Epiphanie after he died, and that there had been a special exhibition of photographs in the museum of the Vaganova Institute.

Rudolf Nureyev, who was not from St Petersburg, but came from a town to the east of the Ural Mountains, had actually been born on a train, presumably on March 17th, 1938, as it rattled around Lake Baikal near the town of Irkutsk. Although he spent the first three years of his life in Moscow, his parents, both Tartars, were evacuated to a small village in the Bashkir Republic when a bomb hit the house where they lived. Having lost most of their possessions, and sharing one room there with another family, life was hard and people went hungry. Moving shortly after to Ufa, life didn't improve. Food was scarcer, the climate harsher and the Nureyev family again found themselves sharing accommodation with two other families.

It was there, however, that his overwhelming passion for dance was born, and where, undeterred by the severe disapproval of his father, he took basic, albeit sporadic ballet lessons in secret from the age of eleven. Despite being forbidden to dance, his sheer determination got him invited to an audition in Moscow with a group of Bashkir dancers. Once there, he bought a one way ticket to Leningrad, his dream destination, where he headed straight for the famous Leningrad State Academic Vaganova Choreographic Institute, to give it its official name. The rest is history.

I left St Petersburg, marvelling once again at how a skinny, barefooted little boy from a poverty-stricken background in war-torn Russia became the most famous dancer in the world, the first male superstar in the world of ballet. His extreme intelligence, glamour and passion breathed new life into the colourless 19th-century princes, bringing huge new audiences to dance, people who had never ventured into a theatre before.

Single-handedly, Nureyev changed the image of the male dancer, making it acceptable for a boy to take dance lessons, opening up possibilities for all the Billy Elliots of the world. Male dancers, worldwide, owe him an immense debt of gratitude, when because of his iron will and personal charisma, they became the equal of the female, no longer a simple prop, there to put her 'en valeur'.

The achievement he most wished to be remembered for, however, was to have broken down the barriers between classical and modern dance. "I hope," he said one day, after an interminable press conference in the Grand Foyer, at the Palais Garnier, "that I have been the link between classical ballet and contemporary dance", while among his last words to the company are those so often quoted, "Wherever one dances, something of me, something which comes from me will dance… perhaps."

From the moment this exceptional man landed in Paris in June 1961, he brought with him joy and beauty, enhancing the lives of thousands upon thousands of people everywhere. And while we can no longer see him dance except on film, his ballets are now in the repertoires of many companies across the world. We can count ourselves fortunate indeed should we only see but one of them.

Meanwhile, as far as Nureyev the man is concerned, I leave the final word to Maude Gosling, the woman he considered his second mother.

"All the world knows of Rudolf the dancer," she told me, "but what many don't know is what a truly wonderful boy he was."

Holiday snapshot in St Bart's, 1988.
Personal collection of Florence Clerc

Epilogue

Since taking up the post of artistic director at the Paris Opera Ballet in December 2022 following eight years at the helm of Spain's national company, José Martinez, a youthful fifty-three, intends on working and transmitting Nureyev's legacy to a whole new generation of dancers. Entering the Paris company himself in 1989, the year Nureyev left, Martinez, one of the troupe's finest étoiles, was a brilliant interpreter of all the leading roles in Nureyev's productions and, as such, arrives commanding the respect of all the company.

In a recent conversation at the Palais Garnier, the new director pointed out that Rudolf Nureyev was his mentor, and that although he's only seen him dance on video, "when he electrified me with his panther-like grace and those eyes full of green fire", he, Martinez, was fortunate to have witnessed the passion and dedication with which Nureyev worked during rehearsals for *The Bayadère* in September 1992.

"I intend to work in the same direction that he did, and I hope to restore the atmosphere of excitement and effervescence that was here when I first arrived in the company," Martinez told me.

"And," in a direct reference to this season's programmes, which has only one classical ballet on offer, "one of the first things I plan to do is present a more balanced repertoire, in accordance with Nureyev's vision. He brought in some wonderful contemporary choreographers, but modern works were never presented to the detriment of classical ballets," he continued. "We are a company of 150 dancers, and to progress, everyone must dance."

Martinez hopes to bring back as guest teachers all those who worked with Nureyev, including Florence Clerc, Elisabeth Maurin, Elisabeth Platel, Charles Jude, and Manuel Legris.

"It's no secret," he said. "The future of the company lies in bringing back all those who respect classical ballet and who can give a solid base to the younger dancers. It lies in the hands of those who danced in Nureyev's ballets during the time he was here, for they alone had the unique opportunity to benefit from him, and they are the ones who remain steadfastly attached to everything they learned. Their main concern must be to transmit their knowledge. I want to be surrounded by those who worked with him.

"Although I'm the second generation, I was fortunate to be taught all his ballets by those closest to him, including Patricia Ruanne and Charles Jude. Jude, together with Laurent Hilaire and Manuel Legris, were Nureyev's greatest interpreters because they understood the movement he was searching for, and how he wished the steps to be danced."

Like Nureyev, Martinez is himself a perfectionist who will work for hours on end to get a role the way he wants. He, again like his mentor, will research tirelessly into the historical background of a story, and will delve into the personality of the character he was portraying, the characters he expects his dancers to interpret. Smiling at my comments, Martinez continued by explaining that, in recent years, there had been a lack of motivation which he hoped to rectify.

"I've given lessons and held rehearsals and seen that one of the main problems here is that everyone seems a little lost. We have the dancers, but they have to learn to go past technique to become artists, and that can only be achieved with the correct coaching. There's been too much emphasis on technique resulting in the fact that the heart Rudolf gave us has gone missing.

"A true super-star, Rudolf gave us another idea of what dance is about," the director continued, "and I hope to work in the same way. One of his favourite sayings was, 'Wherever one dances, something of me, something which comes from me, will dance… perhaps.'"

Further Reading
Books I have enjoyed

Nureyev: His Spectacular Early Years

An autobiography edited by Alexander Bland, the pen-name of Nigel Gosling and Maude Lloyd Gosling. Published by Hodder and Stoughton Ltd, 1962. Reissued 1993.

Initially reluctant to write it at the age of twenty-four, Nureyev did so, believing it might help his career. His English at the time being rudimentary, the Goslings wrote it with him, basing it on a series of interviews. Covering the years from his birth to 1962, Nureyev relates the difficulties of his early childhood and his overwhelming passion to dance against all odds. He gives a succinct account of his time at the Kirov, and states clearly all the circumstances leading up to his defection, describing how it actually happened.

Beautifully written, the book also contains some of the finest early photographs of him by Cecil Beaton and Richard Avedon.

The Nureyev Image
(published by Studio Vista in 1996)

Fonteyn and Nureyev
(published by Orbis Publishing in 1979)

The first, on Nureyev himself, gives one of the best pictures of Nureyev the artist and Nureyev the man, and Bland says it all in his statement, "Nureyev's commitment to dance was total". The second recounts the extraordinary partnership of the Tartar dancer with Margot Fonteyn, one of the most amazing in dance history, alongside over 200 photographs chosen by the dancers themselves.

Rudolf Nureyev: Three Years in the Kirov Theatre
Pushkinsky Fond and Mol Ltd, 1995

This fascinating book, with exceptional shots of St Petersburg, was compiled by Tamara Zakrzhevskaya, Liuba Myasnikova, and A. G. Storozhuk, three of Nureyev's closest friends from Russia who knew him when he was a student at the Leningrad ballet school. They welcomed him with joy on his return to St Petersburg in 1989.

Three Years in the Kirov Theatre contains refreshingly different information on the little-known Leningrad years. Honest and sincere, it is a collection of anecdotes and reminiscences by those who knew him well, and loved him for the person he was. They clearly establish that when Nureyev requested political asylum in France in 1961, he was already a star in Russia with an army of frenzied fans who would shower him with flowers at every performance.

Space is also given to his detractors, and there were many among those who had toiled all their life at the school and were rewarded by seeing this 'uneducated upstart' from the back of beyond being given principal roles while they were still in the corps de ballet. They viewed this virtually untrained boy who arrived at the Leningrad school at the age of seventeen with envy, jealousy and resentment.

The book succeeds in bringing the youthful Nureyev back to life for a short while. He is alive, brilliant, complex and indefatigable, dancing across every page.

The Dancer Who Flew: A Memoir of Rudolf Nureyev
by Linda Maybarduk, Tundra Books, 1999

In this eminently readable and thoughtful biography, the Canadian ballerina Linda Maybarduk, who knew Nureyev as a colleague as well as a close friend, tells a compelling story. *The Dancer Who Flew* is one of the best biographies yet written about him.

She recounts his career, from his birth and early years in Ufa when he was forbidden to dance by his father, to his untimely death in Paris from Aids. And while she has nothing but love and admiration for the man she and her family adored… he was her daughter's godfather… she nevertheless gives anecdotes of his legendary temper, always when his work was being interfered with and when anything or anyone stood in the way of his art.

Comments and anecdotes from dance friends, partners and critics put much of the Nureyev legend into perspective, focusing on Nureyev's work and achievements, which changed ballet forever.

Nureyev: Aspects of the Dancer
by John Percival, 1975, new edition 1979

A remarkable, informative book beginning with a brief account of Nureyev's early years, and continuing with a comprehensive account of Nureyev's productions up to 1979 based on Percival's detailed conversations with the dancer himself. Percival has enumerated Nureyev's roles from 1957 to 1979, giving not only the version danced, but the place and company he appeared with.

All Nureyev's productions are listed with the greatest possible accuracy. John Percival, one of Britain's most important and distinguished dance critics, travelled the world to watch Nureyev's performances with countless companies, and spoke to numerous colleagues and friends, including Erik Bruhn and Rudi van Dantzig. While not always in agreement with Nureyev's often controversial ideas, Percival nevertheless admired the Tartar's intelligence and sincerity in staging the great 19th-century works.

Acknowledgements

While the early parts of this book are written from memory, from a selection of the countless occasions I saw Rudolf Nureyev dance in the 1960s, as well as by my own notes and diaries, I have also included many of my own rewritten published articles. Any confusion or inconsistencies in dates are my own.

The later chapters, however, owe everything to Rudolf Nureyev's friends, colleagues and dancers who generously gave me so much of their time. I am extremely grateful to all of them.

My deepest thanks must first go to the late Douce Francois, a wonderful woman, whose help, guidance and trust made this book possible, sadly, rather later than sooner. I trust I have not betrayed a word she told me. I would also like to give an enormous thank you to Charles Jude and Florence Clerc for generously sharing so many of their private memories and personal stories with me, which bring the Rudolf they loved and knew so well to life within these pages.

My gratitude also goes to so many of Nureyev's friends, colleagues and dancers who gave me their time over the past thirty years. They include Patrice Bart, Claude Bessy, Mario Bois, Etienne Bretel, Yann Bridard, Janine Burdeu, Paul Clarke, Sasha Davis, Hugues Gall, Nicholas Georgiadis, Ivry Gitlis, Sabine Glaser, Maude Gosling, Laurent Hilaire, Martine Kahane, Ninel Kourgapkina, Brigitte Lefèvre, Manuel Legris, Jean-Marc Léri, Agnès Letestu, Monique Loudières, Francis Malovik, José Martinez, Elisabeth Maurin, Dominic Meyer, Hervé Moreau, Pascal Payeur, Genia Polyakov, Elisabeth Platel, Wilfried Romoli, Patricia Ruanne, and Marina Vivien.

I would also like to acknowledge the early encouragement to write about dance given many years ago by Paul Clarke, as well as by Jacqueline Cochet. It was, however, Rudolf Nureyev, who, recognising my passion for dance, gave me the push I needed to begin writing. I hope this book does not betray the confidence he had in me in any way.

My thanks must also go to the late Mary Clarke, editor of *Dancing Times*, the first editor to publish my work, and to Manon Mauguin, at the CNCS in Moulins, who, at the bequest of the Nureyev Foundation, guided me to many of the photographs in this work.

I would also like to express my gratitude to two of my dearest friends, Susan Mackenzie, who first 'introduced' me to Nureyev back in 1964, and Sally Lecomte, for her continued questions, encouragement to keep writing, and genuine enthusiasm for the book as well as to Myra Woodrow for her invaluable help in proofreading.

And not least to my own family, particularly to my daughter Lucy, my first reader, who kept saying, continue, continue, I want to know more, write more, and to my husband, Yves, who, tirelessly and without complaint, uncovered all my past notes, features and recordings, which, unbeknown to me, he had kept over the years. His help in obtaining copyrights for all the photographs has been invaluable.

About the Author

Looking across the Neva in St Petersburg in March 1994

Patricia Boccadoro was born and educated in England, but moved to France aged twenty-four. Encouraged to write about dance by Nureyev himself, her features have been published in *The Dancing Times, The Guardian/Observer* and culturekiosque.com, a webzine based in the US, where she was Dance Editor. Patricia lives near Paris with her husband and two cats, and any free time is spent with her nine grandchildren.